MIRRORS OF THE JEWISH MIND

By the Same Author

FOLKLORE OF MANY LANDS

Mirrors of
the Jewish Mind

A GALLERY OF PORTRAITS OF EUROPEAN
JEWISH WRITERS OF OUR TIME

By

LOTHAR KAHN

Thomas Yoseloff
New York • South Brunswick • London

Thomas Yoseloff, Publisher
Cranbury, New Jersey 08512

Thomas Yoseloff Ltd
18 Charing Cross Road
London, W.C. 2, England

6670
Printed in the United States of America

In printing, the notes to the chapter on Edmond Fleg have been inadvertently omitted, and are given herewith:

EDMOND FLEG

1. **L'Enfant Prophète,** p. 69.

2. **Ibid,** p. 143.

3. **Why I am a Jew,** p. 5.

4. **Ibid,** p. 6.

5. Fleg was never to have this grandchild whom he so lovingly addressed. His older son was killed in action in 1940, a soldier in the French army. His younger son, Daniel, was to commit suicide in the same year. See Daniel Fleg, **Journal.**

6. **Why I am a Jew,** p. 10.

7. **Ibid,** p. 13.

8. **L'Enfant Prophète,** p. 12.

9. **Ibid,** p. 118.

10. **Ibid,** p. 81.

11. **Why I am a Jew,** p. 26.

12. **Ibid,** p. 37.

13. **Ibid,** pp. 77-78.

14. **Le Juif du Pape,** p. 149.

15. **Ibid,** p. 182.

16. **The Land of Promise,** Introduction by Ludwig Lewisohn, p. 17.

17. **Ibid,** p. 124.

18. **Ibid,** p. 139.

19. **Ibid,** p. 182.

20. **Ibid,** p. 183.

To Lore

Preface

THE QUESTION "Who am I?" did not greatly concern Jews before the French Revolution. They were, at that time, a clearly defined social unit, set apart from the community at large. The Revolution dissolved this unit by offering Jews entry into the Western world. The choice of identity became troublesome. Some remained Jews and considered the Western heritage an alien element; others saw themselves as all Western, with Jewishness but the vestige of a disagreeable past; still others felt themselves both Jewish and European and sought, not always successfully, a mode for both elements to coexist.

If the problem of Jewish identity was serious before our time, it has become even more so in recent years. The destruction of European Jewry and the establishment of a Jewish state have added new dimensions to the problem. This book tries to illuminate the dilemma of Jewish identity by tracing the Jewish attitudes of some prominent European writers, all of whom witnessed the two capital events of modern Jewish history.

The answer to "Who am I?" invites other questions of importance: the relationship of Jews to themselves and others; the sense of Jewish mission and destiny; the vision

of Zion as ideal and reality. In describing the attitudes of
the writers to these issues, an attempt has been made to
categorize their particular brand of Jewishness, ranging
from total assimilation to Western values to an equally
firm commitment to the Jewish past. The attitudes reach
from Jewish self-hate and doubt on the one hand to passionate involvement in Jewish destiny on the other. But
between these extremes of rejection and advocacy are the
prevalent eclectic positions.

This book has no didactic goal. Its purposes are to explain and interpret. It aims neither to make bad Jews
good nor good Jews bad. It tries to serve as a mirror of the
modern Jewish mind, puzzled and even tortured by the
complex problem of Jewish identity.

Acknowledgments

The following articles appeared in various periodicals in a somewhat different form. The author gratefully acknowledges the permission of their editors to reprint them here.

The Reconstructionist: Max Brod (April 17, 1961)

Judaism: Julien Benda (Summer, 1958) ; Josué Jehouda (Summer, 1962)

Chicago Jewish Forum: Arthur Koestler (Summer, 1960) ; Edmond Fleg (Spring, 1962) ; Arnold Zweig (Winter, 1960–61) ; Elie Wiesel (Summer, 1965)

Contents

Preface 7

Acknowledgments 9

1 The Drive Toward Sameness 15

2 Sameness Reconsidered: Between Two Wars 30

3 Julien Benda: Assimilation with Self-Acceptance 52

4 Max Brod: Ethical Zionism 68

5 Alfred Döblin: Indictment and Apostasy 83

6 Lion Feuchtwanger: Historical Judaism 95

7 Edmond Fleg: Messianic Judaism 111

8 Josué Jehouda: Integral Judaism 127

9 Arthur Koestler: Dejudaized Zionism 146

10 André Spire: Romantic Judaism 160

11 Elie Wiesel: Neo-Hasidism 176

12 Arnold Zweig: From Zionism to Marxism 194

13 The More Recent Writers 210

14 Conclusion 237

Notes 247

Bibliography 259

Index 269

MIRRORS OF THE JEWISH MIND

1

The Drive Toward Sameness

Two SEEMINGLY IRRESISTIBLE forces joined to launch the Jewish intellectual on the stage of Western European literature. First, there was the Enlightenment which admitted fresh air into the stuffy house of the ghetto dweller, creating a climate for new and daring ideas. Secondly, there was the French Revolution which offered the promise of new status in return for abandoning old ways; the Revolution provided the means by which new ideas could be advanced and developed. The promise was made; fulfillment was not long in coming.

Moses Mendelssohn was the foremost spokesman of the internal revolution wrought by the Enlightenment. By demanding that Jews rationalize their religion, purging it of its empirical mysticism, that they learn German and enter the stream of German culture, Mendelssohn breached forever the walls of cultural isolation. He helped make possible increased personal contact with non-Jewish intellectuals and his friendship with Gotthold Ephraim Lessing afforded a splendid example of cultural cross-fertiliza-

15

tion. Increased fraternization became itself a source of concepts for integrating the Jew into the general community. As compared to the lucidity of liberal and rational Western thought, Jewish traditionalism appeared narrow and parochial. Thus was created, at least in part, the Jewish intellectual's wish for assimilation in culture and customs.

But the actual change could come about only in the wake of general political and social transformations. The new order could not tolerate within the national midst groups with separate status and restricted privileges. At the same time, however, it had to insist on a measure of integration and assimilation.

Thus, the internal desire and the external demand coincided at a given point. Yet in some nations Jewish status was neither clear nor consistent. In France, after the lengthy revolutionary debates it remained fairly constant. But in the Germanies there were advances and reverses with citizenship alternately granted and withdrawn. The Prussian Edict of Emancipation of 1812 was followed three years later by the revocation of rights and full citizenship was not to be bestowed until decades later. Its very elusiveness at a time when it seemed so near may well have intensified the craving for assimilation in the German states.

But there can be little doubt that the doctrines and pronouncements of the French Revolution had an electrifying effect on Jews. For the first time in centuries Jews were permitted to leave their restricted areas. Like prisoners with a life sentence suddenly suspended, they ventured forth, cautiously at first and then with abandon. Here began the modern struggle for Jewish survival. Yet the emancipation generation was too busy finding its way in a new world to assess intelligently and dispassionately its new freedoms and positions. Despite the warning voices

of a few elders, many flung themselves headlong into the
new adventures. Led internally by the thinking of Mendelssohn and his disciples and encouraged outwardly by
the preachings of revolutionary thought, the young Jewish
intellectuals took the lead in forsaking ancestral ways.
There were valid philosophies to justify conversion or integration; the temptations were numerous, the perils min-
imal, and many of the young intellectuals quickly succumbed. At best there was a residue of remorse over hurt-
ing the feelings of traditionalist parents.

Despite setbacks in Alsace and the German states, the
optimism of the emancipation generation remained intact. To most young Jewish thinkers the upward trend in
the material destiny of Jews seemed assured. The prejudices of centuries would perhaps not be eradicated at once.
It was admitted that certain myths, deeply rooted, would
survive for decades. But newly gained rights and privileges,
codified in the laws of Western nations, would guarantee
Jewish safety as well as the promise of growth. The nascent
public school systems would, in the long run, overcome
both prejudices and myth. For the Jew, however diluted
as Jew, a new millennium, a strong, bright future, was in
the offing. Gone forever was the cycle of expulsions, reset-
tlements, persecutions and pogroms. There was now an
end to bowing and cringing, to filth, dirt and squalor.
What were spiritual joys of the ghetto, if such they were,
compared to the bright new world opening up for Jews as
worthy and equal members of the human race?

Certain developments appear to bear out this prog-
nosis. Jews saw before them opportunities inconceivable
to earlier generations. In France and some of the Germanies, they gained admittance to the finest and best
schools; there was ready access to most of the professions;

institutions previously closed to Jews now willingly opened
their doors. For the first time since the Golden Age of
Spain, Jews were given an opportunity to display their
mental wares. The nagging, gnawing, pent-up feelings of
inferiority were begging for release after centuries of humiliating confinement. The Jewish intelligentsia only too
willingly accepted the challenge thrust at it. In fact, the
vigor with which Jews responded in unveiling their mental
prowess acted negatively on the Christian psyche. Within
a few decades this intelligentsia, with a strong Jewish professional class at its core, found itself heavily under attack
for little more than its aggressive achievements.

The chief difference between the new and old Jewish
intelligentsia was, of course, its secular outlook and detachment from Jewish sources. In their manifest desire to
live up to the rational, liberal-national ideals of the Revolution, the new intellectuals were zealous in shedding
vestiges of the old ways. Some carried their rationality
and universality of outlook—their integration into a line-
less humanity—to the point of symbolic though insincere
conversion to Christianity; others disdained even this
measure of group allegiance and remained nominal Jews.
Some discovered a greater residue of Jew-hatred than anticipated and hoped by assimilation to remove it. Most of
them remained within the faith into which birth had cast
them, but mostly as a matter of personal pride, ancestral
loyalty or filial duty. Toward the Jewish past and heritage
they felt neither appreciation nor love. They would continue to regard Judaism as their religious confession, but
were fully cognizant that their rationalism could not admit
of any genuine religion.

Thus, these sons or grandsons of Talmudic scholars and
ghetto shopkeepers converted or adhered to a Jewishness

that was greatly diluted. Practices were abandoned as atavistic; the centuries-old struggle for survival was judged with Voltairian skepticism as the primitive will to live. But while they consciously reduced their attachment, they did not know how to discard certain Jewish characteristics —socially transmitted traits deriving from a ghetto psychology of defense and reaction. The legacy of a long and commonly shared past, these distinctive behavioral marks were ambition, a loud if uncertain confidence, aggressiveness, nervousness, tenseness. Not infrequently, their intense ambitions and basic insecurity drove them to vie with their hosts in displays of patriotism and national loyalty. In this ostentatious attempt to be more German than the Germans and more French than the French, they failed to perceive the effect of their stance on Christian neighbors, the source of a new anti-Semitism.[1]

The nineteenth-century Jew could justly point, however, to shining examples of accomplishment in a very brief span of time. By 1848 Adolphe Crémieux had become a minister of France; the Rothschilds, Milhauds and Foulds had become the financial rulers of their nations; Heinrich Heine, Ludwig Boerne and Rahel Varnhagen were making an impact on the world of intellect. In the light of such quick and impressive achievements, the attacks on Jews by nationalist-reactionary forces as alien, undesirable and disturbing elements could be dismissed as insignificant and temporary. Even the political Right would come to recognize them as human beings like all others, with a capacity for accomplishment that was second to none. They would be a credit to Germany; they would be a credit to France!

Nearly all of the Jewish writers of the nineteenth century mirrored these attitudes and developments. Nearly all reflected the promise of emancipation and the yearning for its realization; with few exceptions they were beholden to the Great Revolution and aligned themselves proudly with its ideals. As they desperately sought to relegate to oblivion the confining atmosphere of the ghetto, they strove increasingly to associate themselves with the doctrinal positions of the Left. They stood for a patriotism which had liberty, equality and fraternity inscribed on its banner. They envisaged a future moulded by the revolutionary Trinity.

Ludwig Boerne, born Loeb Baruch in Frankfurt in 1786, exemplifies many of the distinctive features of the early-nineteenth century writer. Boerne was a direct descendant of the Enlightenment and thus a firm believer in natural human rights. Raised in Frankfurt's Judengasse, Boerne witnessed in his youth many scenes smacking of a virulent anti-Semitism. In the Christian's attitude toward the Jew he recognized the erstwhile relationship between aristocrat and commoner. Both negative attitudes, Boerne determined early, would have to make room for more enlightened ones as the knowledge and spirit of Man improved through education and wisdom. Thus, Boerne's experiences in anti-Semitism did not greatly disturb him. Manifestations of it were but the last flickering light of ancient, moribund attitudes, to be eradicated at last by the forward movement of Man. This movement would adduce a cosmopolitan sophistication which he saw as a true though veiled ideal of the Jews. Boerne had little trouble reconciling Jewishness with his rationalist, revolutionary outlook. The former, however, as the smaller and sectarian element should be absorbed by the larger human unit. Hence he converted, hoping for the flow of Judaism into a universal Christianity, a mere extension of Jewish ideals. Despite his own conversion, however, his creed demanded the right of every Jew to be himself—with full and equal rights—in any modern state of Europe and America.

The great poet, Heinrich Heine (1797–1856), did not subscribe to all of Boerne's beliefs. In fact, the two converts, both voluntary exiles in Paris, feuded long and bitterly. Nevertheless, there were as many similarities between them as there were differences. Both men were baptized; but where Boerne converted out of a desire for a common humanity, Heine's baptism was lacking in conviction and meaning. Both men were ardent admirers of the Great Revolution; but where Boerne lived and breathed its ideals, Heine loved the people in the abstract and shunned them in practice. Boerne and Heine fearlessly championed the rights of Jews to be and remain Jews, but with the former any emotional attachment played second fiddle to socio-political consideration; with Heine the emotional ties to Jewish customs and ways were never broken and their beauty was hailed in immortal lyrics.[2]

Heine is thus the more complex character and mirrors more truly the confusion of the emancipation generation. He was a bundle of contradictions.[3] He converted to a Christianity he never ceased to despise and denounce. He was a liberal, who attacked other liberals: to wit the hateful book on Boerne. He loved freedom, yet worshipped Napoleon. He was at once a romantic and an heir of the Enlightenment, i. e. an anti-romantic. He willingly and greedily accepted money from his wealthy Uncle Salomon, but at the same time wrote pro-communist articles. Heine's verses were filled with nostalgia for Germany although he attacked the German national character and the reactionary regimes of the nation. He had a romantic world of his dreams, but nurtured a ruthless irony which destroyed them.[4] He was a republican, who yet advocated success for various monarchs. At the same time that he was especially active in a Jewish cultural society, he already contemplated Christian baptism.

Judaism as a religion both attracted and repelled him. Finally, in the closing years of a tormented life the attraction seemed to carry the day. Yet there is good reason to suspect that he never understood Judaism. He grouped Judaism and Christianity under the common heading of Nazarenism, i. e. an attitude of self-denial, the rejection of the pleasure principle and the apotheosis of otherworldliness. He sometimes jeered at the Jewish "creed" by opposing to its mournful tenets the marvelous, exquisite cooking of the Jews. In fact, it was the Jews' culinary achievements to which, alone among things Jewish, Heine was consistent in paying tribute. It is more difficult to understand this ironist's praise of the ways of Polish Jewry, so alien to him spiritually. On the other hand, he never ceased to direct his ironic pen against the Jewish Reform Movement, then making headway in the German cities.

It is not easy to explain the phenomenon of Heine. He has baffled critics whose opinion of him is hopelessly split along political and religious lines. More than most writers he must be viewed against the background of his time. He stemmed from a people about to engage on a new and uncharted course; the period in which he lived was itself an age of transition; he was between generations and systems; in a real sense he existed between the no-longer and the not-yet. He appears to have viewed everything from the outside, never really daring to step inside any house, developing loyalty to none, but mocking the follies of all. More than most writers Heine built on his intelligence and imagination, ignoring or eschewing known models. The view of the outsider, the absence of continuity, the refusal to be attached account for the contradictions, the distrust of system and ideology, the remarkable absence of prejudices, and the equally astounding capacity for predictions. By his rootlessness and inner dividedness, Heine epitomizes the Jew of the transitional era of emancipation and choice.

Heine's and Boerne's entries into the arena of European literature were met with as many hisses as with applause. They came under immediate and heavy attack from those who repudiated the Revolution. The alliance of popular sovereignty with liberal patriotism was even then giving way to the more permanent marriage between reaction and nationalism. To the children of this marriage, the emancipated Jew was the very symbol of the hated Revolution. He was the reminder of abolished privilege; the Jew's benefit and profit was their loss. Heine especially, the irreverent scoffer, was part of the vermin gnawing at the very intestines of European civilization. His distrust of authority, militarism, Christianity, tradition and privilege clearly revealed him to be a traitor: a dangerous, subversive force. Although Heine recognized the nature of his enemies, he was not overly afraid of them. As the gains of the Revolution found firmer roots in European soil, the position of the underprivileged—Jews among them— would become tightly secure.

Thus, most of the nineteenth century was marked by a strong optimism about the future of the Jew, whatever degree of Jewishness might be retained. Events tended to suggest the beginnings of a new era, beneficial to Man in general and to the Jew in particular. Despite an occasional setback the Western Jew experienced a new sense of freedom. He was free to choose a profession, a political party, an economic arrangement, a fraternal order. He could remain all Jew, be a Jew-in-name only; he could assimilate; he could convert. But choice made many, and often contradictory, demands upon his person. It was not always easy to be a German and Jew, even if one desired to be both. There was less conflict in being a Frenchman and Jew, but some conflict there was. The new Jewish intellectual became more divided, uncertain, than his forebears. As he entered the free world of competition, with Judaism removed as a central and guiding force, he strained all his energies, unleashed his pent-up powers to follow the secular, Western course. He became increasingly nervous, sensitive, aggressive and defensive. This was the psychological portrait of Jewish author and hero alike and it has remained dominant into the Jewish literature of our time.

This representation of optimism, assimilation, dividedness and ambition held true for the Jews of France as well as the German-speaking nations. Yet there were differences. France as the nation originally offering emancipation was both more generous and hospitable to her Jews. Also, French and Jewish cultural elements, perhaps because of their common Mediterranean origin, had fused more harmoniously than German and Jewish ideas. But apparently the relative harmony of French-Jewish life was less conducive to the development of important literary figures than the greater conflict in Germany. The more complex and demanding choices before the German-Jewish intellectual invited at once greater thought, perception and resourcefulness.

All was going well for the Jew in the closing decades of the century. The following portrait painted of the young

Jewish intellectual—anno 1892—though based on France would also hold true, in its essential features, for the young German intellectual. It reflects the distance traveled from the ghetto, the drive toward sameness and its achievement: the Jew's integration into Western society:

> The young Jew, clerical or anti-clerical, conservative or radical, once he found himself under the banner of a party, no longer had any other program, no longer professed other philosophical concepts than those he received from the group which was willing to receive him to its ranks. To raise the Jewish question would have been tantamount to antagonizing the militants of both parties, an inelegant gesture. The indifferent ones (politically) threw themselves headlong into business and devoted themselves to the pursuit of earthly pleasures; their dream was to merge with the milieux of the haute bourgeoisie and the aristocracy. Judaism for this generation was neither a religious conception, nor a social or political one.[6]

But then, suddenly, the roof fell in on the house of optimism and assimilation. A Jewish officer on the French General Staff, the first ever to hold so exalted a position, was charged with selling secrets to the hated Germans. Alfred Dreyfus himself was a near-perfect example of the nominal Jew wholly integrated into French society. He issued from the very middle class which at first believed him guilty and refused to intervene in his behalf.[7] After all, this was France: a nation in which trumped-up charges against Jews were no longer conceivable. Dreyfus had to be guilty. But as the flimsiness of the evidence was uncovered and an anti-Semitic wave spread through France, an ugly suspicion finally took hold of even the most confident and secure of French Jews. Had they misjudged their status, overrated the historical changes which had occurred? Had they been blinded by revolutionary rhetoric, by their own social and professional advances? Before long, Jews across the Rhine began to draw their own conclusions. If this could happen in France, then a thorough reappraisal of their position was in order. What they found out was not altogether pleasing.

Suddenly it appeared that, with modern mass communications, Jew-hatred could be nurtured more rapidly and efficiently than ever before. Literacy could be as dangerous as it had been judged beneficial. With newspapers and pamphlets able to disseminate rumors and lies in record time, an anti-Semitic climate could be created in a matter of hours. One other dimension had been added to the peril: at one time the Jew, in crisis, could move to another town, another region. Now the threat was nation-wide; there was no place to go. Jews everywhere were aghast at the confrontation with a new reality.[8]

But once the French intelligentsia had taken stock and recovered from the initial jolt, it could do something no previous Jewish generation had been able to do. It could—and did—fight back. Where the vast body of the French Jewish middle-class—if we are to believe Léon Blum—timidly stood on the sidelines,[9] praying to be ignored and for time to heal, Jewish writers and journalists threw themselves wholeheartedly into the melee. Even if previously they had but the barest link with the Jewish past, they were now tempted to reinforce that link and let it become a strong and lasting bridge. The Dreyfus Case left an indelible mark on nearly all young Jewish writers: on Léon Blum, Edmond Fleg, André Spire, Jean-Richard Bloch, Bernard Lazare, the Reinach Brothers. Henri Bernstein's dramatic masterpiece *Israël* was a Jewish reaction to the anti-Semitism of the time. The half-Jew, Marcel

Proust, was provoked sufficiently to become a Dreyfusard and to remember his Jewish ancestry.

Yet initially it had been as Frenchmen of a liberal, democratic bent that they had taken up the cudgel for Dreyfus's defense. A *Frenchman*, Alfred Dreyfus, had been victim of an injustice unworthy of the nation. An individual was being sacrificed to the demands of reactionary institutions. The old alliance of throne and altar was re-emerging in modern garb. But in fighting the Revisionist cause, they became in some way Jews again. When others would deprive them of their Frenchness because they were Jews, they proclaimed themselves Jews, out of honor, spite, pride and idealism. In some what was at first only reactive Jewishness developed later into a positive and conscious position. Thus, what neither dogma nor ancestral loyalty had been able to accomplish, rejection and disillusionment managed to achieve almost at once.

Therefore the Dreyfus Case was the decisive experience in the lives of many young writers. It made irrevocably clear that the anticipated forward march of revolutionary ideals would not follow a straight, upward line; that the millennium had not arrived for Jews; that emancipation had taken *from* the emancipated as well as given *to* them; that the Jewish situation was in many ways as unstable and insecure as ever.

A close observer of the Dreyfus events was a Viennese journalist then stationed in Paris. A true product of his century, Theodor Herzl had been a casual, disinterested Jew. The anti-Semitic outbursts accompanying the *Affaire* had an immediate and shattering effect on him. The Jewish situation, he resolved, had to be normalized. This could not be achieved by sameness, as previously believed, but by the Jews' acquiring a state of their own. Herzl's

The Jewish State outlined a Zionist program which was by no means original with him. Moses Hess in *Rome and Jerusalem* had previously advocated a homeland for Jews. But it took the renewed outbursts of anti-Semitism to give such a Zionist program meaning and impetus, preparing it for popular acceptance and support.

Bernard Lazare, one of the heroes of the Dreyfus Case and a major figure in French Judaism, summed up the post-Dreyfus mentality and outlook of Jews. They wished "to participate in the human task while remaining themselves, while preserving their personality, to develop noble character, the best qualities. To abandon all that repression has produced, to become again free men and not slaves. Being a Jew, one has less difficulty being a man. That is why one must remain a Jew."[10]

Thus, the Dreyfus Case arrested, at least momentarily, the mad push toward sameness, and raised questions that needed to be asked. At the same time, the Dreyfus episode was the immediate cause for the rapid ascent of the Zionist ideal. Both effects of the Dreyfus Case complicated further the question "Who am I?" by underscoring the need for subtle greys amidst the blacks and whites.

But if the Dreyfus Case was a reminder that Jews were still Jews, World War I had the opposite effect. In 1914 Jew fought Jew across the trenches, in French or German or British uniforms. Jew killed Jew because he thought of him only as a hostile national. Rabbis on both sides, pledged to the Torah of peace, invoked divine aid for the success of national arms. Similarly, writers became spokesmen, if not propagandists, for Kaiser, Czar, His Britannic Majesty or the lovely Marianne. With anti-Semitism then as now casting doubt on the patriotism of Jews, many felt duty-bound—at the front or behind it—to go to extra effort. Arnold Zweig's Jewish hero, Bertin, enthusiastically takes up arms for Wilhelm's Germany. Edmond Fleg, to preserve French culture, enlisted in the service of France. André Spire, a socialist and humanitarian, wrote a treatise in which he imputed to Germany the sources and progress of anti-Semitism. But the intellectual in the trenches was frequently to become disillusioned. Bertin was quick to realize that the Jew had more to fear from the German anti-Semitic officer than the French *poilu*. Zweig's Jews at Verdun and the Russian steppes experienced a vast insecurity not previously encountered as civilians. Again, overtures toward sameness and integration were vitiated by the sense of difference and rejection from without.

Thus, Jewish optimism had twice been ground to a halt. It was difficult to be a German and Jew. It was only slightly easier to be a Frenchman and Jew. The gate of acceptance, previously believed wide open, was at least partly closed. The gates of Zion, to be sure, were open; but was one Jewish enough to pass through with confidence? Jewish identity was formed in a knot that was hard to untie. Adolf Hitler untied it, neatly and quickly; but, as we now know, only temporarily.

2

Sameness Reconsidered:
Between Two Wars

TWO SHARPLY ETCHED tendencies manifest themselves in the writers who reached maturity between the close of World War I and the Nazis' assumption of power in 1933. One is an extension of the rational, universalist tradition of the previous century. On the conscious level Jewishness here plays a minor role. The other permits the Jewish writer to be pulled back into the orbit of Judaism. True universalism, according to this school of thought, cannot occur without each human family contributing its individuality to the whole race of men. The Jew can best become a Frenchman or German—a citizen of the world—by perfecting the Jewishness in him.

While these were the broad, dominating trends, there was a wide range of Jewish attitudes. There were the self-haters like Otto Weininger, or to a lesser extent Karl Kraus and Rudolf Borchardt. These men scorned their origins and displayed contempt and dislike for the Jewish past.[1] The suspicion of a serious pathology in Weininger was

Jewish. But Kafka has delineated with exceptional insight and power qualities that have been inherent in the Jewish situation: impotence before temporal power, loneliness in a hostile society, uncertainty about the morrow. His curious mixture of skepticism and faith has been judged as another Jewish characteristic. Although there is in the Kafkaesque hero a trace of universal man as well, the portrait fits more specifically the genus judaicus. Gregor Samsa and Josef K are veritable mirrors of the haunted, persecuted, defiled and debased Jew of the Diaspora. Yet, Max Brod's interpretations notwithstanding, it is questionable whether Kafka consciously used the Jew as model. Brod has labeled as Jewish not only Kafka's sources, especially the tales of the Talmud, but even the nature of Kafka's visions and dreams. To be sure, Kafka's knowledge of Judaism was greater than many critics have believed. But he was not a practicing Jew and his Jewishness probably did not play the major role which Brod has assigned to it. Brod's own strong Jewish identification may have prompted him to overrate the dedication of his friend. In spite of undeniably Jewish components in his work, it is unlikely that Kafka would have answered "I am a Jew" if he were to have responded to the question "Who am I?"

Franz Werfel, also a native of Prague, was a friend of Brod's and Kafka's. Exposed to many of the same social and cultural influences, Werfel's thought developed along altogether different lines. Werfel, too, was a searcher for God, but his emotional makeup required the warmth and love of divine presence. It was not the rational, distant God of the Jews whom Werfel ultimately reached in his quest, but the nearer, more accessible and compassionate figure on the Cross. Nevertheless, Werfel's religious journey did not cause him to abandon completely the Jewish course;

like other exiles in the 1940's, he suffered as a Jew. It was owing to personal pride and integrity, perhaps also a measure of social identification with Jews, that he abstained from formal conversion. Thus, of the famous three of Prague Jewry, it was Brod who adhered fully to Judaism, Kafka who used it artistically, and Werfel who found it wanting—craving as he did for a nearer, more compassionate God.[4]

Besides the self-haters and the famed Prague trio, the two decades following World War I catapulted to prominence two men who bore some resemblance to each other, though this would hardly manifest itself on the surface. Jakob Wassermann and Stefan Zweig, earnest humanitarians, aimed for loyalties and values beyond the merely Jewish.[5] They were the indomitable champions of the weak, the oppressed, the needy; in an age of ultra-nationalism, they dared preach the glories of peace. For Wassermann, the larger unit of loyalty was the German culture of which he felt himself an integral part and to which he assigned priority over his Jewish roots. To be sure, he strove to achieve a synthesis, as suggested even by the title of his autobiographical *Mein Leben als Deutscher und Jude* ("My Life As German and Jew"). But in the relationship of the two identities, the German clearly carried the day. The calmer, gentler idealist Zweig extended his loyalty to humanity itself. Wassermann feared conflict between Jewishness and Germanness; Zweig feared less a clash than the possibility that a frozen, stagnant Jewish culture, with its demand for apartness, would preclude genuine integration into a broader humanity. Wassermann and Zweig, as much as any two authors, embody the contradictions and distortions that have surrounded the Jewish intellectual since he was granted the right of choice.

Wassermann's life discloses the uncertainties, ambivalencies, and consequent *Schmerz* of a man tragically divided. There are in his makeup distinct traces of the self-hating Jew; there are also strong suggestions of an abiding Jewishness. His portraits of Jews are singularly unflattering. They are painted as an unpleasant group of people, with an annoyingly stubborn streak; they thrive only amidst success; their ranks are full of hate and discord; "Jewish eyes now flare with passion, now lose all their glow in melancholy."[6] Yet Wassermann is aware that there are reasons for distinctive Jewish ways and attitudes. According to one critic, Wassermann's Jews have "the eyes of the tracked tiger that turns its gaze fearfully and feebly toward its pursuers or stares with trembling longing out into the distant land of freedom."[7] On occasion, the Jew's defensive psychology has permitted him to reveal a great potential for beauty; but instead of realizing this promise, the Jew has more often been ugly, a charlatan, a fanatic or slave.

It was Wassermann's exposure to anti-Semitism, especially as a soldier, which accentuated the German–Jewish duality. At one time the problem had seemed simpler; his ancestors had dwelled for centuries on German soil, inhaled German air, lived German history—he sensed deep roots in Germanic soil. To the German language, especially, he felt tied with every fibre of his being. Without it there was no psychological and spiritual food, no intellectual nourishment. The attachment to soil and tongue outstripped in significance the accident of religion recorded on a birth certificate. But try though he would, Wassermann could not reach German critics with these convictions. They stubbornly persisted in regarding his work as that of an alien spirit impressing itself on German matter. Wassermann's problem was intensified further by the repulsion he felt for many of the Jews he met. He lacked all sense of kinship with them, although they were writers and Jews like himself. This alienation manifested itself especially with Eastern Jews. For them he experienced actual physical revulsion, as well as intellectual dislike. "What have I to do with them, I whose ancestors on my father's and my mother's side have for six hundred years lived and worked in the heart of Germany?"[8]

Wanting to be German, but rejected by Germans; wanted by Jews but rejecting Jews, Wassermann recognized before long one curious fact: Jews understood his books whereas Germans did not. This, however, Wassermann attributed less to their common Jewishness than to the Jewish propensity to value highly the creative and the new. It appears that Wassermann never comprehended that the psyche of his Jewish readers was closer to his own, that Jewish readers identified more readily with his characters than Gentiles. Wassermann's characters were often men and women who had lost their anchor in life, were psychologically adrift and painfully in search of a new personal dignity. Sometimes, however, Wassermann's puppets attained a goal which proved worthless and illusory; genuine contentment and an integrated life proved way beyond their reach.

Without clearly felt linguistic, cultural or spiritual bonds with other Jews, Wassermann quite understandably could not conceive of the Jews as a people. They were, at best, an association of individuals. Hence the Zionist doctrines of Theodor Herzl seemed preposterous to him and he assailed them continuously and bitterly. The long years of dispersion, he charged, had made Jews unfit for common action. Their strength lay not in united political activity, but in their individualism, their capacity as servants of the spirit. Here, not in political nationalism, resided their true uniqueness. With a state of their own and acknowledged status as a people, they would no longer be Jews. Hence Wassermann believed it better for them to suffer and be scorned than to lose their historic, prophetic mission.[9] Thus, rather curiously, it was in the name of traditional Jewishness that Wassermann publicly objected to Zionism. One can only speculate as to a possible deeper motivation: the heightened conflict, and threat, offered by a spreading Zionism to his cultural identification with things German.

Wassermann, on the whole, foresaw a gloomy future for the people of Israel. Western Jews, being devoid of faith, would gradually disappear as Jews; Eastern Jews, prone to become Zionists, would also cease to be Jews.

Yet in one way Wassermann appeared to regard himself as still and distinctively Jewish: in his intense search for the truly moral. Like the prophets of old, he cried out fervently against injustice wherever it appeared; like them, he was committed to bettering the lives of his fellow-men. Except for his last year or two, when the Nazi waves had already engulfed Germany, Wassermann's thought was permeated by a strong Messianic sense. In some ways he always remained Agathon, the hero of *Die Juden von Zirndorf,* who wanted to lead Jews toward a kingdom characterized by a strong, inner life of its people. Agathon possesses the earnestness of purpose, the warmth and sympathy, and the good will of the redeemer. It is a more perfect moral state toward which Jews are to be guided, not toward the political state of Zion.

Wassermann's tragedy was truly that of Byronic dividedness. At one time he believed that he could be both German and Jew. Others, however, forced a choice upon him; and still others would not let him be what, in his deepest subconscious, he probably wanted to be. When Hitler finally exposed the farce of his wanting to be a German, Wassermann's bitterness knew no bounds. He cast his erstwhile ideal in the mud, but without having cultivated a replacement. Death in 1933 proved a merciful release from an inner agony which had progressively gotten worse.[10]

Stefan Zweig's personal tragedy stemmed from a comparable yearning for something that could not really be. Like Romain Rolland, Zweig aspired to a transnational ideal in which ethnic and other group distinctions had no part to play. But humanity, Zweig learned with increasing dismay, insisted on being divided and each national segment demanded more adherence and patriotic fervor than ever before. When Zweig's dream finally exploded in the nightmare of the thirties, he had few other spiritual reserves from which to draw. It was ironical that in his final years the man who had wished to shed ethnic differentiations in favor of larger loyalties was now increasingly reminded of his Jewish origins.

Stefan Zweig owed his literary beginnings to Theodor Herzl, who as editor of the distinguished *Neue Freie Presse* accepted one of his contributions. Between the then nominal Jew Herzl and the equally nominal Jew Zweig there evolved a friendly, though never close, professional and personal relationship. After his conversion to Zionism, Herzl urged Zweig to endorse his new movement. Zweig refused, perceiving in Zionism just another restrictive nationalism. The European in him always caused him to reject the doctrines of his erstwhile benefactor.

Yet Zweig did on occasion turn to Jewish sources. In voluntary exile in Switzerland in 1917, he courageously penned his anti-war drama, *Jeremias*. Later, when his humanitarian, transnational ideals were pitifully smashed under the heel of the Nazi, Zweig wrote what is one of the most touching affirmations of Jewishness in our time. But it came as an epilogue and preceded by only a short time Zweig's decision to end his life. He wrote:

> It is an ancient road on which we go; our fathers and forefathers too have gone on it. For we have been a people of wanderers for endlessly long years; we are now again on the march and who knows whether it is not our fate that we remain eternal wanderers? Unlike other peoples we cannot call the earth we sleep on our own. Nor do we have fields of our own whereon we grow seed and fruit. Only as exiles do we go over the lands, and our graves are rooted in foreign soil. But scattered as we are and thrown like weeds amidst the furrows from the morning to the midnight of this earth, we have nevertheless remained a people, a single and solitary people among the nations, because of our God and our faith in him. An invisible something binds us, preserves us, and keeps us together; and this invisible something is our God. . . . All our troubles stem from our urge not to tie ourselves to concrete objects but to be and remain seekers of the invisible. Whosoever attaches himself to the invisible is somehow stronger than those who hold to the visible, for the latter passes away and the former endures. It is for this reason . . . that we have outlasted all ages; for we are dedicated to what is ageless, and since we have kept faith with God, the invisible, he has kept faith with us.[11]

Although Zweig put these words into the mouth of the Wandering Jew, they are also, unmistakably, the words of a wandering Zweig. They came too late to help Zweig reorder his life; but they reflect insights which had eluded him before. Herzl's request for support, had it come in 1940, might have met with more sympathetic ears. . . .

Ernst Toller was, like Zweig, a dreamer whose views clashed hopelessly with the time and the place. Like Zweig, Toller was a suicide. Only forty-six at the time of death, Toller's life had encompassed a war—he was seriously wounded in it—a role of leadership in a revolution, and a five-year prison term for active participation. His perennial foes were militarism, capitalism, mechanistic civilization, and social and economic inequities. He had proudly erected himself as a dauntless champion of justice and peace. When these ideals were buried by the Nazis, Toller saw in extinction the only possible solution.

As willingly as he became enmeshed in Europe's burning issues, that studiously he bypassed those confronting Jews. Toller's youthful adjustment to minority status had been poor and he detested the origins which produced his problem. Only by underscoring his *Deutschtum,* by adopting the stance of the superpatriot, could he blot out the shame of Jewish ancestry. At the outbreak of war, Toller eagerly volunteered. But the horrors of war demonstrated the perils of his patriotism. He now changed allegiance to a transnational, cosmopolitan ideal to which he was soon to add a social ingredient. By the end of World War I he was deeply immersed in Communist thought and action. To the intense German, Jewishness had signified alien and minority status; to the avid Marxist it meant exclusiveness, apartness, bourgeois conservatism. It took a whole series of Nazi victories to extract from him the first expressions of receptive awareness of his other identity. Reiterating that by language, culture and education he was German, he also asked, "But am I not also a Jew? Do I not belong to that people which, for many thousands of years, has been persecuted, hunted, tortured, murdered, whose prophets first uttered in this world the cry for justice, a cry which the miserable and oppressed took up and handed down the ages, whose bravest souls never bowed and preferred death to faithlessness. I wanted to repudiate my mother; I am ashamed of myself. That a child was compelled to resort to such lies, what a horrible indictment against those who drove him to it."[12]

Even as he belatedly recognized himself as a Jew, he cautioned himself about paying excessive heed to his origin. Blood was no more important than the German environment which nurtured him. The question of what was German in him and what was Jewish was both unanswerable and foolish. Such distinctions as this question implied had to be obliterated. Toller was determined not to succumb to the idiocies of his persecutors: he would refuse Jewish as well as German arrogance. As a Socialist, he could claim only that a Jewish mother had born him, Germany had nourished him, Europe had educated him, his home was the earth and the world his fatherland.

But his Jewish mother he had really only now adopted as his own; Germany would not nourish him any longer; Europe had cast him out and the earth was not a safe abode and the World—the New World to which he emigrated—not really a Fatherland.

The tragedy of these men is also mirrored in the life of Kurt Tucholsky, the first of the modern German Jewish writers to commit suicide. Long before Hitler he had chosen to live in France and Sweden. Like many writers of Jewish extraction he opposed nationalism and militarism while feeling a genuine sympathy for the underprivileged masses. But beneath the Heinean wit, as applied to his social bêtes noires, flowed the tears of inner strife and distress. He converted to Protestantism, a step as meaningless as it had been for Heine, to whom he has often been compared. Toward Germany he felt what Harry Zohn has called a *Hassliebe,* a curious mixture of love and hate.[13] Toward Jews, on the surface, his attitude was simple and straightforward enough. He did not feel himself a Jew. His knowledge of matters Jewish was no greater than his interest in them. Violently attacked by Rightists as a Jew, Tucholsky could write, ". . . people who want to hurt the Jew in me are usually wide of the mark."[14] Yet despite this disavowal of vulnerability, Tucholsky admitted elsewhere the burden of being German and Jew. The satirist treated unmercifully both German and Jew, but nothing more than the fusion of German and Jew. He was irritated by many rabbis, assailed Jewish Philistinism, Jewish assimilation. The Jewish upper classes were a common butt of his ironic pen. But he lashed out with particular violence at those Jews who would be more Prussian than the Junkers. Tucholsky, of course, could criticize others for inconsistencies and false poses, never even suspecting these most serious faults in his own being.

When adverse times assigned his universalist ideals to the ashcan, Tucholsky lacked another faith to sustain him. Nor did he have enough attachment to a people or group to bolster his sagging spirits.

The three suicides had one misfortune in common: they lacked a foundation on which to arrest their fall. When their noble ideals proved present-day chimera, offering at best a faint hope for a better future, they kept sinking ever deeper into seas of despair.

Richard Beer-Hofmann (1866–1945), in contrast to these men, was an authentic and committed Jew. Jewish tradition is alive and vibrant in his work. Behind the chaos of the outer universe, the poet senses a mysterious guidance and purpose, the continuity of existence. The centrality of God permeates his writing. In the words of Sol Liptzin, Beer-Hofmann's "visions are reminiscent of the prophets of the Old Testament."[15]

Men, according to Beer-Hofmann, exist to perform a meaningful and worthwhile function on this earth. "This task consisted in upholding both in faith and in deed, at the cost of pain and death, the claim of justice in all ages, especially in generations beset by injustice." In *Der junge David* ("Young David"), significantly published in 1933, Beer-Hofmann extended his moral view to mean that a nation, no more than an individual, could live for its own aggrandizement and exaltation.[16]

Beer-Hofmann had been sympathetic from the first to Herzl's dream of a Jewish state. But a Jewish nationalism, like all other nationalisms, needed to have been of an ethical variety, not the common political species developed in Western Europe. Beer-Hofmann did not live to see the birth of the Jewish state, but he did live long enough to observe the vindication of the Prophecy that God will not permit the destruction of his people, Israel.

THE FRENCH WRITERS

With the exception of Edmond Fleg and André Spire, to be discussed in later pages, the French Jewish scene could boast no major names. Even Fleg and Spire could not measure up in significance and reputation to some of the German names. To be sure, there were oustanding writers like Tristan Bernard, André Maurois and Henri Bergson. But these men viewed themselves so thoroughly as the products of French culture that they experienced little obvious conflict in having the accident of Jewish birth and religion recorded on the *registre d'état civil*. There was neither need nor attempt, in the manner of Jakob Wassermann, to describe their lives as Frenchmen and Jews. Such a duality appeared not to exist.[17]

André Maurois, a member of the Académie Francaise, regarded himself so wholly and securely French that he could endorse Marshal Pétain in the early months of the Vichy Regime. In changing his name from Herzog to Maurois he corroborated—the denials of official biographers notwithstanding—his craving for total Frenchness. In general, Maurois has eschewed Jewish themes and questions, touching on Jewish matters in autobiographies only, when it would clearly have been folly to ignore them.

Yet one would search in vain for those behavioral irregularities, violent loves and disillusionments which afflicted the German-Jewish writers. Henri Bergson (1859–1941), perhaps the greatest modern French philosopher, never seems to have experienced either joy or despair over his Jewish origins. He could not really generate any enthusiasm toward the Jewish tradition. Like Franz Werfel, the philosopher of the élan vital—sometimes called, too, the developer of the modern religious spirit—he was powerfully drawn to the beauty and warmth of Christianity, especially its Catholic variety. He is alleged to have said that his whole life of thought and reflection had led him to see in Christianity the culmination of Judaism. The statement may well be apocryphal as the proposition, besides being debatable, is somewhat alien to Bergsonian thought. Less questionable is the assertion that he was spiritually prepared for conversion when the Nazi occupation halted this plan. In the Jews' darkest hour his sense of loyalty and decency precluded this step which his convictions would most likely have dictated. In fact, Bergson refused to be exempted from the racial laws of the Vichy Regime, preferring, despite lingering illness, to share the hardships of Jews.

In Tristan Bernard there are but the faintest traces of a Jewish sensibility, with his origin largely obscured by his identification with French life and culture. Hence it is not altogether surprising that an irate Jewish immigrant spoke disdainfully of the literary talents of those who professed to be Jewish and regretfully of the "desertion" of the important figures.

The unconcern with Jewish problems on the part of these writers was in many ways astounding. Even in the face of personal disaster in the early months of Vichy, several—like Maurois and the conservative Daniel Halévy—paid enthusiastic tribute to the aged French Marshal and Chief of State (while heaping abuse and calumnies on those liberals—including Jews—who had fled the country). Wrote Halévy in accents as strange as they were naïve: "The voice [Pétain's] was that of a father as well as chief. It seemed to come from the depths of the ages, the reflection of an heroic and generous past. . . . Nothing is lost in a family in which the father is on the job. . . . After so many years of sad anonymity and of endless prattling, again the accent of a human personality, the consolation of a voice. . . ."[18] This same Halévy was sufficiently possessed by patriotic ardor to caution the French against the influx of foreigners, and he distinctly meant Jews. In 1938 he bitterly assailed the toxic "foreign" influences which Léon Blum had injected into the French body politic. In his survey of Jewish attitudes in 1940, Professor Pierre Aubéry quotes Nina Gourfinkel that the French Jewish bourgeoisie—including its intellectual representatives—even approved the anti-Semitic policies of the Pétain government.[19] They were Frenchmen; their religion happened to be Jewish. There was no clash, no conflict. What was the importance of religion?

Jakob Wassermann, across the Rhine, had also yearned to live as German politically and culturally, and as Jew religiously to the extent to which religion concerned him. But outsiders—especially his critics—had refused to let him live by this distinction. A Bergson, Bernard or Maurois was permitted to live as Frenchman without the Jew—what little there was—detracting from the Frenchness. To be sure, there were fulminations against them in the royalist, anti-Semitic *Action Française*. But the *Action Française* was not taken seriously in respectable republican quarters and critics from the remainder of the political spectrum judged their works as Frenchmen in the full sense of the word. (The young Bergson was sometimes taken to task for his British ways, but never for his Jewish ones.) Significantly, too, these French writers of eminence, in many ways more assimilated than their German brethren, did not generally convert to Christianity and were spared this form of spiritual torment. They assimilated, retaining for a variety of reasons—disinterest and unconcern for the most part—the label of "Israelite religion."

Yet there were occasional cries of dissent in this sea of contented integration. Henri Bernstein (1876–1953), a noted playwright, was to tear into this assimilationism which struck him as inauthentic. In *Israël,* perhaps his finest play, he created a fiercely aristocratic anti-Semite who, in the wake of the Dreyfus Case, demands the exclusion from his social set of an upper class Jew. The latter turns out to be his natural father. The Jew is curiously proud of having sired so dedicated an anti-Semite, a young man fitting so perfectly into the higher layers of French society. Bernstein reacted with agonizing pain to the examples of Jewish anti-Semitism he saw in the French bourgeoisie. For his own part, he states in the Foreword to the play, he was quite content to be a Jew. If he is not proud of being a Jew, it is only because it is foolish to be proud of the accident of birth, whatever the origin. But to feel unhappy about one's ancestry would be both cowardly and ungrateful. In addition, he suspects that what artistic temperament he possesses he owes to his Jewish origin. It was this same Bernstein who, several decades later, reminded Maurois that endorsement of Pétain's Vichy was incompatible with being a Jew. "You forget," he wrote, "that you are a Jew, that we are Jews and that there has never been a better opportunity to prove it. You've already forgotten it in changing names, in mutilating the name of Herzog to change it to Maurois. You are forgetting it again in opting for the Marshal's (Pétain's) France when the choice is clear: it is that liberty and democracy which we as proud Jews must defend. . . ."[20] In Henri Bernstein there is an open identification with both Jewish and French peoplehood, a more balanced merger of the elements of both cultures.

Jean-Richard Bloch (1884–1947) issued from a wealthy family of industrialists. His home was Jewishly oriented and the young author displayed a strong Jewish awareness. But soon he became interested in socialism, an interest which gradually gained ascendancy over all others. In his last years, Jean-Richard Bloch was a militant communist. Observing the exploitation of workers in his own and other factories, and living through the war were the decisive influences of his life. With his increasing socialism he combined a rabid pacifism that detested all forms of nationalist fervor. His idealism extended to the moral sphere when he exhorted his fellow-men to work for the sake of work, and not for money alone. In those pre-Stalin years, Jean-Richard Bloch was resentful as Jew to be asked again and again to prove his patriotism. He urged Jews to be frankly Jews, to live as Jews and not to hide timorously under camouflage. With equal vigor he counseled them to maintain a continuously alert vigilance against anti-Semitism, to fight it openly and to the death. World War II convinced him of the futility of all moderate action and an aging, generally disheartened idealist sought salvation in the canons of Stalinist Communism. But Bloch did not live long enough to be confronted with the duality of Communist or Jew. He died mercifully in 1947 before the incompatibility of this dual allegiance became overtly manifest.

It is sometimes forgotten that Léon Blum—socialist leader, Prime Minister of France—made his professional debut in literature, an interest maintained throughout his long and eminent career. Blum was born into an upper-middle-class Jewish family. Like most of these families, Blum's displayed a deep loyalty to revolutionary ideals, especially those of liberty and justice. The Blums regarded themselves as well adjusted to—and fully integrated into—French society. This did not keep them, however, from associating mainly with other Jewish families and seeking out one another's company.

The Dreyfus Case destroyed this picture of contentment. In young Léon, it served not only as a strong reminder of his Jewishness, but awakened his social and political conscience as well. Awed by the intellectual and oratorical power of Jean Jaurès, as also his socialist ideology, Léon Blum was gradually converted to his doctrine. Blum became, contentedly, Frenchman, Socialist and Jew.

In his *Souvenirs sur l'Affaire* (Memoirs of the Dreyfus Case) Léon Blum reaffirms his impatience with those bourgeois Jews who, in the 1890's, would not stand with the Dreyfusards for fear of endangering their status. He is equally displeased with their counterparts in the 1930's who objected to the influx of Jewish refugees for identical reasons. He admonished Jews not to be overly sensitive to anti-Semitism, to feel safe and secure in France, to stand upright as Frenchmen of "the Jewish race." It was as Prime Minister of France that Blum, Jew and socialist, was cast in the difficult situation of negotiating with Hitler. At the Riom Trials, engineered by the Pétain collaborationist regime, defendant Blum declared that he could have refused negotiations both as Jew and socialist. "But it was precisely because I was socialist and Jew that I *did* negotiate."[21] Again and again, Blum asserted in official interviews that it was a privilege to be descended from people who, to him, symbolized the virtues of humanity, social justice, and the critical spirit. Although he himself was too firmly anchored in French life to consider a Jewish state his own, Blum welcomed the Zionist idea as a promise of refuge for the unwanted and dispossessed everywhere. It was only in Jewish Palestine that such Jews could graduate to a natural, free, and bearable mode of living.

As Jew and Socialist, Léon Blum was a favorite whipping-boy of the French Right. Yet he did not flinch before pressures because he was a Jew. Though physically beaten by activists of the Far Right, he stood fast against further threats from the same quarters. Wheedled and cajoled by a French middle-class fearful of blame should Blum fail, pressured even by the Grand-Rabbi of France, Blum courageously dismissed all pleas to resign. He was a Frenchman by culture, taste and nationality; he was a socialist by conviction; he was a Jew by origin, religion and moral outlook. He would brook no limitations on any facet of his being.

Over a generation younger than Léon Blum, Maurice Sachs was as confused and befuddled as Blum was firm and determined. After a short life of paradoxes and turmoil, Maurice Sachs died in his fourth decade, a lover of Germany amidst the ruins of that nation. Sachs, it is claimed, actually volunteered assistance to the Hitlerite conquerors, while yet expressing resentment at the martyrdom to which Jews were being subjected. But perhaps he was not altogether resentful; for Sachs firmly believed that Jewish destiny allowed for greatness only in persecution and disaster.

Maurice Sachs was reared in a milieu of freethinkers from which discussion of religion, any religion, was categorically banned. As a result, he adapted poorly to the sense of cultural, social and religious differences which his lycée years painfully brought to his attention. He apparently sensed an equal distance between himself and upper-class Jewish boys on the one hand and Catholic youngsters on the other. Throughout his tortured life, Sachs would be searching for a group that would take him. In this maddening quest he would largely fail. His despair would finally lead him to Germany and a love affair with a nation in the process of committing mass slaughter of his own people![22]

Where equally rootless German writers had voluntarily chosen the grave, Sachs fumbled blindly into the absurd.

His conversion at age nineteen from a Judaism he never understood or cared to understand to a Catholicism which meant equally little was part of this forward march to disaster. His conversion stemmed, interestingly enough, from his reverence for a man like Jacques Maritain—who possessed the certainties and foundations which he had lacked all his life. If Catholicism had done some good for Maritain and others, perhaps it could accomplish the same for him. Only later did the emptiness of his changeover dawn on him. Then he wrote that if ever he could get himself to pray, he would not do so with the Catholics, but with the Jews who had discovered the notion of God. Further evidence of inner derangement was in his attitude toward the Nazis. Initially incensed by their persecutions of Jews he identified himself more with Jews than he ever had before. But only a little while later he wrote enthusiastic drivel about the Germans and offered them his help.

Talented, gifted, Maurice Sachs remains a frightening illustration of human pathos. He wrote honestly enough *"Je n'étais de nulle part. ..."* (I belonged nowhere) . Basically he was that too perfect example of the rootless Jew who wanted to be all he could not be and was perhaps all he did not wish to be.

It is evident that the French writers between wars, with the exception of Maurice Sachs, appeared unafflicted by that biting torment which drove some of their German confreres to bitter self-hate and ultimate self-destruction. Apparently they knew themselves better, knew who they were, what they were. Perhaps, the fusion of French and Jewish elements facilitated this self-knowledge in France, while the more conflicting aspects of German and Jewish coexistence made choice more difficult in Germany. But of the more troubling problem of identity in Germany were born the greater Jewish artists, the more perceptive writers. The craving for assimilation was irksome and pathological on the German side; but assimilation as an accomplished fact was, in many ways, more representative of the French authors.

Some of the Jewish attitudes examined in this chapter were also those of the writers surviving the Nazi holocaust and who witnessed the establishment of the Jewish state. How these two most significant events in modern Jewish history affected these attitudes, steadying them in some cases, modifying them in others, revolutionizing them in a few, will be dealt with in the chapters to come.

3

Julien Benda:
Assimilation with Self-Acceptance

ASSIMILATION HAS BEEN a much overused term in modern
Jewish history. Like most such terms it has lost some of
its meaning. As generally used it covers a broad range of
attitudes which have but few beliefs in common. Assimilation implies a conscious desire to accept all of the ways
and modes of the host people, and in the process to abandon, consciously or otherwise, one's ties to the Jewish
heritage and people. André Maurois, it has been seen, has
been silent on those ties. Emmanuel Berl, a lesser known
contemporary, has largely rejected them. Julien Benda,
one of France's foremost thinkers, has totally embraced the
culture of France; very Cartesian and classicist in his
thought, his work has been judged one of the most representative expressions of that culture. Yet Benda has retained and even nurtured what measure of Jewishness he
sensed in himself.

The wide gap between the assimilationism of Emmanuel
Berl and Julien Benda merits comparison. There is little

Jewish awareness in Berl. In his many autobiographical works he never stoops to deny his Jewish origins. However, he does appear to look upon them as an evil trick of fate, one which it was futile to counteract. In 1925, he could write about his love for a Christian girl: . . . "I was perfectly happy to marry a young girl who was not Jewish. I abhor Zionism. I do not even understand this problem, considering myself as I do a Frenchman and a man. . . . My memory, in any case, does not extend further back than France. And Jerusalem evokes in me, above all, verses by Racine."[1] In fact, Berl continues—after noting he was glad that Christiane, his girl, was Catholic—"I suffered from not belonging to any communion; for me the Synagogue was not one. I deplored seeing evaporate, for lack of a solid frame, the religious feeling which sometimes seemed to surge within me. . . ."[2]

French in his political and cultural outlook, young Berl's religious yearnings—and they were few and spasmodic—turned toward Catholicism. He had grown up very Parisian, very sophisticated, with a Voltairian, irreligious upbringing that shied away from even the most simple of Jewish observances. Deprived in his youth of even a smattering of Jewish knowledge, and of any of those affective associations that are formed by habit, Berl appeased his later religious craving with an occasional and faint move toward the more accessible Church. Perhaps it was only the experience of Hitler which made him wish in 1952 that he had partaken in his youth of those great religious festivals "which shine with a quiet splendor in the memory of my co-religionists."[3] Now, in the autumn of his life, after the shattering years of occupation, Berl describes with warmth and emotion the customs and rites of the holidays he missed.

But even after the liberation, Berl's distance from any position readily understandible to Jews was considerable. One can still comprehend his wholehearted endorsement of the Munich Pact: Berl put his concern for humanity and peace above democratic loyalty and dread of Nazi expansion. But when his close friend and editorial associate, Pierre Drieu La Rochelle (1893-1945), became the Rosenberg—if not the Streicher—of France, Berl's failure to break with him became incomprehensible. With the collaborationist on trial after Auschwitz and Theresienstadt, all that Berl could say was that Drieu's anti-Semitism, even in pre-war years, had sometimes been annoying to him. Since Hitler, Berl wrote, all anti-Semitism had become intolerable to him, that of Drieu not excluded.[4] This detached view of a social disease that had cost so many lives permitted him to continue his relations with Drieu even after the vitriolic, racist pamphlets had appeared. Berl records this reaction, odd, to say the least: "How I would have liked to have it out with him, but it was already done."[5] In *Prise de sang* ("Blood Test") written after Drieu's trial and suicide, Berl strove hard to rehabilitate the anti-Semite's reputation. If this speaks well for Berl, the friend, it is a sad commentary on the humanity to which he professed loyalty.

But then, had Berl grasped the character and ravages of anti-Semitism? In 1925 he expressed himself in terms which clearly presaged his stand on the Drieu affair. *Méditations sur un amour défunt* ("Reflections on a Dead Love") features a curious scapegoat theory in reverse. The worst effects of anti-Semitism, Berl held, was the excessive credence which Jews displayed toward it. Belief in anti-Semitism is the Jew's way of covering up personal inadequacies. "A Jew who is not invited to dinner believes that he would have been invited, were he not a Jew. A Jew, when someone shouts 'dirty Jew,' imagines that nothing would be said to him, were he not a Jew."[6] Berl recalls a significant childhood experience. He was walking with his parents through an Algerian street when some rabble-rousers shouted *Mort aux Juifs* ("Death to the Jews"). Characteristically, Berl summarizes the experience as follows: "It wasn't the word 'Jews' which concerned me, but the word 'death.' "[7]

Despite a softening in attitude toward his origins in the post-war years, Berl has on the whole looked upon the Jew as a Frenchman: not a Jewish Frenchman, but with the detachment of just any Frenchman. He remains the epitome of the fully assimilated Jew for whom "Jerusalem evokes only the verses of Racine."

Jerusalem evoked more, substantially more, for Julien Benda (1867-1956), one of the most controversial theorists of the intellectual's role in society. Benda was a much embattled man. At the time of his death in 1956, he had alienated much of the world which had once admired him. To some he appeared a heartless rationalist with little regard for the emotional makeup of people; to others he seemed intolerant and vicious toward those holding views distinct from his own. Little doubt that the philosopher's peculiar brand of unorthodoxy had the ill-starred quality of exasperating both sides of a question. He offended French nationalists by his determined espousal of Europeanism; he irritated internationalists with his venomous and often unreasoned anti-Germanism. French traditionalists never ceased to abuse him, but liberals also—especially after *Belphégor*—voiced their displeasure. On most every question Benda's position was so rigidly independent that concurrence on broad points seldom signified approval of specifics. Benda had a predilection for dramatizing himself, often appearing ludicrous in the process. Finally, his fellow-intellectuals resented the strain which Benda's concept of *le clerc* (the cleric or monk) imposed on them. This concept has often been misinterpreted to mean that Benda wanted the intellectual to withdraw from the affairs of his time. Actually, Benda did not argue against participation as such, but that in participating the intellectual must remain an intellectual, considering issues from the standpoint of abstract truth and justice.

Benda, the cleric, worshipped at numerous shrines. He was a rapt member of the cult of intelligence, often mirrored in a Spinozan rationalism. He embraced with fervor the values of truth, justice and logic. He placed the scientific spirit considerably above the artistic frame of mind. He adhered to a "fixist," eternalist philosophy which required a strongly affirmative viewpoint. Methodologically, his "religion" revolved about the "dissociation of ideas," the love of systematization, the tendency to abstract thinking. He revered the memory of Spinoza, Descartes and Renouvier; he detested and battled against Bergsonism, Pragmatism and later Existentialism. Because the sentimental internationalism of Romain Rolland offended his calm rationalism, he bitterly fought it, although he was in sympathy with its overall objective. So rigid was Benda in the pursuit of his various "religions" that he was often accused of striking an intellectual pose.

Benda's Jewish attitudes should be viewed against the background of these intellectual tenets. A man with *so many* religions may not have *a* religion. Indeed, Julien Benda was never a Jew by religion. The Jewishness that was ingrained in him—and it was limited—was due to his sense of cultural and historical pride: partly the reaction to anti-Semitism, somewhat less by temperament, and very slightly by habit. Benda's writings were never chiefly concerned with Jewish themes, but he occasionally alluded to his Jewish heritage, commented on questions of Jewish interest, labeled his actions and thoughts as part of a Jewish mentality. Again and again he voiced an abiding affection and even admiration for the Jewish past. In fact, some of his superlatives concerning the Jewish record have been so un-Bendalike as to expose him to the charge of ethnocentrism, casting a long shadow of suspicion over his vaunted rationalism and sincerity.

The philosopher's thoughts on Jewish matters are found mostly in the autobiographical *La Jeunesse d'un clerc* ("The Youth of an Intellectual"), *Un Régulier dans le siècle* ("A Regulator of the Century") and in Chapter VII of *Le Rapport d'Uriel* ("Uriel's Report"). His observations range from social and political issues to the character of anti-Semitism, from the meaning of the Jewish message to a description of classes and types of Jews.

Benda's childhood in a Parisian Jewish home of the 1870's was largely representative of the time and the place. He observed no Jewish ritual, being completely severed from all Jewish tradition, and for that matter all religious thought. In the years to come, this Voltairian climate sealed off his mind from even comprehending religious sentiment or emotion. The author recalls as his sole bit of religious instruction the negative lesson of being asked not to mock Catholic children walking to confession. The emancipated Bendas had little regard for Jewish culture and learning, which they judged primitive and even barbaric.[8]

On the other hand, their socio-political thinking was

largely governed by the fact of Jewishness. Thus, Benda's calm, impractical father—to whom he was more attached than to his lively, Parisian mother—kept eulogizing the French Revolution, which had freed the Jew and granted him civil rights. In fact, Camille Benda was wont to express dismay that there should be Jews who were not in accord with the Revolution or opposed to its achievements. Julien Benda asserts that the strong patriotism of French Jews of his father's generation could be traced back to their attachment to revolutionary ideas and the gratitude they felt toward these ideas.[9] Jewish patriotism—including Benda's own—was different from that of other Frenchmen, because according to Benda it tended to stress the substance and meaning of the nation rather than the forms and symbols.[10] It was equally distant from flags and uniforms on the one side and nationalist notions of earth, blood and instinct on the other. Instead, Jewish patriotism underscored appreciation of the values of liberty, equality and fraternity.

From his family Benda also gleaned the sources of Jewish ambition. Benda believed that devotion to the young and the full realization of their abilities had always been traditional in Jewish families. With the older generation having failed to produce the Messiah, all hope had to be centered on the younger one.[11] But in the nineteenth century, for the first time, other factors entered into Jewish ambition. For the first time Jewish pride, individuality and self-esteem were given a chance to assert themselves. As though the restraints and humiliations of centuries were suddenly to be swept away with one mighty effort, Jews threw themselves headlong into the new careers open to them. What a challenge to disprove the old contention of Jewish inferiority! Benda recalls that, especially in bourgeois families, children were prodded into academic competition to demonstrate they could be first-rate people if they were only given a chance. They were to display at once their immense capacity for work and their intellectual endowment. As models to emulate, Jewish parents held up the Reinach brothers, who had walked off with every academic prize the French Academy could bestow.[12] But in encouraging their children to exceptional effort, parents may have made a serious error. The Reinachs' triumphs, widely publicized, always struck Benda as one of the latent causes for the virulent anti-Semitism of the close of the century. In characteristically cynical fashion Benda wrote that *justice* may have demanded that the Reinachs receive *all* prizes, but political *interest*—and the self-interest of Jews—required that they receive only *some*.[13] Benda himself was only a mediocre student, preferring other diversions to those of books. He claimed to have been intractable to his parents' entreaties and up to the time of his death was still resentful when Jews, as Jews, told him they were proud of him and his books.

Benda was to remember yet another intellectual condition peculiar to the Jews of his time. They knew but two political organisms, the individual and the state, with all linking bodies outside their mental orbit. Benda believed this a Jewish tendency because, as Jews, they thought of the social in a rational and abstract manner—as distinct from the concrete and historical thinking of others, which revolved about such institutions as church and army. Here again, Benda conceived of the Jews as steeped in the spirit of the Revolution, with its *a priori*, idealistic notions.[14]

In his later years Benda was to claim that it was his parents, without deep roots in the soil of France, who unwittingly set the stage for his own non-historical thinking. Despite their fervent love for France, they did not instill in him a conscious respect for the whole of the French tradition. Undoubtedly, Benda surmised, their own past in France was too recent to lend any genuine meaning to a history-centered patriotism. Nor did his parents, as did non-Jewish parents, bind him to religious traditions or even moral teachings. Finally, his parents removed him from the continuum of history by failing to raise him in any particularist tradition, allowing for a universal rather than specific moral outlook. Benda later wondered about the influences which would explain his cult for values based on an eternal frame of reference and his aversion for those who would only consider them from an historical and transient viewpoint. "I am wondering if the true explanation resides not in the education [given him by his parents] and if God would not have recognized the author of *La Trahison des clercs* ["The Betrayal of the Intellectuals"] in this little boy seated at the table between two adults who were praising the beauties of reason, work and science and never the particularities of his nation, ancestors and people."[15]

If one is to believe Benda, the absence of firmly linked chains to the past was thus helpful in developing the individuality of his thought and did not harm him in his condition of being a Jew. Benda declared categorically that he was never at war with himself or with the Jew in him. There was, of course, only a limited Jewishness with which to reconcile other identities. But, in any case, and for whatever reason, he succeeded uncannily well in accepting himself as he saw himself. "I accepted my mathematical bent of mind, my Greco-Roman culture, my Jewish mentality with what limitations and non-inclusiveness these necessarily entail for a true understanding of the world and my feeling of solidarity with Man. I accepted the fact of my pure *intellectuality* [*ma nature de pur intellectuel*] with what it inevitably lacks in terms of loyal devotion, my love of the idea with what it suggests of the anti-social. I have accepted to be what I am and, above all, not to be what I am not."[16]

Yet while accepting his Jewishness and even making some extraordinary claims for Jews, Benda was continually exasperated with some types of Jews. In his early years, he had often encountered *le snobisme des grands Juifs* and had little use for it;[17] later he was to endure an equal aversion in the presence of strongly conscious or militant Jews who, he knew quite well, returned the compliment.[18] Benda's religions would not tolerate traditionalist Jews, as they excluded traditionalists of any party or faith. His anti-particularism was also responsible for his scoffing at Zionism as a Jewish racism. Basically he regarded himself among *les juifs affranchis,* the assimilated Jews; although he was acutely yet painlessly aware they were detested by Jews and non-Jews alike.[19]

Benda belongs to that rare species of Jewish writer who did not encounter until full manhood the phenomenon of anti-Semitism. To believe him, he did not recognize it until, at thirty, the Dreyfus Case suddenly and pungently drove home its meaning. But once familiar with it, he was never again to underestimate it. He relates in some detail an experience in prejudice. His novel *L'Ordination* had been presented to the Goncourt Academy (named after the Goncourt Brothers, whose name is tainted with anti-Semitism) for its annual prize—one of the most highly esteemed literary awards in France. Benda asserted that it was because of the anti-Jewish sentiment of two key members that the coveted prize was denied him on a late ballot.[20] Paradoxically, this defeat marked the turn in his literary fortunes. Following this incident, after long years of relative obscurity, he found the doors of the publishing houses wide open to him. One may question the full accuracy of Benda's report and allegations, but one cannot doubt his sincerity when he wrote: "The hatred for Jews is one of the rare philosophies which, in this so strongly divided mankind, receives almost unanimous support."[21]

Benda's reasoning here is externalized in *Le Rapport d'Uriel,* a work written in the mock-innocent, mildly satiric vein of Montesquieu's *Persian Letters* and some of Voltaire's short novels. Here Benda differentiates between conscious and subliminal charges against Jews. Among the voiced prejudices Benda lists first those coming under the heading of Jewish capitalism—i.e., theft, usury, exploitation, avarice—all at the expenses of the Christian masses and, especially, Christian workers. The second is that of Jew-based communism, an accusation entirely the antithesis of the former—but, adds Benda, in logic only. In emotion and passion, he maintains, they are one, with both striving to make the Jew odious. The third complaint he labels imperialism, a theory according to which the Jews care only for their own, have no love for the host nation, yet seek high office and power in it to gain control on behalf of the "chosen" people.[22]

Benda's refutation of these accusations is more angry than original. It is interesting only in relation to the claims advanced for Jews. They are especially honest in business; they have a congenital fanaticism for justice which sometimes causes them to appear revolutionary. Jews above all others conceive commands of human conscience outside of the prejudices of historical and national factors and, more than others, treat them in their universal, absolute quality. Jews honor moral values in their eternal, everlasting aspects, independent of time and place and are thus an eminent factor of human liberation. In Benda's persistent equating of Jewish characteristics and values with those he espoused, one may indeed discern a considerable identification with things Jewish. He carried this identification further when he declared that, like himself, Jews have disdain for terrestial grandeur and—again like him—have a cult for the spiritually pure, and for rational intelligence. He quotes from the Psalms: "Other nations have their chariots and gilded arms; you, O Israel, you have your God."[23]

In his exposition of hidden, "unconscious" reasons for anti-Semitism, Benda anticipated some of the psychological theories of prejudice which have come to hold sway in the United States in recent years. Benda realized that there were historical facts in the Jewish situation that were responsible for a particular brand of prejudice. But he astutely recognized that anti-Semitism, like all prejudice, would germinate mostly in those already predisposed for it. There were some who conferred upon themselves a certain superiority and primacy by despising others. By despising the Jew, by speaking and agitating against him, they bestowed upon themselves a patrician title, and also the ability, wealth and other status factors which they were actually lacking. "There seems to be a permanent element in the disdain for the Jew," he concludes, and adds these additional subliminal causes for the perennial disease: scapegoating, especially after a lost war; the need in many humans to discredit social justice and democratic ideals which they associate with the Jew (or does Benda?); the need of those governing to employ diversionary maneuvers when in difficulty.

Benda was no pacifist and strongly approved an army that would truly be in the service of a democratic republic.[24] But the Dreyfus Affair apparently conditioned him forever against the military and the authoritarianism it represented. As a result, he was prone to equate anti-Semitism with the military, and his other personal philosophic and social villains, just as he had linked the Jews to his positive virtues. Benda predicted that anti-Semitism would rise and fall with the growth and decline of militarism.[25] Conversely, he seemed to think the Jews would become apostles of a truly civil society because they were civil *par excellence*. This new society would opt for justice, human dignity, and the rights of the most humble. Above all, it would deny to any man the right to make a tool of another. Writing during the Nazi occupation, Benda pondered over the possible triumph of the military system and its effects upon Jewish survival. Any succeeding civil society, he feared, might come about only in time to honor the *memory* of the Jews.

In those gloomy days of World War II, spent in solitary exile in Carcassonne, writing book upon book, Benda appears to have moved somewhat closer to Judaism. *Souvenirs d'un enterré vif* (Memories of One Buried Alive), written when Benda was well over seventy, contains several passages in which he relates more than ever his values to those of Jews. Above all, he had discovered the Prophets and experienced for them a depth of sympathy which he had previously accorded to only a few religious writers—

and these latter he now recognized as the spiritual heirs of the Prophets.[26] The Prophets endowed him with a sentiment he had never known before: veneration for the people which had produced the Prophets and had thus borne into the world the idea of morality. It was their teaching and their message which the detractors of the Jews had always sought to stamp out. More than ever he conceived of the Jews as the representatives of the critical spirit in modern times; for less deeply mired in the nationalist ideas of blood and soil, they could interpret a problem more freely and independently. Now, too, he imputed to his "race" a special capacity for reflection and thought.[27] He could only concur with the dictators of the thirties who had declared that "To think is to be Jewish." While Benda would not carry this notion to the extreme of claiming intellectuality for all Jews, or that they have a monopoly on it (he specifically denied this), he nevertheless credited them with a specificity in this area. He cited the disproportionate number of eminent Jewish scientists, philosophers, and men of letters. In his attic room, hidden away in safety, the aging philosopher was so overcome by compassion that he allowed his objectivity to forsake him. He imputed to Jews a virtual monopoly on justice. His statements were almost surely the result of powerful emotional reaction to the horrors outside his room. For an assimilated Jew, European and citizen of the world, a universalist rather than particularist thinker, his war-time statements suggest deeper attachment for the Jewish heritage than might have been expected.

Despite his mounting claims for the Jew and his heritage, Benda came closer to neither traditional Judaism nor Zionism. Here his Weltanschauung was in deadly conflict with either the irrational mysticism of the former and the politically oriented nationalism of the latter. The proclamation of Israel as a state evoked both traditional Judaism and Zionism, both areas in which he brooked no compromise.

Some critics have seen in Benda's isolation, his quarrelsomeness, his fundamental pessimism, less the result of reasoned intellectual conviction than of his personal and social heritage as a Jew. Some have even suspected the very concept of the cleric's role as a contemplative figure, apart from partisan strife, as a rationalization of his personal background. But it appears doubtful that this personal factor operated more potently in Benda's thinking than in that of other contemporaries. Benda, to be sure, saw himself as a Jew, but never exclusively as a Jew and certainly not even primarily as a Jew. The complete ease with which his family associated with Catholics in his youth, the perfectly natural manner in which he came to view such contacts, the absence of mainly Jewish associations, his ability to move in all Jewish circles but the most militant and nationalist make the hypothesis of an exceptional personal factor highly untenable. His intellectual formation had multiple origins and they all combined to shape the cleric that was Benda.

History is likely to remember Benda's plan for calm, detached reasoning, for the subordination of emotion to the intellect, for the quest for lasting values. All have struck a clear if unheeded note in a world gone awry with propaganda and emotive appeals to the human ear. History will also record his name for his persistent admonitions to intellectuals not to commit "treason" by overvaluing the temporal, by aspiring to power, influence, and prestige and thus neglect the truly clerical functions of searching for truth and justice. History will certainly not remember Benda as a Jew, for his Jewishness, though real, was minor and undistinguished. It cannot forget, however, the contribution which his Jewish background and the ethical values inherent in it added to his overall thinking. Benda was that rare species, the assimilated Jew, who yet fully accepted himself as a Jew.

4

Max Brod: Ethical Zionism

MAX BROD WAS ESTABLISHED as a writer of note when Franz
Kafka was still an obscure official. Yet it may be Brod's
strange destiny to be remembered chiefly as Kafka's friend
and literary executor. For despite a prolific literary activity, which spans nearly six decades, Brod has failed to
achieve the eminence toward which his early successes
seemed to point. The fault may rest partly in unwise and
even unworthy choices of subjects, especially for some of
his later novels: his nostalgic reminiscing about a Prague
long gone and of interest mainly to those remembering
the city, or to the social historian.[1] It may also be that his
uprooting from native soil detached him from his prime
source of inspiration.

Yet despite his weaknesses, Brod deserves to be remembered as more than Kafka's friend and interpreter, as more
than the man who resolutely ignored his comrade's testa-
mentary wish that his work be destroyed. Brod himself is
a psychological analyst of considerable perceptiveness, a
religious thinker of originality and depth, a scholar with

a vast yet never ponderous erudition, a writer with charm and persuasiveness. Brod's talents as a novelist, historian, biographer, musical and literary critic are as varied as they are impressive. In general, Brod's work is analytical and intuitive rather than creative and imaginative.

Brod thus merits at least a modest niche in general literary history and a more substantial one in that of twentieth-century Jewries. He chronicled their life with skill and insight. As publicist for Zionist ideas, he presented well, to a Jewish and non-Jewish public alike, the broad objectives of the movement. Unlike the Zionism of Arthur Koestler, which could not withstand the lure of Western culture, or that of Arnold Zweig which withered under personal and ideological disappointment, Brod's successfully resisted permanent disillusionment and frequent hardship. Except for an occasional trip to Europe Brod has remained in Israel since his emigration there some two decades ago.

Max Brod's life has followed a straight and simple path. Born on May 27th, 1884, in Prague, he attended—as did most Jewish boys in this triply divided city—the German language Gymnasium. He began to publish in his teens, but had common sense enough to earn his livelihood through another medium. Without any intrinsic interest in law, he nevertheless turned to it for a career. Upon receiving his doctorate, he accepted various administrative positions with the government, his longest association being with the post office. He attained the distinguished rank of *Postsekretär* and received a subsequent appointment to the press division of the Council of Ministers. As such, as was then possible, he was assigned to the post of theatre critic of the *Prager Abendblatt*. He achieved wide acclaim as a critic, a reputation that he made use of in 1918 to form the Jewish National Council.

During the severe anti-Semitic outbursts in the new Czech state in 1918-1919, Brod was in the front line fighting for his fellow-Jews. His Zionism, faint at first but rising steadily in fervor, dates back to 1913, being solidly based on a study of Jewish history, lore and language. By 1924, his reputation as novelist, critic and Jewish leader was sufficiently established to enable him to leave government service. In 1928 he undertook his first journey to Palestine. Ten years later, as the Nazi clouds more and more darkened the European horizon, Brod finally emigrated to Palestine. There he has functioned as an adviser to the Israel National Theatre in addition to continuing his own literary efforts. Much of his thought has centered on publicizing the cause of his new homeland.

While his personal life has followed a rather simple and unobstructed course, his intellectual evolution has been more complex. His first works display the influence of Schopenhauer; Brod denies free will and espouses the philosophy of *Indifferentism*. Since Man could not control his destiny, nothing really mattered, and only an attitude of bland indifference made sense. *Schloss Nonypegge,* which exemplifies this thinking, leads its Indifferent hero to a logical and inevitable self-destruction. His *Jüdinnen* (Jewesses) show the same emptiness without, however, arriving at the same pitiless and inexorable conclusion. The title of this novel is misleading because it totally fails to project the lives of his Jewesses as Jewesses. In fact, they are just women who incidentally happen to be Jewish, with but the barest reflection of Jewish ways and values. To be sure, the milieu is Jewish and perhaps those acquainted with early-twentieth-century Prague Jewish life may recognize here an authentic portrait of assimilated Jewish society.

With Brod's next novel, *Arnold Beer, the Story of a Jew,* Indifferentism is on the wane, its protagonist being patiently guided toward a more positive chain of thought and action. Significantly Arnold Beer is being steered toward a meaningful existence by an old grandmother, who is not only a firm residue of the Jewish past, but speaks the rarely transcribed German-Hebrew-Jewish jargon so common in the Central European village. Brod's full command of this tongue hints at his newly found interest in Jewish life and ways.

There can be little question that his concern with Jewish problems filled the void created by his abandonment of Indifferentism. His interpretation of Judaism and his concept of a Jewish "mission" were to prove of more than transient interest. In fact, they have continually occupied him since his twenties, when he first embraced the cause of Zionism to which he has been committed ever since.

Brod has often called himself a Jewish nationalist. Proud though he is of this position, he takes great pains to differentiate it from the divisive, integral nationalism of Western Europe which Brod had vigorously fought in all its forms. What Brod envisages is an ethical nationalism which would be "an example in setting examples."[2] In fact, in its chief emphasis Brod's Jewish nationalism is diametrically opposed to the varieties that had grown in Europe and evolved into the ugly monster of World War I. Brod's Jewish version places the national in full harmony with overall human, transnational ideals. Brod wants the well-being, the physical and moral prosperity of his people, the taking of firm roots and the free development—independent of outside pressures and considerations—of a Jewish culture. But all this must evolve within a framework of justice and humanitarian conciliation. If ever the narrower Jewish interest should collide with the broader human one, Brod would bravely relegate the former to a secondary position. Thus, Brod finds true national sentiment entirely consonant with true humanity, itself the beginning of a higher level of human existence.

To a certain extent Brod's Zionism should be regarded as the extension of religious emphases. Ethical nationalism requires that the Jews become the first people to begin self-purification at home, and thus cleanse the national idea of the filth that has blemished it in recent decades. By removing social inequities within, by establishing a just order at home, each nation—with the Jewish pointing the way—can achieve its national and universal mission. This is Brod's own partial concept of the "chosen people," with *each* people becoming such a chosen one—and with none forcing its solutions on others.[3]

Jewish nationhood is thus broadly and ethically conceived. It is, therefore, not surprising that Brod in 1918 actually welcomed the idea of Arabs coinhabiting the land with the Jews. The presence of Arabs would challenge Jews to prove and demonstrate the inclusiveness of their national ideal and drive home the futility of violence, force and the will of the strongest.[4] But even in the early 1920's Brod was distressed by the ominous clouds darkening the Palestinian horizon, especially by the expressions of hatred emanating from both Jewish and Arab sources. Yet Brod was still hopeful that Jewish nationalism could assert its own distinctive ethical quality sufficiently, and that peace-

the experiment. Without a land to call its own the national idea has not been able to take root—and may never do so. While other peoples suffered from hypertrophy of national sentiment, Jews have not even lifted themselves to the level of national awareness, or recognition of themselves as a people. Where other nationals, overnationalized, crave bigger territories, larger coalmines, better harbors, Jews must still be taught to want the minima of group existence and the right to maintain their own individuality.[5]

Yet, despite their own doubts and those of detractors, the Jews are a people.[6] To be sure, they do not have a language of their own in the dispersion, but neither do the Irish speak Irish, the Mexicans Mexican, or the Americans American. More than these people, the Jews have had a language which has held them together throughout the ages, and which has been a vehicle throughout this time span for their literature and art. More than most peoples Jews are bound together by common rules and values, by historical memories shared by all. Brod, in fact, once called them a race, a term which must have come back to plague him in later years. Brod's race concept has little in common, of course, with Nazi doctrines, but his strong desire to demonstrate the bonds binding Jews as a people brought him to the brink of a dangerous and untenable notion. What Brod had in mind was an unconscious spiritual community among Jews, owing to certain obvious historical facts. Moreover, since Jews everywhere have tended to marry only Jews, a fairly common and constant Jewish physiological and biological type has emerged, with a pronounced *Blutgemeinschaft*.[7] Writing long before Hitler, Brod stated that the racial differences between Jews and Gentiles were greater than between most groups. "Brod allows a particular concept of 'race' to be applied to Jews, even as he totally rejects the Nazi's concept of Nordic superiority and of non-Aryan inferiority. Brod believes that genuinely scientific studies of race can help Jews in the development of their group selves."[8]

Brod is intent upon differentiating between Jewish Nationalism and Zionism. Here, however, he appears to be guided by practical and physical considerations primarily. Zionism is Jewish Nationalism with the idea of settlement in Israel added to it. In the 1920's Brod believed that the land was so small that it could not accommodate more than two million Jews; hence he did not advocate a total reliance on settlement. Yet the importance of settlement was above question; it was imperative for the very survival of Jewish life. Without the homeland which Palestine would provide, Brod doubted that Diaspora Jewries could long maintain their individuality and traditions against competing influences and temptations.

In fact, Brod is especially apprehensive about the millions of Diaspora Jews who cannot find their way to Israel. For them the national idea, without the Zionist component, offers the greatest promise. It will permit these Jews to remain citizens of their present country and maintain a degree of cultural autonomy, especially if they constitute a sizable minority. Brod makes it clear that their political allegiance to the home nation must be total and without mental reservations. Far from being a state within a state—Brod anticipated the charge of dual allegiance—Jews would enrich the political and cultural life of a country, and at the same time be enriched by the host people. The formula would be a simple one: Jewish life in the Diaspora with a Jewish state as a *cultural* base; total political allegiance to the host nation with utter and complete obedience to any and all of its laws as well as generous service to its people; recognition of the Jews as a People, with a continued cultural affinity for Jewish life and values.[9]

Brod never questions that this people deserves to be sustained as a people and its culture preserved. Like other positive Jews he is not beyond idealizing his group. He concedes readily that individual Jews may be materialistic or grabbing or dishonest. But the Jews as a whole can boast of a long line of idealists and dreamers that belies the charge of materialism. Besides Jews have proven themselves the least bloodthirsty of peoples, the least prone to resort to violence for solving their problems. Far from adopting a narrowly parochial viewpoint, the Jewish intelligentsia has displayed a consistently universalist approach.[10] The Jewish people has provided the world with many of its fundamental ethical canons and is still showing promise of building on these in the future. But Brod mixes veneration for Jewish traditions and values with some mildly caustic and reproachful remarks. The Jews are a people given excessively to criticism, in whom the polemic spirit reigns supreme. He also dubs them an ironical people. In Israel he is frequently perturbed by an ironical noisiness which he imputes largely to their Mediterranean temperament.

His years in Israel have redeemed his faith in the national idea, to which he pledged himself even more fervently in the post-Hitler years. He felt deeply and directly for the victims of the Nazi terror, both during and after the war. The Jews, as usual, were the most exposed of all peoples, pitilessly at the mercy of others. A people perpetually in this situation had to help itself, and only through a national program of strength, self-respect and willpower was this possible.[11] Brod therefore defended moderate Jewish action programs and observed in their progress the increasing "normalization" of Jews in Israel. Mentally, he contrasted these action-oriented Jews in Israel with an image that had long haunted him: the Viennese cafés where Jews played cards uninterruptedly and told each other indecent stories—"those card parties . . . in which a dying people sought to become ironical about its lamentable state and succeeded only in doubling its degradation. The intellectuals of this group were drunk on the stench of decay. . . ." In Israel, the Jew can develop healthily, with a defensive, reactive psychology—the disease of Diaspora—gradually disappearing.

Brod belongs to a small number of European Jewish writers who have attempted to define painstakingly a suitable attitude for the Jewish writer to his host nation. In *Die Frau, die nicht enttäuscht* (The Woman Who Does Not Disappoint) and in his biography of Heinrich Heine, Brod counsels a position of "detached love" for the culture whose language is used. Of course, Brod is cognizant of the contradiction within this term. Nevertheless he uses it because it suggests most clearly the need to eschew both love and detachment and seek a living, mid-way position. To steer this balanced middle-course is a delicate, difficult artistic process requiring great care lest the writer tip the balance to either extreme. Brod himself serves to tip it when he writes that the Jewish writer must find firm anchorage in Judaism. He subscribes firmly to the words of his philosopher friend and fellow-Praguian, Felix Weltsch, "Detachment can only be maintained by standing firmly on one's own ground. Detached love demands a balance of forces; but such a balance can be achieved only by opposing to the blandishments of a foreign national culture one's own secure Jewish self."

In fact, this is where Brod's Central-European Jewishness differs sharply from the pseudo-Jewishness of a Koestler or Zweig, limited to an anemic Zionism. Unlike Arnold Zweig whose Marxism precluded it, and unlike Koestler whose cold positivism did likewise, Brod never viewed Zionism as apart from the Judaic tradition. Far from treading the known path of emancipated European intellectuals, Brod puts the God-idea and the search for the infinite on the highest levels of human thinking and searching. In Judaism, Brod discovers a garden which, when properly weeded and fertilized, can nurture the hopes of suffering Jewry everywhere, even those of humanity itself. Consonant with this thinking, Brod expressed the conviction in an American periodical that, had Gustav Mahler known Judaism, he would not have become a Jewish Christian—that, in fact, the Christianity he admired was a veiled Judaism.

Brod externalized his highly personalized interpretation on the living meaning of Judaism in several volumes. In his best novel, *Tycho Brahe's Weg zu Gott* (The Redemption of Tycho Brahe), it is a venerable rabbi who gives to Brahe the clue to his moral and psychological dilemma.[12] In *Judentum, Christentum, Heidentum* (Judaism, Christianity, Paganism), and later in his briefer *Das Diesseitswunder,* Brod set forth the specifics of his brand of Judaism. In both volumes he distinguished sharply between *edles Unglück* (noble misfortune) and *unedles Unglück* (ignoble misfortune).[13] The former reflects man's inability to go beyond his natural limitations, to be more than he is as Man. They both mirror the difficulty of a finite being placed in an infinite situation, being restricted further in his powers of knowledge and insight. Noble misfortune is thus at once unavoidable and inescapable. Ignoble misfortune, on the other hand, is avoidable; it is of the species of war, social injustice, and national feeling which transcends reasonable boundaries. Ignoble misfortune may seem deeply ingrained in man today, but it may conceivably be eradicated at some future time. Noble misfortune touches on the spiritual, while ignoble misfortune is indeed very earthy and altogether in the realm of the human.

It is the particular distinction of Judaism, Brod finds, to have worked on the assumption that both types of misfortune exist and that religion must concern itself with both. Where paganism was solely concerned with the ignoble, and Christianity mainly with the noble, Judaism early recognized humanity's need for ministry in both. Judaism has always uniquely perceived the interconnection of the earthly with the spiritual, of the worldly with the non-worldly. In fact, Brod sees the Mogan David as the very symbol of this connection: two triangles, one from below, one from above; and so intertwined as to have both parts seem one indissoluble figure. God is one!

Because the spiritual has such close links to the physical, Judaism strikes him as the most concrete of all religious systems. Many facets of daily living are specifically treated in the Talmud; at the same time, these discussions of daily minutiae are more than pagan affirmations of earthly existence. For these very worldly problems are viewed in the light of the holy, the eternal, the supernatural. Here lies for Brod the true significance of Judaism for humanity, a meaning not yet fully explored: the magnificent, miraculous interplay of Hagadah with Halakha, of poetry and action, of myth and practice. Because noble and ignoble misfortune require different attitudes for their elimination, the former passive expectancy and the latter active participation, Judaism ineluctably combines both. Judaism, for example, has never scorned politics because of religion—as has Christianity—nor has it thought little of religion for the sake of politics—as has paganism. In Judaism, there is a happy synthesis: balanced, harmonious, an excellent guide to meaningful living.

The Jews of today are the happy carriers of this tradition without really knowing or understanding it. But they must come to know it and from it derive a more satisfying self-image. This vision of Judaism which must improve the Jew's idea of himself is also likely to adduce a proper attitude toward non-Jews. Politically, this spiritual-worldly union suggests the education of man for humanity. Translated into more concrete terms, it culminates in national humanism: Brod's 1939 religious equivalent of his earlier synthesis of the national with broadly human ideals.

Because Brod admires the intellectual and emotional content of his religion, he is disturbed by its lack of attractiveness to Europe's young Jews. Above all, the relative inaccessibility to, and neglect of, the Jewish "dogmatic garden" is a source of disquiet. Besides, the emptiness and mustiness of the Judaism he has observed probably cannot satisfy the spiritual demands of Europe's young. Brod is sympathetic to the spiritually starved youths who turn to neo-Christianity to meet their needs, and not at all understanding of the religious teachers who voice their surprise and shock. Rather conveniently, but unrealistically, the teachers attribute the conversions to the lure of a better job.[14]

In attaching much blame to the religious teacher, Brod

undoubtedly is influenced by his own experiences which he so devastatingly condemns in one of his autobiographical pieces. Rabbis such as his own, he charges, fail to relate the rich content of Judaism to modern problems and concerns. Why doesn't Western Judaism have something to offer, he asks, which would accept the challenge of neo-Christian art and philosophy, either in terms of seriousness or topical significance? As a result of this failure, the young, sensitive Jew will often turn to Christianity where "they teach a love which does not obligate one to anything; a washed out, diluted notion of kindness which can never be put to the test. . . ."[15]

On this subject of effectively communicating the content of Judaism Brod has remained uncharacteristically pessimistic. Neither the humanitarianism of a Leo Baeck nor the organ music of Reform Judaism nor the prevailing bourgeois Orthodoxy promises a hopeful answer. In better, more meaningful and challenging religious teaching—aimed largely at illuminating the moral and cultural essence of Judaism—he expects at least a partial solution to this problem.

Both in thought and action Max Brod has been a more complete, integrated Jew than many of the other men discussed. He belongs to a small and select group of Western European writers in whom Jewish national, religious and cultural elements are not only successfully blended, but in whom they actually supplement and reinforce one another. His faith in the Jewish religious and cultural tradition enables him to accept more readily the Jews as a people which forms a nation. Conversely, his interest in them as a people forming a nation furthers his interest in their religious and cultural values. Unlike others, Brod calls on his fellow-Jews to stand proudly on their tripartite

Jewishness. This Jewish tradition, he admonishes them, was still capable of spiritually and intellectually feeding a Franz Kafka; surely it bears within it the potential of stimulating and inspiring modern youth. But before it can reach this youth and appeal to it, its communication and teaching programs must be largely overhauled.

World War II, of course, and the near extermination of European Jewry has had its effect on Brod. More than ever he believes in Israel, in the need for creating a strong and natural Jew, a tripartite Jew with a solid national, cultural and religious base. His ethical idealism has remained intact even if it has been modified by experience to include a more politically nationalist component. The exterminations have also been responsible, one may presume, for his slashing and not altogether fair attacks on non-Jewish or anti-Jewish Jews of the ilk of Karl Kraus. But on the whole, Brod's attitude is mirrored most effectively in the words of one of his characters in *Unambo* against a pre-independence setting in Israel: ". . . here only am I free; here only do I not have to apologize for being a Jew. Here I am simply a natural human being like all other human beings. . . . The land is poor . . . it is hard to live in it; at the same time it is unconditionally necessary for us. We have no choice: utter destruction or this land! Thence comes the magic power; it is the power of the ultimate remnant. The world does not understand that . . . in each of us there march to combat hundreds of souls who were destroyed by Hitler in Auschwitz."

An unmistakable note of bitterness, of toughness, born of recent Jewish history, has crept into the speech of Max Brod. Yet in the angry octogenarian there remains a strong residue of the national Jew with the ethical and supra-national ideals.

5

Alfred Döblin:
Indictment and Apostasy

ALFRED DÖBLIN (1878-1954) found little to commend twentieth-century Jewish life and rather early detached himself from it. Yet for one brief flickering moment, this master of the German Expressionist novel plunged himself into the turmoil of German-Jewish existence and the deadly crisis it was facing. Döblin emerged from the experience a badly shaken man, flinging a fearful indictment at Western Jewry. While his conversion to Catholicism reflected mainly an inner spiritual need it cannot be wholly divorced from the emptiness of Western Judaism as he had come to know it.

A mystical current, thinly perceptible from the first, wholly engulfed Döblin as the Nazi hordes swept across Europe. His craving for a nearer God was fulfilled in the discovery of Jesus, in whose divinity he recognized both his own salvation and that of Man. The preoccupation with Cross and Cathedral preexisted his escape from France in 1940, but it took constant danger and flight to push

83

him irresistibly toward them. Finally, in 1943, in Holly-
wood, he took the final step of conversion.

Schicksalsreise ("Fateful Journey") vividly depicts these
physical and spiritual migrations. Döblin's account gives
no hint of any inner struggle such as finally deterred Bergson and Werfel from converting at this particular moment
—the lowest ebb of Jewish fortunes. Döblin's only doubts
pertain to Jesus himself: Is he true as his image suggests?
There are no further expressions of concern for the afflicted Jew; there is no last and final search for spiritual
fountains in Judaism. He no longer criticizes Judaism for
any special shortcomings nor does he express specific discontent with it. To judge by Döblin's own story, he did
not convert *from* a faith, but mainly *to* one. Paradoxically
it was at the moment of his own most serious persecution
as a Jew that he determined on his religious apostasy. But,
beneath all this quiet, Döblin felt a sad hopelessness over
the state of disrepair into which Western Jewries had
allowed themselves to fall.

Döblin's entire Jewish history is an unhappy one. At no
time did he find anything that was emotionally or psychologically satisfying in Judaism. His Jewish friends, by and
large, were as detached as he from the ancestral faith.
When Hitler's rising star caused an awakening in Jewish
matters, Döblin thought it necessary to go to Poland to
meet a real Jew. But if Döblin's Jewish history is a pathetic
one, he was yet as much its maker as its victim.

He was born in Stettin on the Baltic in 1878, the son
of a tailor.[1] His mother came from a highly regarded, well-
to-do family. But home conditions were poor, with a self-
centered father pursuing his own pleasures and generally
neglectful of the family. The ensuing burden proved hard

for Döblin's mother, who fully enjoyed the children's love. "We had horrible scenes at home," reminisces the author. Then, one day, his forty-year-old father took off with a twenty-year-old female employee. In 1888 the abandoned and impoverished family moved to Berlin, where Döblin was to live until 1933. His early poverty was to help shape his social and moral philosophy. ". . . I belonged to the poor. This determined my whole nature. To this people, to this nation I belonged: to the poor."[2] Having been deprived of a happy home life and secure family ties, normally pillars of Jewish life, Döblin's vision of the powers of his faith may have been undermined from the start.

Döblin's home offered little in the line of Jewish beliefs and practices. Somewhere and somehow, Döblin writes, he had heard that his parents were of Jewish origin and he a member of a Jewish family. On the outside, he encountered the usual forms of anti-Semitism. But this appears not to have affected him greatly. He describes what he learned of Jewish life: on Christian holidays he was permitted to stay home from school as well as on the High Holy Days, which even his parents observed. The adult Döblin could still see them walking to the Synagogue on Rosh Hashana and Yom Kippur dressed in their best clothes and refraining from work. He did have some religious instruction, but it was scanty, consisting of a little Hebrew, some study of literature and early Jewish history. Considering the many other languages he studied at the Gymnasium—none of which intrigued him— he was little disposed toward the study of yet another. Also, he felt, between the Odyssey and the Nibelungs he had learned enough of primitive history and legend and wanted no more. "And for the teaching of the actual religious element—I read it and listened to it. It was and remained a superficial reading. No real feeling was aroused and no permanent commitment [Bindung] developed."[3] The most affirmative image of Jewishness retained by him from childhood was that of his mother praying by herself, quietly, in Hebrew, in a semi-audible voice.

The limits of this type of religion were evidently too narrow for him. His literary tastes, at this time, clearly suggest this. He was enamored of Heinrich von Kleist's bloody and violent romantic drama *Penthesilea*. After Kleist, his idols were Hölderlin, then briefly Nietzsche and, finally, Dostoyevski. It was in reading these authors, not through the Judaism he had observed, that he sensed God. But even then the phrase, "Thou shalt have no other God for I am the Lord, your God," impressed him as vacuous and uninspired.[4] Döblin wanted a less distant God, more easily within the reach of Man. Later, through Kierkegaard, this longing deepened yet further.

Döblin was well established as a physician and writer when the 1920's produced the first pogrom-like outbursts in Berlin. These initial activities stepped up the activities of Zionist leaders. Döblin was invited to one of their meetings to help assess the situation and become acquainted with Zionist goals and programs. The leaders invited Döblin to visit Palestine, an idea entirely alien to him. But Döblin became sufficiently concerned to want to know more about Jews. "I discovered I did not really know Jews. I could not label my friends who called themselves Jews as Jews. They were not, either in their faith or language; they were the remains of a vanished people who had been assimilated into their new environment. I, therefore, asked myself and I asked others: Where are there Jews? I was told in Poland. . . . Thereupon I traveled to Poland."[5]

Before his Polish journey in the mid-1920's, a critic was justified in asserting that "Jewish questions do not exist in Döblin's books." Following his mission, however, Jewish problems concerned him more and more. The most important book issuing from this period was *Flucht und Sammlung des Judenvolkes* ("Flight and Settlement of the Jewish people").

This book, and others, foreshadow the eventual course of Döblin's spiritual travels. They leave no doubt whatever as to his discontent and frustration with German Jewry. They had no Jewish values.[6] Curiously, the future convert chides his co-religionists, not for their Judaism, but their ostensible lack of it. He is struck especially by their scorn, and even hatred, for it. Döblin's indictment of German Jewry is possibly the most harsh by a Jew. To be sure, his criticism is not directed against the still practicing village-Jew, but only at the sophisticated and cosmopolitan Jews.

He charges German Jews with multiple failings. They have been foolish in keeping their part of the emancipation pact with a German state which abrogated this agreement, after pulling away from Jews all the underpinnings of a secure and rich existence—traditions, values, their very way of life. German Jewry had failed to learn what to expect from the state.[7] Willingly, faithfully, humbly, with an absurdly docile psychology, they suffered rebuff and abuse in an unrealistic hope of better acceptance. They did not recognize that their perennial flight could not possibly end in emancipation. They shied from the obvious lessons of a readily available history. Again and again it was made clear to them that they were not welcome: they had their privileges suspended or withdrawn, heard themselves described by prominent and responsible men as the

most contemptible of peoples, found positions of stature
and importance denied to them. But their optimism born
of the emancipation pact and the desire to escape the
memory of the ghetto were so powerful as to make them
disregard new forms of humiliation. They persisted in the
folly that sooner or later, through peace or war, they could
prove their *Deutschtum* by the sacrifices they were willing
to make for it. The more forcefully they were rejected the
more eager they became to show their deference to the
Prussian master and his "superior" culture. Their brief
experience with civic rights and the tantalizing promise
they held were stupidly allowed to eclipse all historical
examples and consciousness.

Döblin charges that the flight toward *Deutschtum* ineluctably signified a flight from *Judentum*. As a result,
Judaism in Germany fell into a state of disrepair. What
was left of it was a falsification of its nature, a Christianity
without Christ.[8] When they dissolved as a people with
distinct practices and values, they also lost their God—the
real center of their religion.[9] Similarly, having lost their
social cohesion and religious mainspring Jews were faced
with a situation in which their diluted religion could no
longer command respect, and even less reverence. It had
become a burden, a stumbling-block to a career, to full
social and professional equality, or to natural and normal
living. Hence, the waves of conversions, the drive toward
increased assimilation and finally, what Döblin calls the
Jew's secret prayer: "Oh Lord, liberate us from being
Jews."[10] If another man was a Jew, it meant regarding him
as a distant relative; but it was a relationship which was
unwanted, irksome and secretly regarded as a punishment.

As a physician with a strong background in psychiatry,
Döblin understood the psychological consequences of such

attitudes. Since the old, positive content of their religion is unknown to them, ". . . they [Jews] have no longing for it . . . they know the mighty words and teachings of their faith only as the songs of slaves . . . they would rather belong to the masters of today . . . they view their Jewishness as a basic curse." This conviction, mostly subconscious, generates family disturbances, hatred for parents, a shattering and often suicidal inner dividedness. Addressing himself to his fellow-Jews, Döblin wrote with more than a grain of truth: "However many reform temples you build . . . your most beautiful temple would be the one in which one would announce to you 'Beginning today, you are not Jews, you have never been Jews, all your birth-registers have been blotted out . . . you are German, Swiss, Austrian. You may now leave.' " Döblin adds sarcastically that real prayers would be heard in this temple, following such an absolution, prayers by old and young. And a magnificent Hallelujah would follow.[11]

Thus, as Jewish nationality, traditions and the God-centrality were destroyed by emancipation, the conditions for the willing and meaningful survival of Judaism and Jews were also removed. Döblin adds that these were the very conditions which only a few centuries before had enabled Spanish Jews, forced to convert to Catholicism, to continue in secret their practices as Marranos.

Döblin's view on Western Jewry's internal state was hardly edifying and undoubtedly helped pave the way for his apostasy. Though an ironic and even angry tone is readily detectable, on the whole Döblin's look at contemporary Jews is that of the outsider peering in. Döblin may wish to become more deeply involved because his concern over the impending Nazi threat bids him to, but he is not really capable of it. At best he manages the posture of the scientific observer who occasionally becomes heated up over what he sees. Only Arthur Koestler has shown a similar combination of interest and detachment. But with Koestler there has been a much stronger involvement in action. Despite Döblin's keen if overstated analysis and his expressed concern, one must suspect that even at this moment of greatest interest he could not really feel as a Jew.

Though he makes it clear that because of background he can have little in common with them, Döblin speaks warmly and respectfully of the Eastern Jews he has observed on his Polish journey. The latter *wants* to be a Jew, and hence he *is* a Jew. The old ways have meaning for him, his idea of God is still richly alive and meaningful to his every day living. Jewish peoplehood has been kept intact. For Eastern Jews it is still possible to be Jews;[12] for Western Jews disintegration has gone too far. The same applied to him personally: he had grown in a Western environment, his Jewishness had become faint; he could not fit into the Eastern Jewish habitat, however much he might admire its Jewish climate.

But, even Eastern Jewry, especially its liberal wing, seemed to Döblin well on the road to secularization and the denial of traditional Judaism. The potency of Western ideas was such as to preclude any hope of arresting this process. Although the Orthodox appeared least exposed to the influence, there were, even here, evidences of intellectual infiltration. Döblin suspected that Eastern Jews, their desire to be Jews notwithstanding, would follow in the footsteps of their Western brethren and that only one generation stood between them. Little did Döblin sense at this time that Hitler's final solution would totally supersede his own vain speculations.

Yet, Eastern or Western Jew, authentic Jew or Jew in name, had something in common: the external enemy. Reference has already been made to Döblin's denunciation of the Western states which robbed the Jew of his nationality without keeping their part of the emancipation bargain. But the Jewish difficulty antedates by centuries the emancipation era. The Jewish misfortune stems from a defeat suffered two thousand years ago and from which the Jewish people have never recovered. It imposed on them a *Dauerflucht,* an eternal flight, a Diaspora, which is characterized by an historical pattern so obvious it has been unnoticed. It is the pattern of flight from an old and search for a new home. Soon the enemy reappears. First the Jews try, through whatever means available, to soothe or appease him. If they fail in this, they rely on time as their chief ally. They hide, hoping that anti-Semitic manifestations will disappear in due course. If they don't, the flight is resumed; they look elsewhere for a new home and the whole process is repeated.[13] The cycle cannot be broken. Few writers have put the despair of the Jew in the Diaspora in more hopeless terms. The irony of the Jew's situation is unique:

When they (Jews) are poor, they are hated because they are in rags and offensive to the eye.

When they are rich, it is claimed they have robbed the host nation.

When they are religious, they are unwanted because theirs is not the religion of the land and their religion is full of dangerous elements.

But if they are irreligious, they become corruptors, subversives, destroyers, *Kulturfeinde.*[14]

Whichever way they turn, their prospects appear equally

poor. They are the only people without power, without land, without a state. Yet, this is not a divinely decreed destiny. Far from it! God had once chosen them to be proud and strong on their own soil. But it is the Jews' own weaknesses, the misery of their resignation, their dog-like obsequiousness, in trying to find themselves a temporary abode, which has been at fault and a source of displeasure to God. With other peoples, as with individuals, suffering has been a stimulus to indignation and revolt. With Jews, suffering has lost its natural and customary meaning. For them, too, it needs to become a signal for change. Jews must learn to recognize their historical situation, the process characterizing Jewish history, the intrinsic nature of the dispersion and the particular weaknesses this has imposed.

Döblin's pessimistic outburst continues. Contemporary Judaism is not only Christianity without Christ; its spirit runs contrary to the Torah, its basic text. The Jews of the Diaspora do not live Torah which enjoins upon man to maintain his dominion over earth and beast. The Jews, like all slave peoples, do not assert this dominion. They read the Torah, but do not live it. Their reading thrives on the knowledge of a great past. But the descendants of once proud Jews merely read, nod their heads, are proud of the past, and read again. Instead of *Juden* ("Jews"), they are *Judenanbeter* ("Jew-worshippers") .[15] Döblin asks Jews to return actively to the proud spirit of the Torah, not practice a ghettoized, inactive worship of it. Jews should follow the example of Abraham, claim free land and occupy it. But he holds out little hope for the Galluth Jews, who are not Torah Jews, but Torah readers and theoricians. Normal impulse will return to Jews once this dichotomy has been resolved.

Normalization of existence, Döblin maintained in those stormy prewar years, can come about through the acquisition of land, the implanting and execution of the national idea, the establishment of a Jewish nation on Jewish soil. This program would be reactionary in Western Europe and there he would judge it severely. But for the Jews it is a liberal idea, new and vigorous, a genuine step forward. A Jewish nation so conceived will again afford Jews the chance for a truly progressive development and put an end to the pendular pattern of expansion and contraction, flight and settlement. Once Jews have become a united people, owning their own land, they can assimilate without losing identity and retreat without drying up in the process.

"In Palestine," Döblin wrote, "the Jewish shadow can fall normally, a Jewish plant grow straight."[16] Palestine offered the ultimate hope for Jewish security and renewed life. It is the yesterday of Jewish history and the tomorrow after the flight. The Jewish State, writes Döblin, is the chief promise and guarantor of meaningful Jewish survival.

Some writers favoring the Zionist solution visited the land of their dreams. But for Döblin Palestine was not a personal dream; he felt no yearning for a distant Zion and he was not sufficiently attracted to venture even a visit. But he was aware that for others it was more than a dream: an outright necessity. As the youthful Arthur Koestler concluded his Palestine adventure with the realization that he was too much the European to thrive on Asian soil, so Döblin started his Zionist advocacy with that assumption. Döblin's own assimilationist disease had progressed too far to permit the cure which he had prescribed for others.

The novelist's preoccupation with Jewish problems was relatively short-lived, ending even before his conversion to Catholicism. But, describing his program in 1935, he addressed himself to a question of relevance in later years. The Zionism of the 1930's depressed him as a half-way measure which mobilized only part of the people, and not the whole Diaspora. Such a weak effort could not end the dispersion, and without its end there was no final solution. If the land of Palestine was too small, then other soil would have to be picked for Jews to call their own.[17]

Döblin converted in California during the hard, unbearable days of the war after much personal illness and sorrow, physical peril, years of exile, and separation from the cultures that fed his pen. Long before conversion he had written that the Jews believed in a Messiah who would bring salvation to the whole Jewish people; the "Rabbi of the New Testament," however, stressed the "I" and individual salvation. Döblin hoped to find this salvation through his fellow-victim: the man on the cross.[18]

Judaism, he must have felt, did not offer this to him. What he had seen of it had not touched him; what he had observed were the ruins of a religion, the remnants of a people. The practicants of Judaism appeared to gain little comfort from it and even less strength. Yet they suffered—and continued to suffer—in its name. Döblin could and would no longer suffer for it.

6

Lion Feuchtwanger: Historical Judaism

THE MIND OF LION FEUCHTWANGER ranged the world in time and space, much as the Jews whose destinies he pursued in so many of his novels. Feuchtwanger could mentally transpose himself to the biblical times of Jephta, the Rome of Josephus, the Spain of feudalism and later of Goya, the Germany of the absolute princes, the France of Rousseau and Beaumarchais, and finally, the modern Europe of Weimar and Hitler. For historical erudition, psychological perceptiveness and original insights into the mind of a period, and sheer narrative power, Lion Feuchtwanger was unsurpassed in the genre of the historical novel. Perhaps he lacked the sense of romance which distinguished Scott and Dumas, but he overshadowed them in social seriousness and purpose and lent to the historical novel a dignity and respectability it possessed neither before nor after him. Although a refugee in his late fifties under conditions resembling those he wrote about in his fiction, Feuchtwanger remained a prolific writer to his final days. Yet his best work was done in Germany and he never fully regained the heights that he attained with *Power (Jud Süss), Josephus,* and *Success.*

Lionel Trilling once remarked that he could not understand why Feuchtwanger was not a great writer. The answer may well lie in the unevenness of his later work and the mediocre prestige enjoyed by the historical novel. At his worst, Feuchtwanger's erudition subordinated characterization and movement, shoving aside the novel's focal points, and resulting in a length that invited skipping and slurring. But the best of Feuchtwanger will be remembered. *Jud Süss* will live as will his Josephus trilogy; *The Oppermanns* merits rereading as does *Paris Gazette* and *Success.* Significantly, all four are concerned with the basic Jewish situation in the Diaspora.

It is on this theme that Feuchtwanger wrote with consistent understanding and compassion. Here, too, he managed more circumspectly to curb his tendency to write history at the expense of novel. Moreover, Feuchtwanger established an identity with his Jewish protagonists which he did not build with all his characters.

His excursions into Jewish history had convinced him of certain constants in that history which had made an unmistakable imprint on the Jewish psyche. The latter bore the stamp of the social inheritance of a humiliated, insecure minority group, with a reactive, defensive psychology the inevitable result. But there were also positive components. Feuchtwanger associated Jewish values with a fearless, noble and even heroic sense of justice and a love and fear of God that lent Jews uniqueness in history, just as a sense of history was unique with them.

Lion Feuchtwanger was born in Munich in 1884, the

son of a wealthy manufacturer. As befitted a youth of his class, he attended the Gymnasium and later the university. Although he had broken with his parents over their insistence on orthodoxy, his Jewish consciousness even in his early years is mirrored in his choice of a doctoral dissertation: Heinrich Heine's fragment, *The Rabbi of Bacharach*. Upon completion of his studies, Feuchtwanger wrote a number of plays which were widely performed, but have not stood the test of time. Then there followed in rapid succession those historical novels which established his international reputation and immense popularity. In the late 1920's and 1930's Feuchtwanger's name was a frequent entry on the best seller lists of many nations, his total work having sold nearly 60 million copies. In *Success* (1929), Feuchtwanger had mercilessly satirized the attempted putsch of a ridiculous, foolish figure, Rudolf Kutzner. Readers of this bulky though fascinating tome experienced no difficulty recognizing in Kutzner the rising figure of Adolf Hitler. This satire alone would have given him high priority on the Nazis' extermination list; coupled with his non-Aryan status it made imperative an early departure from Nazi Germany. Though cut off from his source of intellectual nourishment, Feuchtwanger appeared reasonably contented in exile in Southern France, surrounded as he was by German writers like Thomas and Heinrich Mann, Arnold Zweig, and others. But then, in 1940, the shadow of Nazism fell upon him again. When war broke out, the French indiscriminately placed Nazi refugees and sympathizers into internment camps, subjecting them to the humiliations recorded in *The Devil in France*. Many fellow-internees commented on Feuchtwanger's indomitable calm and courage, which served as a source of energy to others less happily endowed. Then the Nazis arrived.

Disguised as a woman, he was smuggled across the border into Spain and slowly found his way to the United States, a nation he had frequently teased on humanistic grounds. Feuchtwanger spent his remaining years in California and died in 1958 at seventy-four.

Nearly all of Feuchtwanger's Jewish protagonists sense their insecurity in the host nations and are conscious of many enemies surrounding them. But in spite of their traumatic fears, they lose neither courage nor serenity. Whatever peaks of power and prestige they achieve, however close they are to the rulers they serve, they can never forget that Jewishness is their Achilles heel. They cannot forget it even at the moment of greatest glory and acclaim. Jud Süss is the virtual dictator of Wurttemberg, yet receives showers of abuse from the duke who cannot rule without him. Yehuda has restored financial soundness to the Kingdom of Castile and has ably and nobly served his king, only to suffer humiliation and, finally, death. In ancient times, Josephus is patronizingly addressed as "My Jew," both by Vespasian and Titus, despite his seeming closeness to the throne. At the other end of time, the Oppermann brothers have enjoyed wealth, prestige and even power in Weimar Germany, but stand helpless with the advent of Hitler.

Feuchtwanger's historical Jews comprehend more clearly than their descendants the source of peril and exposure. Their Jewishness precludes acceptance as either a full national or a whole human being. Whether they choose to identify as Jews as Süss and Yehuda, or seek absorption into the general society, as some of his latter-day Jews, or aim to live more peacefully in both worlds as Josephus, the outside reaction is not terribly different. Nearly all of

Feuchtwanger's Jews are intent upon proving their solidarity with host-king or people, while retaining a modicum
of Jewish identity. They all fail. Full Jew, half Jew or
nominal Jew—any degree of Jewishness automatically
makes them suspect and exposes them to the whims of
masters and fortune.

They also discover that they are at the receiving end of
ancient and fearful prejudices and superstitions. Josephus'
Roman and Egyptian contemporaries viewed the Jews as
a quaint, stubborn and willful people whose symbol of
pride, the Temple, had to be destroyed. While the Moslems of Spain treat Yehuda with respect—he is normally
one of them—they are yet aware of a distance between
them; the conquering Christians display all the religion-
based prejudice against which there is no defense. To the
religious bias were grafted on other hates all culminating
in the demand of exposing Yehuda as a malicious conspir-
ator. Jew Süss was specifically labeled a devil and murderer.
In this same work, a duchess who has never seen a Jew,
asks, "Does he murder children?" To the Wurttemberg
court, Jews are werewolves, usurers, murderers and devils.
Like Feuchtwanger himself, his Jewish heroes own sump-
tuous homes and Süss's palace and Yehuda's villa come to
symbolize a dark and evil Jewish power.

The historian's portrait of the Jews themselves borders
on idealization. Their history is replete with moral heroism for the cause of principle and the human spirit. He
finds his co-religionists in the forefront of movements for
social justice and progress. Because of the Jew's religious
distinctiveness and commitment to advanced ideas, he has
enriched the societies he has joined, though often serving
as a disturbing element. Wherever he went, he brought a
message of peace, law and justice, often showing a willing-

ness to die for his message. Perennially exposed, the Jew has stood morally erect. Even when he has seemingly left the fold, as Dr. Geyer, the lonely attorney of *Success,* the ancestral teachings are still within him. Feuchtwanger lets it be known that Geyer is a Jew, that he is defending the unjustly incarcerated art historian, Krüger, that Geyer is writing a book exposing Bavarian justice and that this cold rationalist knows nothing but the pursuit of law and justice. He is single-minded in his preoccupation with his book and its overriding theme. Geyer's illegitimate son, a Nazi bigwig, who financially exploits the father's guilt feelings, is killed during the Nazi Putsch of 1923. At this moment of greatest tragedy, the words of the Kaddish iron-ically pass the just man's lips. Although Feuchtwanger never alludes to Geyer's relationship to Judaism, his mum-blings of the Kaddish hint at the strong underpinnings of early Judaic teachings which probably played a major, though consciously repressed role in his adult life and values.

Feuchtwanger singled out several other traits as common among Jews. He frequently depicts their cunning and in-telligence, prudence and wisdom, and their enormous capacity for charitable and collective action. In whatever period of history, all sacrificed in concentrated effort in behalf of the oppressed and imperiled. Josephus originally came to Rome as a deputy of the Jerusalem government to save three Jewish prisoners; co-religionists offered to shelter Yehuda; they banded together to save Süss; they lent one another support in Hitlerite Germany. Yet it is more than just fear and social awareness that has held them together. It is as much and more the meaning, knowledge and the lesson of the Book. In an eloquent passage, Feucht-wanger wrote:

They had no state, holding them together, no country, no soil, no king, no form of life in common. If, in spite of this, they were one, more than all the other peoples of the world, it was the Book that sweated them into unity. . . . They bound it with phylacteries round heart and head; they fastened it to their doors; they opened and closed the day with it; as sucklings they learned the Word; and they died with the Word on their lips. From the Word they drew the strength to endure the piled-up afflictions of their way.[1]

Feuchtwanger spells out yet one other distinctive trait—their ability to recognize the futility and transience of power. This almost mystical knowledge, Feuchtwanger believes, often produced an enigmatic and even supercilious smile which provoked their enemies.

Despite his admiration for the Jewish heritage, Feuchtwanger was too Western and cosmopolitan to indulge in any narrow parochial praise. Except perhaps in the darkest days of Nazi terror, he would never lend himself to Jewish publicism. Yet, because of the vast sales of his novels Feuchtwanger did much to shed light on Jewish history and its implications.

Feuchtwanger supported the Zionist solution from the start.[2] He had endorsed it for a variety of reasons: first, it would offer persecuted Jews a place of refuge; secondly, it would give those Jews who had decided on the desirability of living with like thinkers a place to do so; thirdly, it would offer a cultural center to world Jewry; and finally, it would instill in Jews everywhere the feeling that they could be like other people. Feuchtwanger was frequently incensed at the prejudice that Jews were not fit for agriculture or competent in the military, or too individualistic to organize into a state. A Jewish state would put an end to these defamatory notions. It was perhaps because of his impatience with these ideas that Feuchtwanger inserted several battle scenes into the *Josephus* to demonstrate how a poorly equipped Jewish Army distinguished itself most heroically against vastly superior and highly trained Roman legions. At the same time, he took great pains to show the collective defensive spirit which then animated the Jewish people.

Feuchtwanger did not become an avid fighter for Zionism, despite his known sympathies. His skeptical humanism never permitted his dedicated participation in any cause or movement—unless it was the fight against Fascist terror. It is also doubtful that Feuchtwanger, deep inside, fully surmounted his reservations about the political nationalism of the movement, resembling in this respect his close friend, Arnold Zweig. Thirdly, while he recognized in Zionism a defensive rather than offensive brand of nationalism, he kept being drawn to the idea which Johanan ben Zakkai first expounded in his *Josephus*, before, during and after the Fall of the Temple. Johanan and other Rabbis believed that a nation could be kept together without the material base of a state. They were confident that certain common rites and convictions, a certain "consensus omnium" on the vital questions of Man, were sufficient to bind a group of people into a nation. Indeed, it appeared throughout the millennia of their history that the Jews' sense of history would almost alone provide them with this welding sense of unity. In a brilliant article on this sense of history,[3] Feuchtwanger commented that "All the deeds of the Jewish people have been wrought in the name of their history, and it is by this rather than by race that they have felt and still feel themselves to be united." Jewish nationhood without statehood was partly made possible because "No other people has felt so deeply the flow, the dynamics of what they experienced as a community, nor has any other people experienced as intensively the ever-enduring, the permanence within this eternal change. The waves roll on, the river remains the same."[4]

For a long time, this unique Jewish phenomenon of nationhood without statehood—founded on a unique sense of commonness and a sense of history—lured Feuchtwanger and kept his Zionist sympathies alive, but within cautious boundaries. In 1940 Feuchtwanger admitted that he had long wondered whether Johanan's successors had not been right after all, and not the partisans of the state. But then, he declared, the war decided him. It proved to him "that no nation, no large group of men, can exist in airless space, where only ideas are housed, without endangering their bondage. A nation must have a ground on which to stand, a State."[5] In his *Josephus*, a leader of the Jewish rebellion had stated that "as sure as Juda cannot be without God, God cannot be without Juda." The war caused Feuchtwanger to return to this more materialistic conviction.

In his final years Feuchtwanger referred to the state of Israel as "the proudest event of contemporary Jewish history."[6] More than ever he believed that this "third commonwealth in the land of Israel" had its source—like so many Jewish phenomena—in the living consciousness of historical continuity. For what other reason could Jews have ignored the British offer of Uganda in place of Palestine? History pointed uncompromisingly to Zion.

In an interview shortly before his death, Feuchtwanger —a cautious sympathizer with East Germany, which has glorified his name—expressed the wish that they—the Israelis—"were a bit more neutral."[7] But he added that he was hopeful Israel could survive whatever would happen.

In these closing months of his life, Feuchtwanger predicted that Israel would become a central point for Jews
and Jewish culture throughout the world. At the same
time, he remained certain that most Jews would continue
to live elsewhere. He restated the hope of Johanan ben
Zakkai that a Jewish center of learning—now more specifically the Hebrew University of Jerusalem—would fulfill its mission of becoming a spiritual focal point for Jews.

To gauge by the Nazis' hatred of him, Feuchtwanger
would appear in the main a political writer. But as Feuchtwanger asserted in *Devil in France,* this was far from the
truth. After living through the German Revolution and
Counterrevolution, he had made up his mind "to look at
the world as a spectator." Long after writing such tenden-
tious books as *Success,* he denied the allegation of being a
political writer. "The fact is," he wrote, "that I, of all men,
am not at all interested in politics. I am not a man of action. The pushing, the scrambling, the hustle and bustle
apart from which politics is inconceivable, utterly disgust
me. My delight is contemplation and delineation."[8]
Feuchtwanger did, of course, abstain from active political warfare. But his contemplation and delineation were
mostly directed at socio-political issues. He never concealed his generally leftist sympathies, and while he seldom
participated in a leftist cause or endorsed a party, he was
less hesitant to actively oppose the right, both before and
after Hitler's seizure of power; but on the whole Feuchtwanger sought to eschew excessive attachments which
would silence the individualist's voice within him.
He was in the habit of painting himself in at least one
character in every novel. Perhaps the best full-length self-
portrait is his characterization of Jacques Tüverlin, the

Swiss novelist of *Success*. After lengthy debates with Kaspar Pröckle, the Communist engineer—most critics believe Pröckle to have been a benevolently satirical portrait of the youthful Bert Brecht—Tüverlin writes himself notes of political independence, such as ". . . Jacques Tüverlin. Don't ever forget that you are not in need of support, and so you have no need to be class-conscious. Don't ever forget that your mission in life is to express yourself, and yourself only. Yours very respectfully, your most candid friend, Jacques Tüverlin."[9]

This note of Tüverlin's has bothered Feuchtwanger's Marxist admirers—East Germany awarded him her highest literary prize in 1953—who have unsuccessfully attempted to place Feuchtwanger squarely in their camp. They have sought to counteract it by "proving" that a more mature Feuchtwanger had moved from this overbearing individualism and independence to a more modest position of human kinship and collectivism. They have seen him abandon contemplation in favor of activism.[10] Actually, Feuchtwanger kept hovering most of his life between Gandhi and Lenin with neither one ever wholly able to bring him into his orbit.

Feuchtwanger's political sympathies may be gleaned both from his historical and contemporary fiction. In his novels of the past Feuchtwanger was forever searching for meaning for the present; in a real sense he tried to locate the nowness of history. The character and doings of Josephus did not alone intrigue him, but the relevance of his positions to the present: the issues of nationalism versus cosmopolitanism, the problem of being caught between cultures, the perennial presence of anti-Semitism. Jew Süss was not intended exclusively to retell the life of a ruthless, power-hungry eighteenth-century usurer, but to explain the growing power of money in the modern world, the power it brought to its possessors and clever manipulators, the hatred enveloping a Jew in power. (Some of the problems facing Süss bore more than a casual resemblance to those of the then recently assassinated Walther Rathenau.) Similarly his Rousseau novel deals as much with the modern intellectual's dilemma of contemplation vs. action, or the problems attendant upon twentieth-century revolutions, as with the quizzical figure of Jean-Jacques. It should be stated in passing that East German critics were dismayed by Feuchtwanger's greater closeness to the moderate Voltaire than to the radical, activist Rousseau.

In his contemporary novels, Feuchtwanger's socio-political inclinations come more incisively to the fore. They stamp him as a man of the moderate Left. In *Success,* based on Hitler's abortive 1923 Putsch, the author castigated the sacrifice of Bavarian justice to enable traditionalists to sustain the success of their person, class, institutions and parties. It is their uneasy yet conspiratory union which drives beer-drinking Bavarians to join or follow the absurd figure of Kutzner, the Führer. In *Simone,* the tale of a modern French Joan of Arc, distressed by the German conquest, Feuchtwanger again indicts the greed and treachery of the middle-class.

Even if involvement had not been his inclination, abstinence became academic with the advent of Nazism. Forced to flee from Germany, to make a new life in exile in France, to flee again after prolonged incarceration and humiliation to find a new exile, made political disinterest impossible. It no longer even permitted his concerns to remain, as they had often been, on the theoretical and contemplative level.

Where then did Feuchtwanger stand in the postwar years? He stood, where he had basically always stood, on

Social-Democratic ground, in the current Western sense of that term. To be sure, he was with Marxists in his dislike of a money-grabbing, hypocritical selfseeking bourgeoisie; he advocated alongside them greater social justice, a better deal for the beleaguered everywhere, and was often impatient about achieving these; his report in 1937 on his Moscow visit was, in the main, favorable, in spite of numerous criticisms.[11] This positive attitude appears to have been transferred to East Germany. His approbation of the latter was a least partly occasioned by West Germany's failures to purify itself, on the governmental level, of former Nazis, and his fear that present bourgeois contentment had produced apathy to past guilt. Nor was he overly optimistic regarding the "democratic" German future.

But if Feuchtwanger wanted Eastern emphasis on economic and social equity, he did not want them without Western political and intellectual freedom. Feuchtwanger never did forget Tüverlin's memo to himself, that he did not need class consciousness but only express himself and to do this freely. Moreover, the author was too much a lover of the expressive and the beautiful; he treasured his untrammeled freedom; he was too skeptical of simplicist solutions such as the Marxist; he was too humanistic to accept an unqualified materialism or to want his socioeconomic gains without the protection of individual rights. But he was visibly frightened in the 1950's by the witch-hunts in America and in the ignorant or self-seeking partisans of McCarthy he must have seen some of the same creatures who had catapulted Kutzner to power in *Success*.

Feuchtwanger should be placed in the camp of social democracy in which German Jewry—and perhaps Jewries elsewhere—had been lodged virtually since their emancipation. Essentially, social democracy is the secular God of modern Jewish intellectuals—the ethical credo into which many of the ancient Mitzwoth have been transferred. His stance of distance and abstinence notwithstanding, the evidence would net Feuchtwanger the label of a pious secular Jew—i.e. a man seeking to improve the physical lot of man without depriving him of any of his spiritual and personality needs.

Throughout his fiction Feuchtwanger demonstrated a consistent respect for the Jewish religious tradition. His religious Jews are honorable human beings and his allusions to Jewish holidays and practices, beliefs and commandments, are filled with awe and reverence. His respect for the values and courage of Eastern Jews found frequent expression placing him, in this regard, beside Döblin and Arnold Zweig. Yet Feuchtwanger himself, the product of an observant home, fell increasingly into the orbit of Western secularism. Unlike so many other German Jewish intellectuals, he made the transition without ever developing any disrespect for the inherited tradition.

Feuchtwanger was learned in Jewish religion, history and lore, and was apt to remark often that the Bible remained one of his favorite books. One can only wish that *Jephta and His Daughters,* based on solid biblical scholarship, had been written earlier and with the full force of his powers. His intensive study of Kabbala and reverence for its teachings is mirrored in the portrait of Rabbi Gamliel whose love of God ultimately flows from him into Jew Süss, the power-drunk financier. Feuchtwanger had a reasonable command of Hebrew and delighted in its revival in Israel. He frequently delighted in employing a biblical passage or Talmudic saying. The range of his historic fiction amply attests to his vast erudition in Jewish history.

If Feuchtwanger's secular Gods were social justice with dignity, wherein lies any residue of a Jewish component? Are not these also the Gods of countless non-Jews, a Romain Rolland, for example—as well as thousands of decent lesser lights? Many rightly contend that the secular transformation of Christian beliefs will somehow be different from those of Jewish origins. Whether Judaism itself is the cause of difference, or the teachings by Jewish parents (with Judaic influences no longer on the conscious level), or associations with other Jews, cannot be determined. An ethical Jew and an ethical Christian, neither one observing the demands upon him of his religion, will have had indefinable differences and emphases in the ethic they share. So it is with Feuchtwanger and numerous others. Their secular emphases are in some manner distinctive from the same beliefs held by people of other origins—no better, no worse, not radically different, but different nonetheless.

Feuchtwanger's Jewish positions are characterized by a deceptive simplicity. Acutely conscious of Jewish insecurity, he has never despaired of life in the Diaspora. Yet he supported from the first, though without genuine dedication, the Zionist cause. The ancient dream of a Jewish nation united by common spiritual values fascinated him more than an ordinary nation with the physical base of the state. Nazism and the war convinced him that this physical base needed to be added, however noble the ancient vision. In his politics, Feuchtwanger veered sharply to the left, but without the loss of those political freedoms on which the bulk of Jews have insisted, as they housed themselves in social democracy. An exciting interpreter of the Jewish past, Feuchtwanger maintained a clear, but selective loyalty to the Judaic tradition. In a broad sense, he preferred to see the ancient God transformed into more effectual modern divinities. With other modern Jewish intellectuals, Feuchtwanger was willing to accept the complexities inherent in this transformation. Like most others, he met with only fragmented success.

7

Edmond Fleg: Messianic Judaism

MORE THAN MOST consciously Jewish writers, Edmond Fleg
has felt the lure of Western culture. At the same time he
has experienced the rich emotional and esthetic power of
Catholicism. On all issues pertaining to Judaism, Fleg's
voice has been one of moderation. It has always been a
gentle voice which only rarely reached the point of anger.

In the manner of the poet, Fleg personalizes all Jewish
problems. He will not argue in the abstract the duality
of Jew and Frenchman. It is the experience and the attitude of Edmond Fleg which concerns him. Because of this
personal note, it is relatively easy to trace through his
prose and poetry the reaching for a mature philosophy.

His most cogent comments on Jewish problems are to
be found in the autobiographical *Why I Am A Jew,* the
partly autobiographical and highly revealing novel *L'Enfant Prophète* (The Prophet-Child) and the historical play
Le Juif du Pape (The Pope's Jew) . Fleg's work is tainted by
unevenness, reaching peaks in *L'Enfant Prophète* and *Le*

Juif du Pape and descending to occasionally sophomoric efforts in his biblical lives of *Salomon* and *Moses*.

This most Jewish of French poets is a Jewish apologist who yet grasps the grandeurs and beauties of Christianity. With the exception of his adolescent years, when his faith faltered, Fleg has been a God-seeker all his life: an interpreter of divine will and ways. In Judaism Fleg has recognized the chief and best marked road to God, but he can see in Christianity a valid, though less clearly conceived, alternate route. Like Alfred Döblin, his German-Jewish contemporary, Fleg has been powerfully attracted —and repelled—by the compassionate figure Jesus. If we are to believe him, there was a time in his youth when he was on the verge of embracing this figure. But where Döblin in his advanced years finally succumbed to the lure of the personal God, Fleg in his later years increasingly turned away from him. But even during his most Jesus-conscious period, parts of the dogma surrounding the Galilean preacher repelled him. One of Fleg's characters steps in front of the Host, asking innocently, "Are you really in there, little Jesus? Tell me, please just whisper it to me. . . ." This mock naïvete was superseded in later years by greater acrimony as anti-Semitism decimated European Jewry. Reflecting then on the symbol of the Cross, he could not help asking, "How many hours did you suffer? And Israel, how many centuries?"[2]

Edmond Fleg was born in 1874 in Geneva. His father was a devout Jew, his mother "the joyous priestess of her home." His whole childhood impressed him as a recollection of observances of do's and dont's, with every daily act sanctified in the prescribed manner. His was an observant, almost pious home. Curiously, it was these very observances, this very piety, that induced the first reactions of doubt and negation. Why should the peace of the Sabbath be violated for the sake of business, for those "practical and necessary reasons" of which his parents so often spoke? Fleg was not satisfied: "Thus, like all children of all time, I began despite myself to scrutinize my parents, and drawing conclusions from their inconsistencies I very slowly began to break their idols."[3] Soon the young Fleg applied the same critical spirit to his religious teachers and found them wanting. Fleg is as merciless and slashing in his appraisal of Jewish teaching and officiating personnel in Geneva and Paris as was Max Brod in Prague. Jewish values were poorly presented; the Hebrew language, under their teaching, appeared without structure and was curiously untranslatable. The methodology was aimed at discouraging, if not silencing, the inquisitive mind. Even as a child Fleg was dismayed by the intellectual shallowness of his religious instructors as contrasted with the splendid, stimulating presentations of comparable courses at the lycée in language, literature and philosophy. The cynicism of one particular rabbi whom yet he admired for his gentle humanity completed the cycle of disillusionment.[4]

The combination of his parents' pragmatic deviations and ritualistic, rigid, unintelligent teachers frustrated Fleg's early quest for God through Jewish institutions and their servants. This frustration predisposed him unkindly to all his Jewish surroundings. These impressed him as musty, creaky and downright unwholesome. He was especially disquieted by any comparisons he drew with the free atmosphere of French-Genevan life.

Fleg makes these caustic disclosures in *Why I Am a Jew*, a book addressed to his yet unborn grandchild.[5] In this same fascinating education of a serious Jew, he describes his rather revealing introduction to the life of a Christian family:

> Our Ghetto was not shut in by chains, but none the less it was a Ghetto. I had come out of it for the first time. I looked upon free air and free sky, and my spirit liberated itself not only from the rites of the Jewish family but from the family itself.[6]

It led him to a study of the life of Christ, and Fleg experienced for his passion an ever mounting sympathy. His thoughts of the distant and more unknowable God which he had privately nourished in the privacy of his bed, after saying his nightly prayers, were now largely transferred to his more knowable son on the Cross. As his enthusiasm spread, his love for his own religion—and even its adherents —declined markedly. Fleg actually recalls that he indulged in the habit of dubbing his own co-religionists *sales Juifs* or "dirty Jews." It is interesting and surely significant that even in a Jewish child, love for Jesus involved in some way a corresponding dislike for his "killers" and their descendants. But the God-starved soul of the young Fleg was also losing its God:

> . . . this God of my prayers, the only gift and the most precious which was left to me of Israel, this God whom I already so coldly called the Good but who so vitally dwelt within me that I still addressed myself to him as to a living person, even this God was to forsake me.[7]

In *L'Enfant-Prophète* Fleg expounded further on the inner struggle of that time. His very description of the book is revealing. It is "the history of a temptation, of a great burst of love achieved by doubt, repentance and frustration . . . [It is] the inner crisis of a young Jew tempted

by the earnest face of France and the mystery of the Cross."
Fleg's hero is a Jewish youngster, Claude Lévy, from a fully
assimilated home, who one day overhears a passing priest
tell the family maid that the boy is truly a "little Jesus."
To this the maid replied, "But no, M. le curé, he is a little
Jew."[8] The discovery of being different, of being special,
has often been interpreted in fiction, but seldom with
greater power than in these pages. For young Claude is
ostensibly shaken by the mysterious revelation. What is a
Jew? He commissions his Christian girl friend to find out
what she can. She reports back first of all that it is nothing
very good and then submits that the Jews were the ones
who had slain the Savior. The Jewish child is distressed and
laden with guilt, especially after the girl tells him just
how beautiful this little Jesus—whom yet he resembles—
really had been. Here in opposition to his own Jewishly
rooted childhood, Fleg analyzes the plight of a youngster
without roots or anchor, left to the fluctuations of chance,
in discovering his identity.

A Claude Lévy, Fleg knew, was representative of a large
segment of Western Jewry which felt itself lost in a seemingly alien world. From his parents Claude received no
guidance at all. They had abandoned all faith and, truly
Voltairian, mocked their son's search for a God. The father was the very epitome of the emancipated, assimilated
Jew: a roughly hewn delineation, a sardonic caricature.
This Cartesian, Voltairian rationalist was more concerned
with his son's use of *juif* instead of *israélite* than he was
with any other facet of the boy's identity. The father expressed his amusement that the son should have qualms or
doubts about marrying a non-Jewish girl. "There are only
men," he informed his son—who had already learned otherwise—"not Jews or Christians."[9] Having secured no help at

home, succumbing ever more to the charms of the pious girl next door, Claude finally resolved to confess himself and his yearnings to a priest. But the latter gave him an answer at once strange and unexpected. "Just be a Jew, be a good Jew!"[10] Claude perceived a dim glimmer of hope for solving the problem of existence. He began to study his own faith and discovered what it could communicate to him. He would never fully forsake the Jesus he loved, but he became subservient to the demands of his Jewishness —a faith he now adopted, but in more enlightened fashion than the Jews he saw about him.

L'Enfant Prophète, which poetically illuminates some of the inner conflicts of Fleg's youth, was written long after Fleg had given himself wholly to Judaism. His conversion —or reconversion—was more a consequence of the shocks and tremors of the Dreyfus Case than the result of inner evolution. Yet his post-adolescent development toward a clear concept of Jewishness followed a course which was neither straight nor simple.

As a student of the famous and intellectually exclusive Ecole Normale Supérieure, Fleg devoted himself in the main to philosophic pursuits, none of which initially propelled him toward the ancestral faith. This was accomplished instead by his friendship for a young man (whom he oddly calls the *logicien* [logician] because of his power for cerebration and rational thought). This friendship coincided in time with the anti-Semitic outbursts emanating from the Dreyfus controversy. As the once Dreyfusard logician sided increasingly with the anti-Dreyfus factions to assert his Frenchness, Fleg sensed a reaction which demanded Jewish identification: "Why then was my irritation against anti-Semitism increasing day by day? What had I in common with those who were being attacked? What

was it to me whether these attacks were justified or not?"[11]
His friend's ever more vocal charges that there was undue
Jewish influence in French life and a Jewish conspiracy
to prove Dreyfus innocent finally elicited a strong response. He bitterly resented the attacks and vehemently
sympathized with those attacked. Every new day strengthened the realization that the fate of Dreyfus was inextric-
ably linked with his own as well as that of the whole Jewish world. He recognized, in the same setting as Herzl—
at the same time and largely for the same reasons—the
light of Zion on the distant horizon. As his Jewishness became more clearly defined and as he aligned himself with
the still vague Zionist ideal, Fleg became aware of the
need to stake his new identity in relation to the old. There
was no conflict, he concluded: ". . . I felt that I was a Jew,
essentially a Jew, but I also felt myself French, a Frenchman of Geneva, but French."[12] Fleg was pleased with this
happy fusion, especially as he compared his evolution with
that of the logician. The latter, reasoning outside the Jewish faith, had opposed humanity to his race; he, Fleg, as a
Jew, was to merge his with humanity. The ideals of France,
he felt, required no sacrifice as great as total assimilation.

Jew-Frenchman-Humanity! This trinity was to dom-
inate the remainder of Fleg's long life, and without apparent conflict. Political loyalty he would give entirely and
unstintingly to France. His cultural allegiance would be
extended to France and Israel alike. But he would let
others write about French culture and about humanity;
there were enough competent poets and critics to do ample
justice to this task. Fleg would devote himself to writing
about things Jewish and relate these to French culture and
humanity. Fleg apparently sensed no dichotomy between
these various goals which were also broad enough to satisfy

. . . because Israel's promise is a universal promise.

. . . because for Israel the world is not finished; men will complete it.

. . . because for Israel Man is not yet created; men are creating him.

. . . because Israel places Man and his Unity above nations and above Israel itself.

. . . because above Man, image of the Divine Unity, Israel places the Unity which is divine.[13]

All twelve of Fleg's reasons—and these nine in particular —reflect the poet's awareness of the unique history of the Jews, of those qualities especially which have set it apart from Catholicism. Fleg's *Leitsätze* are interesting even in their stylistic formation. They contrast what is with what will be, what has been bad with what can be good, what has been despair with what would be hope. From the statement of past meaning Fleg invariably proceeds to the potential of the Jewish message. The first half of each statement reports a negative past to be replaced by a positive future. Even when despair is at its greatest, the Jew hopes; Jewish thought is the oldest, but with its capacity for self-renewal, perennially the newest. Equally pronounced is the humanistic element in Fleg's Judaism. The Jewish promise is the universal promise; for Jews the world is not completed by supernatural forces—men complete it; Man is not created—Man creates Man. Yet this Man-centered world in which Israel believes—in contradistinction to Christian otherworldliness—derives its unity from the supreme unifying force which is God. Israel, Fleg suggests, has achieved a synthesis of this-worldliness with the traditional Jewish idea that God is One and His Name One.

Fleg's twelve avowals point to a thoughtful pride in his Jewishness. Its strength and conviction derive primarily from within. If there had been no Christian world and no millennia of persecution, Fleg would have found the Jewish tradition equally pregnant with meaning. He viewed it as offering Man, individually and collectively, a body of precepts for happy, ethical and therefore satisfying living.

The poet's inner voice and serenity helped him weather the crises of the forties. His optimism remained essentially intact. His faith in God sustained his faith in Man and in himself. Faith was indeed needed. For the war deprived him of his only sons, in whom, in typically Jewish-Messianic fashion, he had envisioned all future hope. It deprived him also of his closest friends and collaborators, and even as he suffered this anguish and witnessed the decimation of European Jewry, his inner resources proved sufficient to produce the post-war *We Who Hope*. It was this book—sad yet hopeful, mournful and gentle—which prompted one critic to comment that personal disaster of the greatest magnitude had been unable to rob Fleg of his basic goodness.

It was probably this same ethical-humanitarian Judaism which prompted him to resume his dialogue with the Christian world. Together with Christian friends he was instrumental in founding a society known as *Amitié Chrétienne-Juive* (Christian-Jewish Friendship). This society, Fleg insisted, should not be built on false, idealistic principles: a vague, misleading do-goodism. For his part, Fleg was willing to fit the warm Galilean teacher into the Jewish tradition. Christ's teachings, it seemed to Fleg, could form a bridge between the two faiths, stemming as they did from Jewish values and lore. In his *Jesus as Told by the Wandering Jew,* Fleg had already reminded Christians of the Savior's declaration that he had come not to destroy the Law, but to fulfill it. But if Fleg was willing to see in

Christ an inspired Jewish teacher through whom, in this limited sense, greater spiritual unity could be achieved, he was adamant about rejecting the theology concerning Christ that had developed within the bosom of the Church.

This quest for greater mutual understanding has marked much of Fleg's literary output. Even in *La Maison du Bon Dieu* ("God's House"), an early drama, Fleg had made a God-centered appeal for men of different faiths to respect one another, despite divisive dogmas. But this youthful optimism was to give way in later years to a greater awareness of the obstacles to such a goal. In a later play, *The Pope's Jew,* this awareness was sharply delineated though hope was not absent. Based on the known meetings between Pope Clement VII and Salomon Molcho, Reubeni's lieutenant, the play cast on the stage two men of good will, each seeking to eradicate hatred, suspicion and prejudice from his respective group:

> The men of Moses and Jesus together
> . . . .
> . . . .
> The Just according to the heart of God.[14]

The entire play was predicated on the notion of unity deriving from the one God and the need for Man's salvation through peace and understanding. But both Clement, the Pope, and Molcho, the ghetto leader, are vanquished men, their efforts foredoomed to failure. The eternal hope of the defeated is voiced through Molcho's mouth:

> One must go forth, be it into solitude,
> And, when one has fallen, rise again
> One must not weary of weariness;
> Whatever the road, at its end there is light;

Let us march toward this day which the shadow an-
nounces—
A future day which the present one remembers;
Every hour of the night prophesies it;
For the blackest of nights is a dawn which comes.[15]

Written long before the Nazi holocaust, these lines yet
presaged Fleg's own inner feelings during the hours of
despair. It was this hope, against a backdrop of realistic
despair, which afforded a chance for physical and spiritual
survival. Fleg, too, was a man of good will, whose efforts
were seemingly condemned, whose every recent step had
been stalked by defeat and failure, who could only pray for
the dawn to follow the night.

Hope for a better day, for an improved human species,
a more balanced society had remained intact and perhaps
been the bulwark of psychological defense. But the Nazi
era had brought another dimension to Fleg's Jewishness:
an intense loyalty to the martyred men of his faith. It
provoked a much greater aggressiveness in the face of
criticism and an almost painful sensitivity to attack. He
now demonstrated a determined refusal to kowtow to
the majority. Thus, Fleg vehemently rejected a Francis-
can's allegation that Judaism was an inflexible, unre-
newable religion. In example after example of splendid
scholarship the now octogenarian delineated the growth
and adaptability of Jewish thought. Although his language
had lost much of its moderation and temperance, his
thoughts were still those of the conciliatory man, the man
of good will.

On the Zionist issue, Fleg's feelings were ambivalent.
To be sure, he regarded himself as a Zionist and had been

a hard worker for the Jewish state. Nevertheless, he sensed
a greater conflict in the duad Frenchman-Israeli than in
the triad Frenchman-Jew-World Citizen. When Fleg finally
visited Palestine in 1931, it was ostensibly to collect material for his life of Christ and not to learn about the
rebirth of the Jewish state. Fleg was evidently aware of
the awkwardness of his attitude, for in his introduction
to *Land of Promise* (1934), he had his yet unborn grand-
son chide him for not having undertaken the visit sooner.
The late Ludwig Lewisohn was probably right in stating
that it was Fleg's love of French culture which adduced
the Zionist dilemma.[16] It precluded at once a firm inner
commitment and the actual physical step of setting foot
on Israeli land. Fleg's deep cultural roots in France were
suggested by his intense, almost absurd, joy in meeting in
Palestine a Dominican monk who spoke French. "What an
air of home we had been breathing," Fleg commented
ecstatically, "far from gesticulations, and from Jewish accents! Never had I felt myself more completely different
from a monk; but what French this monk spoke and how
close he seemed to us, this Frenchman!"[17] While Jerusalem
evoked in him far more than verses by Racine, to recall
Emmanuel Berl's confession, it could, however, never make
him forget these. Fleg remained very French in Palestine,
even as he was very Jewish—perhaps not Palestinian or
Israeli—in Paris.

His inner conflicts abounded during his initial journey.
He would have wished to be like the young, vigorous activists before him, the Jewish laborers, the enthusiastic,
virile idealists, but he could not be like them. With this
recognition there came guilt. Why wasn't he doing something? Why wasn't he participating? "But I, alas, what am
I doing amongst them? . . . I remain inert while I watch

them at their work. And the tower rises toward the heavens without my help!"[18] Fleg experienced an increasing reverence for the noble and selfless building, the perennial optimism of the people, their utter disregard and contempt for crisis. Born and bred in the civilized setting of Western Europe—with its rich sophistication, its cynical attitudes born of centuries of secular experience—Fleg could not partake of the innocence and hopefulness of the builders around him. He did not have enough in common with the new Jew emerging on Palestinian soil. This sense of difference was painfully brought home to him through the presence of Marc Chagall, who visited Palestine with him. The latter could integrate more readily into the new surroundings and eschew the bitter feeling of strangeness. Unlike the great artist, Fleg could only think of himself as a Frenchman "wishing to be conscious of his *Jewish background* [italics his], desiring to choose Judaism as a literary theme, to have some small part in what there is in the world halfway Jewish!"[19] But as he reflected upon this Jewishness, considered rich in France, but inadequate and possibly unsuitable for the new Jewish land, he consoled himself with his status as Jew in the Diaspora. Anticipating the conflicts in Israeli-Diaspora relations of later times, Fleg wrote in self-consolation:

> Those half-Jews who are scattered throughout the world, are they less interesting than these so-called *one hundred percent* Jews who live here? Why? Are they less of men? Have they not, as these have, their cares, and their dramas? If it takes courage to carry earth to the rocks, to make a deserted land verdant again after two thousand years, is courage not also needed to endure under persecution, because of fidelity to one's ancestors and to their God? If it require nobility to be oneself among one's own, is it not equally noble to remain oneself in the midst of others.[20]

Full adherence to Zionism was impossible for yet other reasons. He could not be loyal to a Jewish state. He would render political allegiance only to France, the country which had harbored him. To France also belonged his labor and devotion. And Fleg had one final doubt, Zionist sympathizer and worker though he was. By being a nation like others, would Israel really become a blessing to all the families of the earth? Was there not some merit in remaining a non-national people which by virtue of its unique example could offer hope of unifying others? Fleg, the French anti-nationalist, was not without reservations concerning a Jewish brand of nationalism. But despite these fears and the recognition that for the Parisian poet Israel could only be an inspiration from the distance, his visit was a success. Fleg continued his work in behalf of the promised land.

After two decades, and after the loss of six million European Jews, Fleg returned to the now State of Israel. The "Land of Promise" had now assumed a new significance. In *The Land Where God Lives* he wrote that all must now lead to the realization of the final promise. All that had happened in Israel and all that was happening was but a portent of Messianic days. The establishment of the state appeared to the aging Fleg a partial realization of Messianic promise. He was also convinced despite the recent War of Liberation that Jewish nationalism was of an ethical species quite different from that which had plunged Western Europe into repeated wars.

Thus, in the twilight of his life the national Jew in Fleg was finally to complement the ethical and spiritual Jew. The issue of emigration had become academic. As it receded more firmly into an unimportant past, a more determined and aggressive Jewish national stance, with

8

Josué Jehouda: Integral Judaism

PERHAPS MORE THAN any other European Jewish writer, Josué Jehouda epitomized the authentic and integral Jew. Where for other writers the Jewish topic is but one, for Jehouda there existed no other. Even in his novels Judaism took precedence over all else, his characters being thinly veiled abstractions. Jehouda's works revealed an organic concept of the Jewish mission, the Jewish state, the solution to long-standing problems. The doctrine which he preached tirelessly for half a century he has labeled, perhaps unhappily, the "doctrine of monotheism." Unhappily because Jehouda's use of "monotheism" embraces far wider scope than the term usually implies and also because its meaning is often stated with greater force than clarity. Yet this Swiss-French Buber, as he has sometimes been called, belonged in the front ranks of contemporary Jewish theorists. His considerable output was awarded the Leven Prize for Literature, a recognition limited to the Jewish field, and in Jehouda's case long overdue.

If full recognition has been late in coming—and only

now are English language translations beginning to appear—it is because Jehouda was more an interpreter of the old than an innovator. But to his reinterpretations he brought all the fire and warmth that so much of Jewish writing has lacked. In his condemnations and praise, his admonitions and exhortations, he displayed the fearless strength of his convictions, many of which have run headlong against the moral and social forces of our times as well as deeply entrenched Jewish mass opinion. He was an independent and suffered some of the anguish of a lonely and embattled man.

Josué Jehouda was born in 1892 in a town near Kiev in Russia, the son of a Hasidic father to whose influence the son was later to pay glowing tribute. It was from him that the young Jehouda apparently derived that sense of the divine and of spirituality which was at odds with the excessive ritualistic and legalistic concerns of the time. The warmth of his home and the meaning of the customs observed were to remain with Jehouda throughout his life. In fact, his finest pages are aglow with descriptions of Jewish home life and vibrant accounts of festival moods. On the whole, Jehouda was reticent about other phases of his Russian childhood. Like a hero of his *Royaume de Justice* ("Kingdom of Justice") , he emigrated to Western Europe, still a young man. He pursued his studies in the arts and letters first in Zurich, then in Geneva—a city in which he has dwelt ever since. A dedicated Zionist virtually since adolescence, he was preparing in 1914 to emigrate to Palestine when the First World War required his services in the Swiss Army. This did not prevent him, however, from assuming the secretaryship of the political committee *Pro Causa Judaica,* which was instrumental in arranging the transfer of the Zionist executive from Berlin to The Hague and contributed to the realization of the Balfour Declaration. When, at the end of the year, a serious illness struck him down, he was compelled to withdraw from Zionist political activity. After that time he devoted himself entirely to his writings.

Jehouda's long-postponed trip to Palestine finally materialized, and in 1924 he published *La Terre Promise* ("The Promised Land"). Between 1923 and 1932 he produced a series of novels under the collective title *La Tragédie d'Israël* ("Israel's Tragedy"). Much of his literary effort from 1932 to 1939 and again from 1945 to 1958 went into the publishing, under his direction, of the *Revue Juive de Genève*. The hundred-odd issues of this periodical fought the growing German racism with a firm and dignified spirituality. Most of Jehouda's postwar volumes, which constitute his more important work, have been published under the auspices of the Center for the Study of Monotheism. The Center was founded in 1952 by Jehouda's friends, including among them the distinguished Parisian psychiatrist Henri Baruk.

The more important titles in the series are: *Les Cinq Etapes du Judaïsme Emancipé* ("The Five Stages of Jewish Emancipation") ;[1] *La Vocation d'Israël* ("Israel's Calling"), a major volume interpreting the perennial existence of the Jews; *Le Monothéisme, Doctrine de l'Unité* ("Monotheism, Doctrine of Unity") which examines the doctrine in the light of modern knowledge; *La Leçon de l'histoire* ("The Lesson of History"), an appraisal of the providential conception of history; *L'Antisémitisme, Miroir du monde* ("Anti-Semitism: Mirror of the World"), an analysis in spiritual terms of the disease of anti-Semitism. It is for his entire work officially, but in the main for these efforts, that Jehouda was awarded the Prize of the Leven Foundation. *Le Marxisme, Face au Monothéisme et au Christianisme* ("Marxism Against Monotheism and Christianity"), one of his last published works, studied the crisis of our times.

All Jehouda's ideas on Jewish issues stem from his doctrine of Monotheism. But what is Monotheism?

At best a descriptive definition may be attempted. According to an official statement of the Center for the Study of Monotheism, which quotes from Jehouda, it is

> not solely a religion in the current sense of the word. It constitutes the common basis of Judaism, Christianity and Mohammedism. It also comprises a precise mental discipline, derived from a knowledge of the Law of Moses and the Oral Tradition. Its conception of life rests on a mode of thought uniting all branches of human knowledge so as to raise the consciousness of believers to the height of a synthesis. Its appraisals of value are based on one and the same common denominator applicable to religion as well as to politics and sociology. Its purpose is to bring about unity between peoples by uniting knowledge and action.[2]

Thus Monotheism, in a broad sense, is a doctrine which defines and seeks to achieve spiritual unity. It purports to fuse the secular with the religious, the profane with the sacred; it aims at a synthesis of all human forces through the spiritual unification of mankind. Monotheism places Man on the road to the messianic age, to be constructed on justice and love.

Two words recur on every page Jehouda has written: *spiritual* and *unity*. The One God, symbol of unity, on which Jews, Christians and Moslems can unite, has assigned to the Jews a special function: that of spiritualizing the world. To maintain and further their own spiritual qualities, to enrich their heritage, and by example teach it to others is at once the meaning of the "Chosen People" and the particular duty and obligation of the Jew. If the Jews allow themselves to be corrupted by the materialist temptation which lurks on every side, they will lose themselves, and moral and even physical disease will strike them down. "For, above all, the Jew wants to live, live to bless God . . . to live and rejoice in God. To make divine the least daily act in order to glorify His name. To attest to His Power, is this not the very goal of life?"[3]

As with some other philosophic doctrines of this century, Jehouda's is best explained by the concrete elements of fiction. Grouped together under the heading of "Israel's Tragedy," Jehouda's novels depict those debilities in modern Jewish life that run counter to the spiritual needs of Monotheism as well as its insistence upon unity and harmony. The evils he outlines are those of materialism, uprooting, assimilation, disregard for authority, and false intellectualism. The penalty for yielding to these evils is mental and physical disease. Disease can be cured and tragedy averted when there is a return to the spiritual.

Jehouda's novels generally follow an identical pattern. Invariably the story projects a young man or woman from an observant, God-centered home. While these youngsters remain within its protective walls—or seek to perpetuate its values and practices—they are secure and well launched on the road to human and spiritual contentment. But often, when they leave its confines and are irresistibly attracted to the lures of Western culture, they succumb (usually through the influence of a lover) to the goddess of success—be she money, intellectual status or artistic fame. The early background of his heroes is such that they only *sense* they are tempted, without fully comprehending the perils involved. Intuitively they know that they should not yield, but they always do. Once the first wrong step has been taken toward the embrace of the seductive goddess, the road back to sanity is heavily obstructed. At first, Jehouda's youthful heroes enjoy their wealth, their prestige, their honors; but the enjoyment proves to be illusory. For underneath the external happiness there already spreads the cancerous ailment. The diagnosticians and healers of the disease are usually *Schnorrer*-like figures, clad in rags, devoid of earthly riches, and though they lack the attributes of Christian saintliness, are strongly endowed spiritually. It is they who effect the cure.

The temptations of materialism thus constitute the chief source of Israel's modern tragedy. They are the primary threat to that spiritualization of life which monotheism exacts. Yet care must be taken to point out that Jehouda's denunciation of the physical materialist emphasis are in no way part of a Christianized dualistic concept of Man. Spirit and matter, mind and body are one, and weaknesses in the one will inevitably adduce difficulties in the other. It is not love of comfort and pleasure that Jehouda's healers denounce; nor is it wealth in itself. Instead, it is the single-minded pursuit of the material, to the detriment of the spiritual, with which they find fault. Again and again his sane characters say to those less sane: "But don't you have enough to live on, enough on which to enjoy life and build a meaningful existence?" Preoccupation with the material precludes that respect for the Jewish spiritual heritage, that love for the one God which Jehouda regards as the Jew's primordial task.

The second source of Israel's tragedy is that of uprooting and the consequent lack of continuity. Jehouda is not alluding to that forced uprooting in the Diaspora which has come from without; he is speaking mainly of the lack of continuity from father to son. In the "good Jew" of Jehouda's novels the father lives on as a guiding force, a permanent inspiration. He lives on in the heart of the son. Conversely, his unhappy protagonists have broken with the paternal example and have markedly deviated from the ways of the father. Thus, Jehouda censures one of his characters for not having become a *Shochet* like his father and that he was instead drawn to the alien life of the city. This initial uprooting was to lead to his personal disgrace and, later, to the restlessness and discontent of his own children. In another novel, a rabbi's son becomes a physician and marries a Christian who converts to Judaism; but this satisfies neither the father nor the author. The rabbi's daughter becomes a vain, aggressive would-be pianist, fluttering about Paris in search of "contacts." In fact, the intellectual or artistic female is a frequent target of Jehouda's satire. Apparently she represents to him the extreme departure from Jewish continuity and is even more than the males the victim of her own folly. But in the modern relationship between parents and children, the author fears an invitation to chaos. "Today, under the guise of liberalism," one of his characters in *Miriam* informs us:

A father causes all differences to disappear between himself and his child. He treats the latter as an equal. And the child becomes an idol to his parents. It is the child's reasoning which dominates; it is his reasoning which supplants the authority of the father and the love of the mother. . . . Men hurt themselves and struggle convulsively, for lack of an authority capable of uniting them toward a common goal. The World will perish from this, for without [authority], anarchy establishes itself everywhere and destroys.[4]

Compare the current confusion, dislocation and uprooting Jehouda tells us about in *De Père en Fils*, with the relationship of Moische, one of his simple and sane Jews, to his father:

Leibl, his [Moische's] father, good and pious, long deceased, lived on in Moische, permanently engraved in his heart. Happy is he for whom the father remains a living example. For his entire life, Moische will always remain the same docile child of his father, Leibl, whose memory cannot be effaced. For, during prayer, he identifies himself with his father through the same attitude, the same undulation in the voice and the same swaying of the body. Thus, he is attached to the unbroken chain which links him to his ancestors. And the soul of Leibl, an obscure drayman in some forgotten village of the Ukraine, is immortalized and continued in his son, Moische, the tailor.[5]

His uprooted characters lean, of course, toward assimilation. Again, Jehouda is less concerned about the depletion of the ranks, or weakening of Jewish peoplehood; he is concerned because assimilation implies the rejection of those values which, in the life of the Jew, should be dearest to him. Even more lonely, confused and pathetic than Jehouda's heroes are the minor characters who are blind worshippers of Western culture and, concomitantly, scornful of their Jewish traditions. Again, it is not a note of national or cultural protest that Jehouda sounds, but regret at wasted lives, lived out emptily, purposelessly, without benefit of divine love and direction.

Jehouda's assimilated characters are more often than not intellectuals whose passionate attraction for Western thought, science and culture precludes respect for the monotheistic tradition. To Jehouda they are false intellectuals and he treats them with compassion rather than

contempt. True intellectuality and the monotheistic tradition complement each other; at no point need they clash.
One of his foolish intellectual women is taught the meaning of spiritual life by the Christian archaeologist she has
married. The latter is one of Jehouda's very few intellectuals who places life above science and strives for a serene
and selfless existence. Significantly it is through the English
Christian that the wife renews herself as a Jewess: "Jews
had removed me from Israel and here my John [the
Englishman] has brought me closer again, so much so that
I have begun to study under his direction the history of
my people whom he revered and whom I began to know."[6]
The true intellectual comprehends the unique strength
and proven guidelines provided by the monotheistic tradition.

In defining the tragedy of Israel in his novels as the
materialist temptation, thoughtless uprooting and the lack
of continuity, the heresy of assimilation and the shame
of false intellectualism, Jehouda has hit sharply at the
chief threats to Judaism in the post-Emancipation era. But
there is another tragedy on which he does not dwell at
length, because it is the anguish of the few, rather than
the many. Jehouda treats with warmth and sympathy his
fictional patriarchs, those venerable fathers who helplessly
watch their children veer from the prescribed course.
Whether simple tailors or distinguished rabbis, they experience sorrow and guilt over their paternal failure. They
are only dimly aware—and care less—that theirs is a battle
against overwhelming forces in contemporary civilization.
They themselves are rocks of the spirit for whom temptations do not exist or are easily conquered. They will not
excuse themselves for they view their failures as personal
rather than social. Back in the confines of the ghetto the

conflict between the generations had loomed less large. Once outside these confines, their sons had not hesitated to inhale freely and quickly the air of material success and social liberalism. Thus Jehouda at no time blinds himself to the difficulties impeding either a return to—or renewal of—his God-centered Judaism. His patriarchs symbolize the strength of the monotheistic tradition, eroded by the failures of the sons. Israel's tragedy is at once collective and personal.

At first glance Jehouda's doctrine seems stolidly conservative and even unsuitable to modern man. But deeper penetration permits a more liberal and correct view. He is far removed, indeed, from any ascetic or other-worldly notions. Again and again he reminds us that the Jewish tradition means above all the valuing of life, treasuring it for its beauties and urging that it be lived richly and to the fullest. The Jewish religion, as Jehouda writes in *De Père en Fils,* is entirely consonant with the nature of man, the demands of life, and one's physical surroundings:

> The Jewish religion, more than any other, cannot weigh on a conscience. It asks nothing that runs contrary to common sense or reason. Our religion does not ask us to believe blindly, but to study, to reason endlessly, in order to know. To understand the beauty of divine creation, that is what our religion asks of us. What optimism in the Jewish religion which makes only God divine! It does not know the cult of individuals. Our prophet Moses is a man like any other, whose tomb we do not even know.[7]

Although Jehouda denounced a mad search for comfort and pleasure, he added there was nothing inherently wrong in these qualities. It is not through abstinence from them that God can be reached—it is only that God must come before pleasures, or better yet become a part of pleasure. Even Jehouda's patriarchs are not mere Torah students, but actively preoccupied with the questions of life. The sexual relationships of his characters are neither all physical nor repressed in a mystical etherealism. On food and drink, Jehouda enjoys seeing his protagonist partake of a festive meal, and his healers are not beyond encouraging a penchant for drink in their patients. There is a humanistic defense of earthly joys. "God," Jehouda tells us repeatedly, "can only live in a joyous heart."[8]

Ritual is at best of secondary importance. In fact, Jehouda's characters frequently cry out against ritual hyprocrisy. He is fearful of stifling the spirit by absurd precepts. Though he recognizes the need for ritual, he is forever fearful that Judaism may shut itself up, as in the past, in a formalism which is deadly to both spirit and intent. He has little taste for Talmudic controversies. He admonishes against the tyranny of books and scholastic disputes—both of them toxic for spontaneous religion, which must be partly of heart. One of the reasons for the formalistic preference has been the absence of an elite to guide the people. The modern rabbi, receiving as he does a salary, has surrendered his freedom and unwittingly betrayed the people. Jehouda views with disapproval the situation of the modern synagogue and the compromises it has been compelled to make with its most holy value.

Jehouda's novels thus purport to reveal the multiple modern tragedy and failure of Israel. His fiction shows Jehouda as a modern Hasid, advocate of a meaningful, joyous religion of the heart. Through his pages there shines brightly the sense of the divine. His novels disclose a doctrine which is basically traditionalist, but which underscores in the traditions those facets which give it meaning for the present day. His thinking provides guidelines not only for the bewildered Jewries of modern times, but for confused, undirected people anywhere. In a true sense, Jehouda's fiction is genuinely, authentically Jewish, even if in terms of art it falls short of quality. But few novels of Jewish origin and treating of Jewish concerns suggest as effectively the possible roads for a return to God and pleasure in His existence.

Since a complete doctrinal examination cannot be within the purview of a single essay, suffice it to examine briefly Jehouda's attitude toward two of the most vital forces affecting twentieth-century Jewry: anti-Semitism and Zionism. Jehouda delves into both against the backdrop of monotheistic Messianism. His views are found chiefly in two works of his maturity, *L'Antisémitisme, Miroir du monde* and *Sionisme et Messianisme*.

The real function of anti-Semitism, which Jehouda regards as the Achilles' heel of Western civilization, is to oppose Israel's Messianic vocation. Anti-Semitism is the negative pole of monotheistic Messianism. Israel has remained alive in order to remain loyal to its Messianic calling. Its Convenant with the Lord commits it to a watchful position over the Messianic certitude which serves as a compass to the monotheistic people in their advance to the Messianic era.

Israel's universal monotheism, whose goal is Messianic, is different from Christian Messianism, which is over-spiritualized and fed by Greek Gnosticism. Because of these elements the Christian world is as much in crisis as the Jewish world. Christians have been wrong in directing their missionary effort toward the Jews; they would have done better to return to the original monotheistic principles of Judaism and to purify the Judaic content of Christianity of its corrosive Greek pagan elements. The results of the internal struggle within Christendom of Jewish Messianic notions and Greek-pagan ones has led to a perpetual dualism, indecision, elements of incompatability and even hatred. When this discord within Christianity erupts with particular force, when the mutually exclusive components clash, the result is war or an historical monstrosity such as the Nazi epoch. Jehouda vigorously assails the idea, propounded by well-intended Christians, that Christianity continues Judaism and is an extension of it. Far from it: by making a man divine Christianity broke the fundamental tenet of Judaism, that of the one and only God.

The struggle within Christianity has also been responsible for the Christian role in the history of anti-Semitism. Jehouda advances the thesis that even Hitler's virulent racism was merely a modern anti-Semitism grafted on—and also the result of—the old split in Christianity. Jehouda claims that the world does not really know authentic Jewish values, but only those which were passed by Christianity through the channels of the Greco-Roman world, mangled by it and then falsely attributed to the Jewish people. To be sure, the conflict between the Greek and Jewish spirit well antedates the birth of Christianity; however, the falsification of Jewish ideas occurred only with the advent of Christianity. From this confusion and mistaking of values has stemmed one of the major sources of the conflict between Israel and the world. What has developed is the anomaly whereby the Jewish tradition has come to represent the same values as its heresy. Very often, too, Judaism has been used as the easy-to-hit target when the veiled, but real, target was Christianity. In the vaunted

Jewish stubbornness which Christians have for so long castigated, Jehouda recognizes only Jewish loyalty to their history and calling. Thus, Jews have been persecuted for different and opposing reasons—but, because of the inner Judaic-Greek split of their religion, by two distinct and even contrary types of Christians: by the devout and those others who would prefer to be pagans.

It is thus the repression of monotheism and the hope this repression gives its enemies which has opened the way to anti-Semitism. Jews have been wrong—as have been other analysts of the phenomenon—in regarding anti-Semitism as merely a surface phenomenon caused by economic and social causes. They have erred in believing that education will cause prejudice and fanaticism to disappear. The latter are symptoms. An improvement in economic, social and political conditions will not touch the cause. Anti-Semitism will lose some of its power only when the millenary dialogue between the monotheistic conception and the dualistic ideologies of paganized Christianity achieves a measure of clarification on both sides. Jehouda chides the Jews for having been reluctant ever since the Emancipation to engage in a full explanatory dialogue with the Christian world. This grave omission, he asserts, has enabled anti-Semitism to spread despite the undeniable progress of human institutions.

In a broad sense, then, Jehouda looks upon anti-Semitism as at least partly a Christian problem, but also as a fatal reaction to the spiritual bankruptcy of the time. The havoc wrought by anti-Semitism exists in proportion to the spiritual abdication of the Jews themselves. Jehouda thus has hinted that anti-Semitism fulfills a mystical, supernatural function: it eliminates the weak and awakens the monotheistic consciousness in the survivors, bringing them closer to God. From the monotheistic standpoint then, anti-Semitism ceases to be a "mystery." For neither Judaism nor Christianity can move toward its Messianic goal of peace without spiritual understanding between the two monotheistic faiths.

Israel's guilt has been its failure in modern times to go beyond a *theoretical,* spineless, meaningless commitment to monotheistic Messianism. But besides Israel's guilt there has also been its glory. This glory has been in shunning the successive imperialisms—an achievement that has allowed it to remain free of compromises. Not so with Christianity. Christianity's failure has been twofold: its development with two self-exclusive currents, the providential and the imperialistic. Christianity's initial dualism has made the peoples refractory to the message of monotheism. Mutual understanding of all these weaknesses—and the resultant increase in self-knowledge—will eventually lead to the realization that Judaism, Christianity and Islam represent, under the Law of One God, different expressions of the same Messianic aspiration. International unity in the political sphere will become concrete once the Christian and Moslem peoples recognize the immense sweep of the monotheistic message. They will then be cognizant of their debt to Israel and fully comprehend its message of unity for the peoples of all origins, since all men are brothers, sons of the same One God.[9]

Monotheism likewise points the way to ending the Zionist crisis, which has become more acute since the establishment of the state of Israel. With a Messianic goal and a monotheistic basis, Zionism can harmonize its often contradictory features and bring about a workable Jewish unity. Although Jehouda has always been a Zionist in a broad sense—he believed Jews had a right to a national life and prayed for the return to Zion—he rejects the notion that Jewish unity can be achieved on the political and national level alone. There are simply too many Jews, dispersed all over the globe and belonging to too many nationalities. On the religious plane, however, unity is possible, not as a confession or observance, but as a doctrinal conception. *Sionisme et Messianisme* is largely devoted to the thesis that spiritual indecision threatens to destroy the inner peace of the Jewish people and may actually, in the long run, compromise the unity of Israel.[10]

Jehouda casts doubt on the theory that politically oriented nationalism can long sustain Zionism. Political Zionism can only respond to the external misery of Israel while at the same time intensifying the ever acute problem of dual loyalty in the Diaspora. Also, political nationalism is incapable of providing the Jews of Israel and the Diaspora with a common goal. In the struggle between the political-nationalist Zionism of Pinsker, Herzl and Nordau on the one hand, and the cultural-universalist Zionism of Salvador, Ahad-Ha-am and Buber on the other, Jehouda finds himself siding wholeheartedly with the latter. This conflict, evident since the earliest days of Zionism, has become intensified since the promulgation of the Israeli Constitution. From this conflict derives the incapacity of contemporary Zionism to define its goals after its political program of statehood had been achieved. A formula is needed which can encompass the interests and needs of both the Jews of Israel and the Diaspora. The Herzl-Ahad Ha-am controversy, continued by Weizmann and Buber, is a Jewish dualism which can best be resolved by the unifying force of monotheistic-Messianic Judaism with its ethical-universalist base. On their common Messianic doctrine the Jews of Israel and of the world can successfully unite. Jehouda is fully aware that Zionist culture, so conceived, is still in its infancy, but he envisions its steady, forward movement. After its liberation from political tutelage, Zionism is destined to direct the spiritual regeneration of Jews everywhere.

Much though Jehouda admires Jewish monotheism—and by and large the Jew's loyalty to it—he displays little charity for the weaknesses of Jews. He is ever prone to allude to them with irony and sarcasm. Jews strike him as an absurdly independent people with no one Jew ever willing to accept the authority of another; they are highly critical and their propensity for debate and disagreement is at times terrifying.[11] Endless discord and argumentation are the inevitable consequences of such critical independence. Jehouda also sees the modern Jew as basically an insecure person who possesses confidence only in the bosom of the family. The family replaces all for those persecuted from without: country, honor, politics. The distrust and envy Jews show in interpersonal relationships are consequences of their pride, not of their religion. Jehouda wonders that perhaps, despised by outsiders, Jews seek revenge by treating one another with the least possible esteem. He is keenly aware of the continued existence of Jewish self-hate. Jews, he believes, generally admire only non-Jews.

Despite this self-hate or self-depreciation, especially pronounced since Emancipation, Jewish spirit is yet deeply entrenched in the modern Jew. "A Jew is a Jew whatever he may say, whatever he may wish to be. . . ." This cultural ingrowth may well be the result of the Jew's amazing vitality, his deeply embedded love of education and learning, his earthiness and realism.

Jehouda, like others, has interpreted the Jewish psychological pattern as a largely defensive one, weaker in those Jews in whom the Jewish heritage is fully alive and functional. Adherence to the mainstream of the tradition is essential in the Diaspora Jew who wishes to live a spiritually rich and psychologically free life.

Thus, more than any European Jewish writer—including Fleg, Spire and Brod, the other "positive" Jews—Jehouda developed an organic, if not altogether original, theory of Judaism. In fact, in the eyes of some critics his doctrine was Judaism.

It was a doctrine which abhorred splits and dualisms, which saw the salvation of man in the unifying, synthesizing power of a central force: the One God of the Jews. It demanded recognition of the spiritual side of man while not divorcing it from the material and while wholly rejecting overspiritualization. But, while it insisted on the unity of spirit and matter, it was fearful of wanton materialism even more than excessive spiritualization. Monotheism is a doctrine which stands for Jewish renewal within Jewish tradition. It synthesizes diverse and even conflicting elements within religion, ethics, Zionism and the relations among the more or less monotheistic peoples. Jehouda united soul and body, the individual and the social, the political and the cultural. Only through such unity afforded by monotheistic Messianism can a cataclysmic, materialistic, self-seeking world be returned to sanity. Judaism can help achieve this. For the world of today, as for that of yesterday, it bears the most significant message of all: spiritual unity.

Jehouda left much to be desired as a writer. Writing perhaps the closest thing to an authentically Jewish novel in a spiritual and ethical sense, his lack of artistry and preoccupation with doctrine limit the effectiveness of his fictionalized demonstrations. Yet the novels deserve to be studied by more effective—and perhaps more interested—craftsmen, if for no other reason than to recognize the need for such novels. Unfortunately, his limitations as a writer —he was disturbingly repetitious—have also limited the appeal of his philosophical works. And yet there was always the essence of Judaism, positively, richly and intelligently presented.

Despite his personal dissociation from the modern Synagogue, which he mercilessly criticized, Jehouda was a God-obsessed Jew who demanded more than a theoretical commitment to His Covenant with Israel and mankind. Do we mean to be Jews—and human beings—Jehouda asked; or do we merely think we are? Quietly, without much recognition, the Geneva sage for nearly forty years called for a revitalized, meaningful Judaism from which would follow the solution of many Jewish as well as non-Jewish problems.

9

Arthur Koestler: Dejudaized Zionism

ARTHUR KOESTLER IS A BRILLIANT dealer in ideas and a masterful dialectician. Even his titles suggest the intellectual preoccupation: *The Yogi and the Commissar, The Age of Reason* and *The Age of Longing, Promise and Fulfillment.* Koestler's ideas probably range over a wider terrain than those of any other writer of our time. Few contemporaries have treated ideologies more analytically and in more original fashion. Few have lived their ideas—and their opposites—as fully and few have become so frequently their victim. Koestler's work is largely circumscribed by our time and to many seems lacking in universal components. Silone and Malraux, to whom he has been likened most often, have also lived twentieth century ideas. However, more conscious artists, they did not stop there, but delved deeply into the recesses of human personality. The divorce in Koestler of idea and personality is especially sharp and the settlement so strongly in favor of idea that even in his autobiography concepts clearly overshadow personality. Both in his general *Weltanschauung* and his

146

Jewish pronouncements, it is difficult to determine whether Koestler's is a cold heart and a hot head, or perhaps a warm heart and a cold head. In any case, head and heart seldom seem tuned in on the same wavelength.

If Arnold Zweig's intellectual peregrinations took him from a partly dejudaized Zionism to a dezionized Marxism, Koestler's far more extensive wanderings began with assimilation, turned toward a rabidly nationalist Zionism, stopped at length in various cells of the Communist party and Fascist jails, led to a renewed interest in Zionism and, seeing its promise fulfilled, completed the cycle with a return to assimilation. But the restless Koestler has sought refuge also in Oriental philosophies and found them wanting, and in European culture he has encountered too large an estate for him to find a proper place. One cannot help wondering whether his intellectual journeys will not take him, for however briefly, to the protective bosom of the Roman Church. His last reported position on the Jewish trek confronted Jews with two choices: emigrate to Israel, land of the Jews; or go with determination and without regret toward the nation whose ways and culture they share. In this instance, Koestler's choice shows him once more to be rational man, with a cold, silent heart.

Koestler was raised in an assimilated Jewish home in Budapest, Hungary. His autobiographical *Arrow in the Blue* and *The Invisible Handwriting* are coldly, even cruelly, outspoken on his relations with his parents. He appears to have been chronically annoyed with his mother and looked down upon, perhaps even despised, his father. The former's crude and unyielding prejudices and the latter's chimerical grandiose schemes precluded any genuine attachments on his part. He was riddled with feelings of inferiority that made easy and natural associations with other children of his age difficult. This social insecurity plagued him from childhood days in Hungary to early manhood on a Kibbutz. In fact, Koestler's prolonged quest for a haven in a "closed group," the desire to be one among many, the need to feel he belonged, may all be partly traced back to his emotionally deficient childhood. When, upon his return from Palestine, his bourgeois journalism finally netted him status and success—which he promptly sacrificed to Communist asceticism—his friendships became more numerous and acquired some permanence. If several ended prematurely, as Koestler benignly puts it, it was less his fault than that of the times and especially the unfortunate political or religious affiliations of his friends. Many of them died as a result of Stalinist distrust, interparty squabbles, hopeless disillusionment and political necessity. Thus Koestler learned early the power of political commitment.

Koestler was not at first successful in his relations with women. To read his account of his first marriage and of his liaisons with other women, one cannot escape the suspicion that here again he held back, incapable of giving of himself. Koestler has been aware of this need to keep emotional distance, while sensing at the same time a continuous craving for companionship. He could give of himself as a companion, but he could not return the love he received.

Yet, the turbulence that has marked his adult life is only partly the product of inner tensions. Equally if not more responsible have been his socio-political choices, his ideological battles—commitments which exiled him from country to country, propelled him from one all-demanding cause to another, stranded him in jails and camps, and kept him dangling, for three long months, under death sentence in a Spanish prison.[1] Obviously political events and associations were major directing forces in his mature life, crowding personal considerations into subliminal spheres and relegating human relationships to a secondary rank.

All these factors explicate the emotional barrenness of his novels, his inability to create characters that are more than political or Freudian symbols. They account for the failure to generate real warmth even when one suspects it is warmth he is trying to produce. Perhaps Koestler's rationalism and coldness are deceptive. For underneath both there lurks a potent romantic heart, usually kept in bounds, but frantically striving to break out. Both his Zionist and Communist involvements hint at the intensity of this sub-surface struggle.

Koestler embraced Zionism at nineteen. His background had ill prepared him for this cause. As he informs us, his initial interest in it was the result of chance. His mother had been advised that a *Unitas*, a Zionist fraternity, could keep Arthur out of the kind of trouble university students were prone to get into. At this time, he recalls, neither he nor his family had ever even heard of Zionism.[2]

Membership in *Unitas* provided the impetus for his Zionist activity. Koestler admired the camaraderie of *Unitas*. Later he regarded this *Burschenschaft* with all its duels, orgies, and outmoded customs (which his mother's friend had neglected to mention) as the healthiest of the "closed communities" to which he belonged. Being with the group he felt as if he were "emerging from a dark tunnel into a new dazzling light." At last he belonged.

Unitas confronted him with notions entirely alien to his home. Here he heard that dueling and fighting were necessary for Jews in order to discredit the myth of Jewish cowardice. It was here that anti-Semitism, previously a problem "as remote as the Spanish succession," first began to disturb him.[3] Although much of what he heard about the Jews confused him, he identified with them and accepted Zionism. The romantic idea clearly preceded a rational commitment.

But even as Koestler identified, Judaism, to use his own phrase, held little attraction for him. His own home had provided no Jewish roots and his first contact with traditionalist Jews was one of shock. Meeting people who spoke Yiddish and were steeped in Talmudic learning was a distasteful experience. For the language especially he felt total revulsion. "This jargon with its insinuating singsong that turned every factual statement into an emotional one, repelled me. . . . It was not spoken, but sung to the accompaniment of gestures. Nothing said in Yiddish seemed a flat statement to be taken at face value; everything was charged with over- and under-tones, lubricated with sentiment, shrouded in a kind of logical twilight. I disliked this language, and the mentality which it reflected, from the first time I heard it, and I have never lost my aversion for it."[4]

Similarly, Yiddish literature in translation was repugnant to him. It smelled, he wrote, of the unsanitary conditions of the ghetto, of "unventilated bedding, mental inbreeding and tortuous ways."[5] Equally unpalatable was the alleged mixture of servility and arrogance, of cunning and sentimentality, of mysticism and cupidity. When he wrote this vicious indictment, Koestler had as yet little knowledge of the Jewish past. At times he seemed close to accepting the anti-Semitic stereotype of the Jew. With later historical insight to guide him, Koestler attributed these characteristics, where they still seemed to exist, as products of conditions as they prevailed in any hermetically sealed community. He discovered many of the same supposedly Jewish traits in the groups which later enjoyed his allegiance.

Koestler's pet aversion was orthodox Judaism. The intolerance of orthodox Jews was medieval. Their narrowness in not mentioning the name of Christ in the mid-twentieth century seemed incredible. Various practices impressed him as dishonest: lighting a fire on the Sabbath was sinful, but persuading your Gentile neighbors to do so was not; selling your crockery to your neighbor for Pesach and buying it back thereafter was a "pettifogging practice" and, worse yet, a "manoeuvre of evasion." Upon later study, while not condoning the practices, Koestler at least recognized their role in ritual which alone could provide cohesion during the centuries of dispersion.[6]

Jewish learning also scandalized him. The survival of a brand of scholasticism in today's Talmudic schools was an intellectual shock. The acrobatics in logic in which it indulged appeared to aim at the same intellectual and moral evasion as the practices relating to the Sabbath and Pesach. Interpretations of Mosaic Law, specifically devised to evade the original law, struck him as a form of mental corruption.

Finally, he was dismayed by the literal acceptance by traditionalists of the concept of the Chosen Race. Jews could not on one hand protest against ethnic discrimination, and on the other maintain the superiority of their own group. Koestler, who had already fought nationalist teaching in Hungarian schools, was equally intolerant of Jewish ethnocentrism.[7]

Koestler obviously did not think of *Homo Judaicus* as an attractive specimen of mankind. In *Thieves of the Night*, a book which did more for Jews than for Koestler's reputation as a novelist, his half-Jewish protagonist reflects on the faces he sees:

> Joseph was struck by the ugliness of the faces around him as they were lit up in the intermittent, ghastly flash of the search-light. It was not the first time that he had noticed it, but tonight his revulsion against this assembly of thick, curbed noses, fleshy lips, and liquid eyes was particularly strong. At moments it seemed to him that he was surrounded by masks of archaic reptiles. . . . But it was no good denying to himself that he disliked them, and that he hated even more the streak of the overripe race in himself.[8]

Even as Joseph's political attachment to Zionism becomes more absorbing, his objectivity toward the Jews does not lessen. Again and again he ponders over Semitic intensity, the frequency of mental crackups, their inability to stand still, the girls with aggressive laughter and unmodulated voices, without traditions, manners, form or style. He comments upon their ethnic inferiority feelings and nervousness—born of exile and dispersion—of Jewish self-hate, which he ironically labels Jewish patriotism.[9]

The charge of self-hatred has often been flung at Koestler himself. The above would, at first glance, lend substance to the allegation. Examined, however, in the context of his total work, the accusation seems less justified. Koestler's reaction is a form of self-depreciation, common among Jews. Added to this is Koestler's personal tendency to depreciate himself, as evident in his autobiography: he is shy, insecure; he has no confidence; he has not succeeded with friend or foe. Others are more confident, less shy; more secure, more successful. Although his criticisms of what Jews are, believe and look like are unbalanced and exaggerated, they may be only an extension of his personal self-degradation.

Koestler seems aware that even as he fights hardest for Jews and bemoans loudly their destiny, he is displaying emotions about Jews—not affection for them. In an extremely significant conversation in *Thieves,* Reuben, a more representative Jew, accuses Joseph of emotional positivism toward the Jews: Joseph, he declares, loves the Jews only in abstractions. "You are engrossed in Judaism," Reuben explains, "but don't like the Jews. You love the idea of mankind, but not the real man. You have lived with us for six years, and still we are objects to you, not subjects."[10]

Koestler's is the involvement of the outsider looking in, wanting badly to get in, but being held back by an invisible force. The same attitude, one may suspect, was operative in his embrace of Communism. As a Communist, he also fought for the oppressed, but it is questionable whether he was anxious to shake the hand of either a worker or peasant.[11] Koestler's causes are cerebral, his loves abstract. Yet Koestler requires the guise of emotion, if only to give himself the impetus for action.

While doubt is legitimate concerning the quality of his involvement in Zionism, none is possible concerning its existence. Despite his impersonal judgment of Jews, and the absence of affection, there was enough sympathy for the Jew as underdog and a strong enough sense of justice to get him to work tirelessly for a revised status. The more he also learned about Jewish history—the physical and psychological evils of ghetto life—the greater his distress and the more fervent his Zionism.

The Jewish state was the only cure for a sickness which I could not name or define, but which seemed intimately connected with the Jews' lack of a country and a flag of their own. In the absence of these they were paying-guests in the house of strangers; and whether tolerated or beaten up, were always regarded as different; therein lay the root of the sickness. When the Jewish state was re-established, the cure would be automatic and all would be well.[12]

Perhaps in not too serious a vein, Koestler relates his strong attraction to a Jewish National Home to his own youth when he lived mostly in hotels and boarding houses. Himself a "rootless cosmopolitan" with a "polyglot culture" and physically always on the move, he can well comprehend the Jews' craving to "grow roots . . . to create and construct, to build cities in the desert and gardens out of the swamp."[13] The romantic streak becomes more evident as he pursues this theme:

Besides, to resurrect the State of Israel was something like building a George Washington Bridge across two millennia of History—a supreme feat of engineering. Connect; always connect! construct! always construct! Zion was a new version of the song which promises that we would "lift the globe from its axis."[14]

What Koestler wanted from Zionism in those pre-Hitler years was the opportunity for assimilation into humanity. Jews were to be and act like other people: they required a chance to regain the capacity for collective action, to remove from the Jewish psyche those humiliating and tortuous ways which ghetto life had nurtured. Returning to the soil would eliminate the habitual overstrungness and breed instead of the countless neurotic people, a healthy race. To eschew the past evils of persecution, torture, debasement and filth, Koestler expressed a perfect willingness to sacrifice any prospect for future Einsteins and Freuds. Through the Jews' acquisition of a homeland, he hoped to arrest the "deterioration of the hereditary substance through the survival of the nimblest, the humblest, the crookedest, into its final product, the flat-footed, shifty-eyed, eternal tramp."[15] The Jewish homeland is to do away with, once and for all, the sources of Jewish self-depreciation and thus eradicate a disease of long standing.

In support of his argument Koestler cites the difference in observed behavior patterns of Jews in Palestine who have known minority status and those others, Sabras, who have not been burdened with it. The former reflect the physical appearance and tortuous psychology of the victimized Jew; the Sabras are un-Jewish in their appearance: strong and vigorous, with a mentality which reflects the happy and secure native. In his comments on the Sabra, Koestler's admiration is bounded only by his prejudices as a Western intellectual. He misses in the Sabra, as expected, the sensitivity, creativity and culture status of his European coreligionist. Koestler is not disturbed, however, since in Jews he assigns to physical and psychological vigor absolute priority over all other virtues.

A young man's wild romanticism, followed by intellectual commitment, had originally driven him toward the shores of Palestine. It was the emptiness of the developing culture—wholesome for the young native Jews, unbearable for one steeped in European culture—which prompted his return. The harsh, demanding reality of Palestine, alien language and culture, the physical exertions and vigorous discipline of the Kibbutz, ideological hair-splitting—all tended to crush what romanticism was left. Koestler's total apartness from the Jewish tradition did not help; there was no chance to counterbalance with Jewish idealism what had been lost before uncompromising reality. While in Palestine he sensed that the absence of Judaic roots would always make him feel alien in a Hebrew language environment. Upon arrival he had renounced European citizenship, but not European thought. ". . . my mind and spirit were longing for Europe, thirsting for Europe, pining for Europe."[16] Later he was to refer to his three years in the East as the years of cultural exile and starvation of the senses.

Thus ended Koestler's initial experience with the Homeland. In 1937 he returned to Palestine as Near Eastern correspondent for a Western paper. After many years in the Communist Party he had lost all faith in political and social miracles. The Soviet Union as the land of promise had turned out the same mirage as the Promised Land had earlier. The spectre of Hitler, looming ever larger on the horizon, coupled with better self-knowledge and political disillusionment, altered considerably his concept of a Homeland. Palestine was now to be viewed as mainly a place of refuge for the Jews of Europe. The most virulent anti-Semitism was rampant; a Jewish state was needed to offer shelter and protection. A utilitarian Zionism had superseded the earlier species.

The Nazis' Final Solution added yet another dimension to Koestler's Zionism. The Nazis' plans had become an ill-concealed policy and from 1941 on Koestler devoted himself single-mindedly to the establishment of the Jewish state. From 1942 to 1948 he produced two books, numerous articles, and countless speeches, all of which plead the Zionist cause. In *Thieves in the Night* Koestler frankly endorsed the violence and terrorism of the Irgun—a position which, to use his own words, involved him in acute conflict between conviction and inclination. Although he knew this exposed him to new attacks—an ex-Communist was again allying himself with radical causes—he maintained that the situation of European Jewry admitted of no personal considerations.

As an ardent admirer and personal friend of Vladimir Jabotinsky, Koestler had no difficulty in choosing the course of Jewish militancy. Jabotinsky's advocacy of strong methods appeared more justified than ever in the light of the untold suffering of European Jewry. Terrorism alone could overcome the dishonest delaying tactics of the British and the sudden patriotism of the Arabs. But Koestler's willingness to follow Jabotinsky was predicated on distinct attitudes previously expressed by Koestler. Jabotinsky had represented the liberalizing, Western tendency in Zionism. Unlike Weizmann, who stood for the extension of Eastern Judaic thought, Jabotinsky had sought to break with this tradition. Jabotinsky had supported the Westernization of Israel, the Latinization of the Hebrew alphabet, the transformation of the Talmudic school into a streamlined Western institution of public learning. After the establishment of the State of Israel, Koestler claimed—not wholly consonant with the evidence—that Jabotinsky's general program had been vindicated by events and accepted by the dominant Zionism which had once rejected it.[17] But Koestler's own dissatisfaction with Israeli events, in the years following independence, would tend to mean that Zionism had been de-Judaized much less than Koestler—and perhaps Jabotinsky—would have wished it.

As Koestler saw it, the establishment of Israel in 1948 created an unprecedented situation in Jewish history. For the first time in two thousand years the Jew did not need to look upon himself as being in exile, unless self-imposed.

Jews everywhere were now confronted with facts which they could not honorably consider before. In a valedictory message to Jews everywhere, Koestler urged them to settle in Israel, become citizens of the new state, and thus terminate their religious and social apartness, as well as their old and cursed minority status. The alternative was simple: "to go their own way, with the nation whose life and culture they share, without reservations or split loyalties."[18] Emigrate or assimilate; become a Jew and Israeli, or a Frenchman, German or American. The time for pussyfooting, for compromises was past. Israel was an historic reality for Jews to embrace as Jews, or to reject as citizens of a Western state and adherents of a Western culture. For Koestler himself—who had been "a supporter of the Zionist movement, while his cultural allegiance belonged to Western Europe"—the course was clear. He would opt for the latter. Assimilation was no longer escape or flight, as in pre-Israel days, but the only honorable alternative to settling in Israel.

Koestler thus welcomes the establishment of Israel, despite a measure of disappointment with its policies and programs. He is pleased for humanitarian reasons. Jews now have a place of refuge. He is happy that those who regard themselves mainly as Jews now have a nation to call their own. He is equally pleased that Western Jews who feel themselves more Western than Jews now have an honorable way of detaching themselves from the Jewish tradition. Israel itself, he suspects, will become a Levantine state and a very un-Jewish country (again the Sabras). Thus, he considers it perfectly possible that Israel, the fulfillment of Jewish history, may yet in some way ironically become the end of Jewish history. The prospect does not frighten the man with the hot head and the cold heart. "To renounce the Jewish faith does not mean to jettison the perennial values of Judaic tradition. Its essential teachings have passed long ago into the mainstream of the Judeo-Christian heritage." Thus, having helped for twenty-five years to provide a state for others—a state which cannot meet his own needs—he wishes the new State good luck, but going his own way "with an occasional, friendly glance back and a helpful gesture."[19]

The story of Arthur Koestler is that of an incomplete, self-deprecating Jew who, though he leaned over backward to develop a limited facet of his Jewishness, was too deficient in others to achieve fullness in even the one. It was his distance from Judaism, his emotional positivism toward Jews which precluded any lasting or even meaningful relationship. Politically and culturally he has already obeyed his own injunction of choice. Considering his perennial search for causes, a conversion to another faith is not inconceivable. Because he believes that the best in Judaism has already found its way into Christianity, it may not prove too difficult to take this final step.

10

André Spire: Romantic Judaism

ANDRÉ SPIRE'S JEWISHNESS was eruptive, impetuous, sensitive, combative. It had in it much of the romantic. Together with the late Edmond Fleg, Spire, who died in 1966 at the age of ninety-eight, for the last half century was France's greatest Jewish poet and the talented spokesman for much of French Jewry. Because of its heavy romantic overtones, his brand of Jewishness had been assailed as puerile by some and as foolish by others. Yet, in Western Europe Spire's persistent demands for heroic action anticipated by decades the Sabra of Israel and the new activist Jewish hero of fiction. Other critics have placed him in proximity to the Catholic poets whose ranks he probably would have joined if he had been of their faith. Spire could have written, some claim, a *Génie du Judaïsme* ("The Genius of Judaism"), a Jewish counterpart of Chateaubriand's warm, sensitive, emotionalized—though neither pious nor orthodox—interpretation of Christianity. Spire was more vague and uncertain in his vision of Judaism than other writers, but far more than they he would have laid down his life for it. (Spire did, in fact, engage in one duel over an offense to his Jewishness.)

The more significant of Spire's pronouncements on Jewish questions were to be found in his prose rather than poetry. But however he expressed himself, he did so with unparalleled frankness and boldness, with blacks and whites overshadowing the few greys.

André Spire was born in Nancy on July 21, 1868, the son of a long line of prosperous Jews of Alsace-Lorraine. The Spires were without Jewish religious convictions, although they were aware of their Jewishness in an hereditary, ethnic sense which perhaps included the cultural. Young André received no Jewish education. Some childhood impressions were, however, to leave a permanent mark. The Spires owned a factory to which André often escorted his father. The boy noticed how the bright coloring, the lively manner of young teen-agers entering the factory gave way, within two years, to a frightening pallor and emotional drabness. And yet his father, André knew, was imbued with a greater spirit of justice, charity and compassion than most. His family enjoyed an exceptional reputation for kindness and humanitarian enterprise. The boy often accompanied his mother to the homes of the poor and he was deeply touched by the tender understanding which she brought to their problems. It was the system, then, which was at fault. As a result, except for a brief wartime stint the mature Spire could never get himself to manage his father's plant. In later years one sad image would recurrently come to mind whenever he met the wealthy at a party: the squalor which made this wealth possible! Spire's social thinking was to be shaped largely by these childhood recollections.[1]

The values stressed in Spire's youth were not representative of those of youngsters of upper-middle-class Jewish
background. He was a prize-winning athlete—a talent dis-
couraged by his humanistic teachers, but surprisingly encouraged by his parents. His father often took him hunt-
ing, a sport seldom practiced in Jewish families, but one
he loved well into his advanced years. André did not excel
as a student, revealing time and time again that indiscip-
line and revolt that foreshadowed the later romantic. But,
at age fifteen, he was tempted one day to write a poem,
was heartened by his teacher's response, and soon proceed-
ed to compose others. His parents, who had endorsed his
sportive pursuits, were just as eager to encourage his literary effort. But their interest waned markedly; and one day
when a satiric poem of André's was included in a volume
critical of upper class local society, his only excuse was the
truth: the poem had been published without his consent.
But this poem disrupted the smooth course of his life.
André was packed off to a cavalry regiment in which he
served, an unruly and rebellious soldier, who often found
himself in hot, if not steaming, water.

Upon his return to civilian life, his parents refused to
support his literary career, insisting on a more lucrative
and rewarding enterprise. So Spire took up law. This
brought him to Paris, where he earned his doctorate and
then applied for an appointment as *auditeur au conseil
d'état*. Unlike other Provincial Jews in the big city, Spire
was overcome neither by the conformist temptation nor
by the attractions of Parisian culture and wit. Instead he
willingly submitted to the tantalizing influence of Paul
Desjardins, a humanitarian idealist preaching a program
of moral regeneration. This program called for the moral
reform of the army, resistance to socialistic and anarchistic

movements, and the establishment of cultural centers to enable the masses to become enlightened. Spire viewed this platform as a lucid continuation and extension of the charitable and philanthropic effort of his parents. While Spire was thus occupied building adult education centers, the headlines of the Dreyfus Case were beginning to split France into two hostile camps. They also reduced to size most other concerns. Anti-Semitic articles appeared in the Drumont papers which heatedly condemned the presence in the government and state service of Jews like Spire himself. Jews, these articles asserted, were fattening themselves at the expense of French citizens. Spire took violent offense at one of these articles, challenged its author to retract or fight. In the resulting duel Spire was wounded in the forearm. Undaunted by the difficulties Spire extended his efforts to raise the level of the working class. Before long, however, he found these efforts inadequate. Increasingly he came to recognize in socialism the remedy to the worker's plight. At the turn of the century Spire's literary career began to flourish. In 1901 his first poems appeared in *Pages Libres* under the pseudonym of André Voisin. Two years later he published *La Cité Présente,* his first full volume of poetry. From then on his poetic production was fairly steady though perhaps never prolific. His first declarations on Jewish issues also date back to these opening years of the century. A significant forward step in his literary career was made when he became a close collaborator of the idealistic, forceful, Catholic poet Charles Péguy and the then pro-Semitic but later anti-Semitic Georges Sorel. Except for his years of exile in the United States during the Nazi Occupation, Spire lived continuously in the outskirts of Paris, a poet, a statesman, Jewish theorist and publicist. As a poet he was mainly a

solid Jewish milieu and a rather strong Jewish tradition, only then to have been plunged in Paris into a non-Jewish environment."[3] Spire was thus in the main concerned with the foreign relations of a people traditionally in a weak position, and sorely in need of strengthening it.

It was in the wake of Dreyfus Case, and upon reading Zangwill's *Chad Gaya*—a book which he called a revelation—that Spire first expressed himself on a Jewish theme. In his first essay Spire exposed the Jewish condition. To be a Jew meant to be regarded as different. "To be a Jew is that nothing which prevents one from being like others." The anti-Semitic virulence of the previous decade had bolstered his impression that an almost unbridgeable gulf existed between Jews and others. Even as a child a Jew must suffer more disappointments, feel more often left out, fight more frequently than other youngsters. The Jew, having encountered hostility in the small town, is forced to seek refuge in the city. Here his human craving for the companionship of others may finally lead to discovery of fellow-Jews. But Spire recognizes that the frustrations of a saddened childhood negatively affect the adult. The Jew remains *capite diminitus* no matter which country he may move to. He has been made to feel his difference; he increasingly senses it himself; besides, he knows he is not permitted to become like others. Outside the Jewish circle, he feels himself despised and rejected. If the Jew is a brave, courageous man, he will react like a fighter, a man at war. But if he is weak and requires the support of others, he will resort to subterfuge. He will hide his origin and be afraid of his own shadow. In earlier centuries this fearful Jew had no recourse but to the open wallet. For our time, Spire proclaims, this method is both ineffective and wrong. The modern Jew must not open his wallet, but instead close his fist.[4]

Having recognized the unalterable difference in the Jewish situation, the Jew must be able to come to grips with it. He must neither hide Jewish difference nor even reduce it. Again and again Spire mocks the cringing Jew, the Jew afraid to be a Jew, the assimilated Jew. Spire was one of the first to detect and isolate the phenomenon of Jewish self-hate.[5] Often, he tells us, a Jew will find in other Jews attitudes, manners ar habits that pass as distinctively Jewish. He is annoyed by these and he will be frightfully upset if he should discover such traits in his offspring. "Don't do that," he will admonish his child, "this is Jewish."[6] Especially prevalent in the upper and middle classes, assimilationism insists on forgetting the Jewish past, on being merged into the whole of human history, and on stamping out the last tiny residue of Jewish identity. Spire reveals his own disgust at the embarrassment of the Western Bourgeois Jew in the presence of Eastern Jews—those incomprehensible, primitive creatures who actually flaunt their Jewishness for the world to see.

André Spire decries assimilationism as dishonest, plagiaristic, conformist, spineless. In its craving for adaptation it demands and practices self-denial. It is an attitude which is ineffectual even in achieving its false goals. After a century of assimilationism, it is abundantly clear that it offers neither answer to, nor defense against, anti-Semitism. Lacking even this merit, the Jew cannot afford the loss of originality and distinctiveness, of heritage and birthright. Assimilationism can at best breed contempt.

Despite his internationalist outlook, Spire denies hope to the Jew in universalism. He pokes fun at the humanitarian ideals which, it had once been believed, would sweep away all prejudices and lead to the brotherhood of men. Anti-Semitism was much too firmly embedded in the stream of Western civilization to be dislodged, not to speak of being swept away.[7] At best it could be temporarily discredited by such episodes as the Dreyfus Case and Nazi genocide. But a residue of anti-Semitism would remain for centuries. At times, it might be weak, but not too weak to rise and subjugate any ideals of common humanity.

Spire's evaluation of the Jewish situation underwent little change between his first pronouncements in 1900 and the present. He consistently viewed it through dark glasses. The Jew is, has been, and will be insecure in the Western world. In a preface to Paul Giniewski' *Quand Israël Combat* ("When Israel Fights") (1957), Spire returned to the same old theses, more firm in their tone, more secure than ever in their dire convictions. Not even the monstrous war, not the decimation of European Jewry, not feelings of guilt—nothing could eliminate anti-Semitism even from France, the nation most generous to Jews. Although in a wartime document in 1917 Spire had branded anti-Semitism as chiefly a German product,[8] he recognized its true universal scope only after the Nazi episode. The same forces which had always hated and baited Jews were again rearing their ugly head, only doing it more cautiously and discreetly than before.

Like most other European writers, especially those in Catholic countries, Spire singles out the religious factor as primordial in anti-Semitism, which ethnic, financial, cultural elements merely grafted on to this main trunk. "... It is only the loyalty of the courageous, undaunted people, its refusal to melt into the Christian order," that persistently gripes "the Christian soul which sees its prophecies destroyed and its foundations weakened."[9] In the

face of this threat, the Christian churches have used every
technique, every trick, and spared nothing to have Jews
turn to their God. For this reason, too, all modern plans
at a rapprochement between the two faiths are foredoomed to failure. The meetings initiated in France in 1947
to eliminate from Christian teaching the charge of deicide
could only produce noble paper results, but nothing of a
permanently useful nature. In 1945, in the wake of the
Nazi defeat, Spire had a brief, bright glimmer of hope,
but soon events demonstrated to him the accuracy of these
words written in 1913:

> To understand the attitude in the Jewish Question of the
> Catholic Church which can neither completely destroy
> Judaism nor cease to hurt it with its tortures, one need only
> read the prayers (offices) on Good Friday. . . . It is im-
> possible that a sincere Christian after hearing these services
> should not leave full of hatred for the deicide Jew. In any
> case, if the devout no longer perceive the type of suggestion
> which emanates from these imprecations . . . and no longer
> incontinently plunder the Jewish section of town, the priests
> for their part remain inflamed with a holy wrath.[10]

While paying tribute to liberal Catholics who have
labored for more desirable relationships—one does well to
remember his collaboration with the ardent Catholic
Péguy—Spire could not have conceived of a papal policy
which would basically permit a lessening of anti-Jewish
feeling. Church tradition as well as dogma precluded such
a direction. From the crucifixion and the dogma pertaining
to it stemmed also the anti-Jewishness of some Catholic
writers. The opposition to Zionism, a program damning to
Christianity, had its source in the doctrines surrounding
the deicide. Zionism denied the notion that the Jews were a

condemned people and that perennial dispersion was their punishment.[11] Leading Christians had adduced a long list of reasons for their anti-Semitism, but beneath them all was the fear that Jewish resurgence would undermine Christian thought and belief.

Spire knew that his prognostications have been gloomy. Yet he was cautious in warning Jews not to lose hope, not to beat their chests, not to plead guilty to the charges of the anti-Semites. More than ever, in the post-Hitler era, he held to the view that Jews must fight and yield not one inch to the hatemongers. More than ever they must nurture rather than forsake their Jewish characteristics; they must live freely like other peoples; they must not appease the anti-Semitic enemy who will not be disarmed. For, wrote Spire, if you empty the anti-Semitic basket of some refuse, it will soon be filled with other kinds. No Jewish concessions short of total surrender can satisfy the basic Christian dogma that the Jew must suffer eternal punishment. Surrender, however, was one word outside Spire's activist vocabulary and he advised Jews to eliminate it likewise.

There is little of the religious Jew in Spire. Though he had at times experienced a vague need for a God, he never rationally accepted Him. At the very moment that the youthful Spire was willing to die in a duel for offenses to his Jewishness, he penned these words:

> I do not believe in God. I am a pantheist. Thus the religions themselves belong to my religion. If I die tomorrow (this would be quite incorrect; one kills an editor of *La Libre Parole*;[12] one is not killed by him) I desire that a priest of each religion be at my funeral, walking side by side, the rabbi in the middle. While following the body of

a victim . . . of religious quarrels, they will be able to medi-
tate together on the evil which they have done and on the
good which they might have been able to do. . . .[13]

In later years Spire abandoned his pantheism. It could
not survive his continued observations of the cruelties in
nature. Yet he increasingly understood the need for God
in others and perhaps secretly envied those who experienced such a need. "I do not believe in you and my whole
heart feels you" wrote Spire in later years.

Intuition and irrationalism characterized his approach
to the divine as well as to other philosophical issues. (In
his famous quarrel with Bergson he wrote that intuition
was a permissible approach for the poet, but not the philosopher.) Spire sensed the divine, perhaps even craved it;
but was afraid to give meaning to, or even verbalize, what
he sensed. Intellectually he shunned it even as he was willing to assign it some place in the scheme of things. Thus, at
one time Spire conceded the necessity of some kind of God
because a moral order for Man could best exist in relation
to God. That Spire's was a genuine though insignificant
flirtation with God was indicated by his later ironic reference to that "deceitful God" who "has so betrayed us we no
longer believe in him." Spire's evolution was thus neither
clear nor straight. Essentially he was a non-believer who
yet perpetually sought to believe.

Although he himself was not a religious Jew, Spire expressed unbounded admiration for those who were. Again
and again he spoke enthusiastically and even tenderly of
those men of the Eastern ghettoes, with their intense trust
in God, the position He held in their lives, the strength this
faith instilled in them. Spire's look at these ghetto Jews is
that of the wistful outsider, too deeply steeped in skep-

ticism to partake of their faith. But he was grateful for sharing with them certain Judaic values. Even in the West, though shed of its old taboos and paralysing don'ts, Judaism has given many "an armature, even reasons for living."[14] Spire admired this perennial capacity of Judaism to give direction to life. He could even understand agnostics and atheists who, despite this fact, regarded themselves as Jews and transmitted their Judaism to their children.

Spire apparently felt that there was a Jewish way of doing things which was not the result of biological or genetic traits, but of a distinctive cultural pattern that was deeply ingrained. Nor did he mean to imply that there was a specific Jewish position on given problems. The roots of thought reach deep in the human subconscious. In Jews, this subconscious was filled with historic memory, values two millennia old, beliefs and customs of equally long standing, defensive psychological reactions born of centuries of persecution. Moreover, an extraordinary number of qualities in common could be the result of enforced intimate contact with one another, first in the ghetto and later in the Jewish quarters of modern cities. It is thus as the eternal outsiders that they developed into a group with distinctive qualities of their own. *Quelques Juifs et demi-Juifs* ("Some Jews and Half Jews") develops this idea yet further. Zangwill, the willing, integral Jew who wanted to be all Jew; Weininger, the anti-Jew who detested every fibre of Jewishness in himself; Stefan Zweig, the assimilated Jew who wanted his Jewishness to be merged with a broader identity and loyalty—all three had strong ties in common, not racial and yet not at all of their choosing. All three, despite radically differing views, were in some sense Jews, perhaps through the milieu into which they were born, or their upbringing—or the effects upon them of their broader environment. Thus others, like Spire himself, could be real Jews without having clearly definable Jewish beliefs.

Much as Spire abhorred French nationalists, he nevertheless borrowed liberally from them to underscore the need for Jewish identity. He was especially influenced by the doctrines of Maurice Barrès, the sometimes anti-Semitic theorist of nationalism. Barrès had seen in the French soul a Lorraine soul, a Breton soul, a Norman soul.[15] For the French soul to become really strong, it was essential that the regional or provincial soul should fully develop its potential. Being a good Provençal or a good Breton was a prerequisite to being a good Frenchman. Similarly, Barrès had advised Jews to fix firmly their Jewish soul instead of assimilating. Spire listened attentively to this teaching; he was, for once, a willing disciple. Here was a clear voice from the enemy camp urging Jews to be Jews. By truly being themselves, honestly themselves, they could also hope to become Frenchmen.

How did Spire see the Jews in their physical, social and moral aspects? He thought of them, different psychologies and modalities notwithstanding, as similar in essence to other peoples, with their generous share of the good and the bad, the strong and the weak, the happy and the morose. They were men of flesh and blood, with all the assets and liabilities that this entailed. Spire suggested that not even on the highest levels of Christian intelligence had this fact of Jewish humanity been recognized. Either the Christian intellectual had envisioned the Jew as villain, the offspring of a Shylock, or gone to the opposite extreme of idealizing him. Spire maintained that Zangwill was the first writer to introduce an authentic, credible and convincing Jew. In Zangwill the Jew recognizes himself: without pride, but also without self-hate. Here a Jew emerges with all his absurdities, vices, tenacity, mobility, boldness, energy; a Jew with "all those clear and strong traits which make him both repellent and attractive."[16] The real Jew of fiction—and perhaps Spire means the real Jew in life— is the Eastern Jew who eats Jewish foods and is aglow with warmth and feeling on the Sabbath and holidays. The real Jew is also the worker-Jew; Spire loves Zangwill's description of him as "neither resigned nor brutal, more modest than sensual, mocking, sarcastic, and full of respect for matters of the intellect, subtle, having an inner life, the sense of religion, crazy about theorizing on God, the origins and meanings of the universe. . . ."[17]

Just as Jews are individuals and not merely members of the group called Jews, so they are also politically diversified, with opinions ranging from radical to reactionary. Conservative anti-Semites have placed them in the camps of the radicals, while socialist anti-Semites have placed them among capitalist exploiters. Some may indeed belong to such extremist camps, but the majority of Jews will occupy other points in the political spectrum. Spire conceded that many Jews were motivated in their political thinking by Jewish historic memory and the psychology of defense which minority status has instilled in them. However, in practice not even this unifying element leads to any uniform One Jewish position.

Spire's own socialistic predisposition was discernible in his attitude toward fellow-Jews. The Jewish worker apparently can do little wrong and the poet abounds with praise for him. Conversely the bourgeois businessman and industrialist can do no right. It is the Jewish bourgeois who serves anti-Semites as pretext for their activities, but it is the working class Jew who reaps the whirlwinds. Unlike some other Jewish writers, therefore, Spire did not idealize the Jew as Jew; he saw him mainly as a human being worthy of praise and blame alike.[18] Where he did indulge in any grouping, it was between socio-economic classes. Here obviously Spire was riddled with socialist bias.

Given his pessimism on the status of the Jew in a non-Jewish world and his trenchant dislike of assimilationism, it was inevitable that Spire would be attracted to Zionism. His interest was proclaimed as early as 1904.[19] If there was a chance, he wrote even then, for the Jew to develop his culture freely and independent of outside pressures, for the Jew to be natural, stand upright and fearless, then certainly he should avail himself of the opportunity. Among the best known poems in the *Poèmes Juifs* is "Exodus," in which he urges Jews to flee the false homelands in which they are not wanted and where they have suffered periodic persecution. He bids them to detach themselves from the memory of sorrows and humiliations. Cross oceans, he advises, turn to the new Canaan that your chiefs have selected for you. He promises Jews a new pride, a new and vital self-esteem.[20]

Since Spire was not a religious Jew, the Zion in Zionism was unimportant and Spire gladly endorsed Zangwill's Territorialist position. But after the Balfour Declaration, Spire joined the mainstream of Zionism. At the Versailles Peace Conference he served as liaison officer between the French government and the Zionist delegation. In the decades which followed Spire frequently addressed influential professional and student groups. He founded the *Ligue des Amis du Sionisme* and its publication *La Palestine Nouvelle*. These publicist efforts continued until the Nazi Occupation drove him into North-American exile.

In his Zionist apostolate—mainly among the upper classes—Spire repeated the same theories which he had held for half a century. A Jewish state would furnish new strength, new power, new dignity, new prestige, not only to its inhabitants, but to all Jews everywhere. To all he reaffirmed the old belief that Jews must regain their courage and lead plain, simple, unfrightened lives and that their free development as an ethnic group could be furthered best through their normalized situation via a Jewish state.

André Spire at the time of his death would have been able to boast that the two most significant events of contemporary Jewish history had proven him right on most issues. If anything, they bolstered his earlier positions. By 1948, Spire had been forced to ask himself, more pessimistically than ever, whether the old religious-ethnic anti-Semitism would ever die short of the death of Judaism itself. And even Israel, the state of Israel, had found first-rate enemies from the start.

But despite this gloomy view, Spire's words ring forceful as always. "Since they wish to make an insult of the name of this royal race to which humanity owes some of its noblest aspirations, let it be then! Let us take hold of this insult and let us make of the insult a flag!"[21] Spire turned pride in Jewish identity, never firmly founded in reason or scholarship, into a crusade and through the force of his pen draped it in revolutionary fervor.

11

Elie Wiesel: Neo-Hasidism

ON THE SURFACE, Elie Wiesel's Jewish attitudes resemble those of Josué Jehouda. Wiesel, too, is an integral Jew for whom the outside world has a low literary existence value. Both are products of ghetto environments and a strictly Judaic education. Both began with Hasidism and evolved further in that direction. Both used the novel as a tool for religious-spiritual expression and not as an end in itself. But where one looks in vain for many original formulations in Jehouda, Wiesel's books abound with them. Also Wiesel is a highly skilled and moving writer, a talent not shared by Jehouda.

Wiesel has been considered the chief novelist of the holocaust. But it was only in *Night* that he disclosed the horrors of Auschwitz as he had personally experienced them. In other novels, the hero, a former inmate, is mercilessly pursued by past memories. They shape his attitudes toward all later experience. But Wiesel's novels of horror are more searching and penetrating than other writings on the subject. He has approached the holocaust mainly from

176

a moral standpoint, leaving legalistic and political debates to others. He has dealt with Auschwitz, not only on the level of Man, but also that of God.

Wiesel's six books to date have marked him as the messenger of the Jewish dead to the living. The mystic Wiesel appears to have interpreted his survival as imposing two obligations: first, to tell the ugly and unvarnished story of the dead, and to plead for understanding of the unheroic manner in which they perished; second, to attempt to fathom the unfathomable reasons for which they died, to comprehend the human and divine madness behind the deed. Finally, he has unwittingly assumed the role of prophet, cautioning against another Auschwitz, linking the burning ovens to burning Hiroshima, recognizing the infectiousness of evil and destruction, and the callousness of the witnesses, the comfortably uninvolved. But Wiesel is not only the representative of the dead to the living. He is also their ambassador to God. In this capacity, Wiesel has ceaselessly interrogated the Divinity, now begging Him for enlightenment, now castigating Him for his silence, now in despair turning away from Him, or seeking Him out more than ever.

This writer now approaching his forties has considered most of the questions suggested by the holocaust. What is the meaning of absolute evil? How can any faith survive in this confrontation? How could men remain so uninvolved in the misery of others? To what low of animal living can Man descend as a result of untellable suffering? What are the implications for human progress, the human future? Finally, what did the tragedy teach about the state of Jews, their destiny, their guilt and promise? These considerations have lent Wiesel's work an importance far beyond the boundaries of world Jewry, this despite the omnipresence of Hasidic tales, Cabbalistic allusions and Talmudic sayings. Besides being the keenest interpreter of the most bewildering deeds of all times, Wiesel also proffers hope of becoming one of the most authentic and constructive Jewish writers of our century. For he has not been contented with merely posing questions; he has searched for answers within Jewish tradition and found at least some in Hasidism.

Wiesel was born thirty-nine years ago in a Transylvanian village near the Rumanian border—a village which keeps reappearing in some form in each of his novels. His father, a rationalist, seemed skeptical of traditional Judaism and urged the youthful Eliezer to look westward for humanist values. His mother, on the other hand, adhered to traditional modes, inclined toward Hasidism, and was instrumental in securing for her son a thoroughly Jewish upbringing. Wiesel appears to have been more fortunate than the other writers in his religious teachers; he has repeatedly paid tribute to them. Several of these teachers leaned toward mysticism, which in a Western sophisticated garb still marks the mature writer of today.

Then came the great break. The war had seemed remote to Hungarian Jews despite the proximity of the Nazis. But overnight the latter insisted on the final solution for unsuspecting Jews. In 1944, with the Russians within thirty miles of their city, with booming guns clearly heard, they were yet rounded up—Father, Mother, children. They were kept in an alternately hopeful and despairing uncertainty, and finally shipped off in a cattle-train, destination unknown. *Night*, Wiesel's first book—and one of stunning power, an effect achieved by restraint and utter sparseness of style—records the heartbreaking months of agony, horror and guilt. Not the least of his lingering memories was of a little boy who had been hanged, and was dangling, still not wholly dead, from the gallows; another was of the valiant attempts to keep alive his aging and weakened father only, in the end, secretly to wish for his death and see this wish granted. Finally, the towering guilt over the death wish, the gnawing guilt of surviving, the knowledge of having descended to the brutality of sub-human existence. Again and again, Elie has returned to these themes: the dying father, the lost youth, the burden of survival, and the road to spiritual recovery; finally the search for meaning after total emptiness.

Wiesel was his family's sole survivor. While still an adolescent, he found his way to Paris, a city he grew to love. He quickly acquired a mastery of French—the language in which he prefers to write. He studied philosophy at the Sorbonne. Keeping faith with a death-camp vow and struggle, Wiesel left for Israel. From the strife-torn country he reported on the evolving struggle for independence. Thus began a journalistic career which eventually brought him to New York. For the past eight years, he has served as United States and U. N. correspondent for an Israel daily.

These various locales which have been focal points in Wiesel's life also constitute the physical settings for his novels. In the tradition of exile and flight, his characters roam the earth's surface—from Hungary to Paris, from Paris to New York, from New York to Israel and opposite directions. Wiesel has been an impassioned traveler, and has significantly been drawn to the myth of the Wandering Jew. But wherever his heroes are, they are tormented by the ugly memories of the past, the inability to cope with them, the realization that this past—in new and vile forms

—is ever-present and that the negative in various shapes—
Hiroshima, Communist prisons, etc.—has demonstrated a
virulent capacity to renew itself.

Dawn begins in a Palestinian terrorist hideout, with
quick mental returns to Paris and the death camps. The
mood is somber as the young hero, recently released from
Auschwitz, is faced with the grim assignment of executing
an innocent English officer as a retaliatory measure. During the night preceding the execution, the Jewish hero
searches his conscience for any and all legitimate reasons
that will enable him to do his hateful duty. He is acutely
aware that he is departing from the traditions of his people,
which admitted suffering and rejected violence. The hero
would like to hate his victim, but finds that hatred doesn't
come easy ". . . because my people have never known to
hate. Their tragedy throughout the centuries has stemmed
from their inability to hate those who have humiliated
and from time to time exterminated them. Now our only
chance lies in hating you, in learning the necessity and the
art of hate. Otherwise . . . our future will only be an extension of the past, and the Messiah will wait indefinitely
for his deliverance."[1]

The still very fresh memory of Jews being tamely led to
slaughter finally justifies in the hero's mind the legitimacy
of his task and conquers the old aversion to violence. Even
rabbis had now sanctioned terrorism in the light of recent
events. Upon his admission to the terrorist group the hero
was sufficiently a victim of wartime Jewish passivity to
think "that the mission of the Jews was to represent the
trembling of history rather than the wind which made it
tremble."[2] As the hero is gradually propelled to action he
becomes increasingly aware of the moral sacrifice it repre-

sents. The promise made by Elie in *Night,* that he will turn to Zion if ever he becomes free, is fulfilled in *Dawn.*

Dawn is thus inseparably tied to *Night* and *The Accident* (the French title *Le Jour* ["Day"] should have been retained in the English version) is attached to both. Now in New York, the hero, who has become a foreign correspondent, suffers a severe automobile accident that for weeks keeps him tottering on the verge of death. As he ponders over the accident and discusses it with his physician and mistress, he comes to realize that the accident had been no accident, that he had tried to relieve himself of the unbearable weight of guilt. The burden of memory, of living with ghosts, had become too heavy. The journalist-hero recognizes that his articles are those of a man at the end of his rope and that the youth sliced out of his life has turned into an insurmountable handicap of living. He knows that all he touches bears the stamp of death, that even his mistress is compelled to fight the dead through him. His own suffering and the memory of it has opened unbreachable gaps in his relations with others. "Men reject the sufferer, unless they see a God in him."[3] The accident occurred at a moment of supreme conflict, just after he had promised his mistress to forget the past because it precluded any possibility of love.

The hero's physician stands for the principle of life. Where his patient is powerfully attracted to death, the physician is certain of man's limitless capacity for living, of the ultimate victory over doom and death. Day follows night with the hero's final realization that the past must be chased "with a whip if necessary."[4] He accepts the notion that the dead must leave the living in peace and that the guilt for living must be ruthlessly discarded. He has learned that it is man's duty to make suffering cease, not to keep it alive. Despite the glimmer of hope brought on by the day, the hero has no illusions about the obstacles ahead. Forgetting will be a hard task, even as he has found a moral basis and psychological determination to perform it.

Indeed, *Town Beyond the Wall* leaves no doubt that the hero has not forgotten. He has, however, emerged from the night, seen the dawn and benefited from the day. The reliving of his haunting past drives him in an act of physical —and metaphysical—madness to the *City of Luck,* as Wiesel ironically calls the town of his birth. Here he searches for the Other, whose eyes have pursued him throughout his tragic peregrinations. They are the eyes of the Witness, the man who had peered from behind the curtain windows, had seen the Jews rounded up, old and young, herded together in the market-place, thirsty for water, crowded like cattle into the wagon of death. The other had calmly and dispassionately watched the perpetration of dastardly deeds. The hero is drawn back to face this Other, a man without seeming guilt or shame. In a passage of unusual power, Wiesel assails the witness psychology and with it sides with existential commitment and the notion of human community.

But is not the silent, unconcerned witness also the silent, seemingly unconcerned, God who also watched and allowed things to happen? And now, on the hero's return to the home-town, is not the Witness-God still sullenly silent and responsible for denouncing him to the new masters of Hungary?

Yet now the hero's reaction has changed. He no longer addresses the Witness or God through reasoned language, through questions and reproaches. He has given up on that. He now acts. Through a frantic deed of loyalty to a human, a crucial act of affirmation, Wiesel offers the very symbol of rehabilitation. The forces which had hitherto been expended in the struggle for physical and spiritual survival and self-restoration are now channeled into frenzied service to another. In the jail of the *City of Luck,* Wiesel's hero joins the human race even as he languishes in jail awaiting probable death.

The Gates of the Forest once more returns the hero to his Hungarian youth. To escape deportation he is now hiding in a mountain cave. One night he is visited by a strange man whose stories and laughter have an unsettling, if not hypnotic, effect on the youngster. Their hideout is accidentally discovered and the older man ostensibly sacrifices himself for the youngster by surrendering to the police. But the hero, who has given him his own name of Gavriel, is obsessed with the memory of the stranger. In the months of underground existence in the village of their former maid, who has sheltered him and given him a Christian identity, the hero thinks he recognizes Gavriel at a village passion play. Again Gavriel rescues him without clearly revealing himself, as the villagers out of religious fervor nearly kill the hero playing the role of Judas. Once more, years later, he believes he is confronting Gavriel, only this time at a Hasidic festival in Brooklyn. But who is Gavriel? Is he, too, God, who has watched over him, guided him through the tribulations of a perilous existence? Or is Gavriel the Messiah about whom he has told some fascinating and philosophically significant tales? (As Wiesel describes him below.) Or perhaps he is the symbol of the ghosts of the past whose power must finally be broken if they are not be a permanently crippling force in living. The excitingly told episodes of the young hero's adventures lead him to the acceptance of life as it is, with hope being a modest but necessary component. The hero's entente with life has become realistic:

> Whether or not the Messiah comes doesn't matter; we'll manage without him. It is because it is too late that we are commanded to hope. We shall be honest and humble and strong, and then he will come, he will come every day, thousands of times every day. He will have no face, because he will have a thousand faces. The Messiah isn't one man, Clara, he's all men.[5]

In the final pages the hero is found in the synagogue, reciting the Kaddish, "concentrating on every sentence, every word, every syllable of praise." He can now pray calmly for the souls of the dead, for his father, his friends, even himself. Why for himself?

> . . . that the angels, jealous of his strength and, above all, of his purity, cease to persecute him, that he himself cease to cause suffering to those who once loved him and still love him. Yes, the last *Kaddish* would be for him, our messenger to heaven.[6]

The glimmer of unexpected hope in *Accident,* the frantic doings and affirmations in *Town Beyond the Wall,* have been transformed by the end of his latest novel into a quiet and more mature faith. The hero appears to abandon the useless dialogue, the hopeless quest for all-embracing answers, the mad, mad searchings, and perhaps even the guilt and guilt-fixing patterns of earlier years. Although he has now learned the lesson taught him by Pedro, the most intriguing character in *Town* that "You suffer—therefore I am," the hero is not entirely in the clear. The questions have deepened, but the answers forthcoming are still shrouded in fog and uncertainty. Other Wiesel novels are likely to proffer new approaches to existence in a world still contaminated by the stench of burning flesh. Yet the direction of salvation has been indicated. It lies in the commitment to humanity and justice on the one hand and the joy in living and God on the other. Under the aegis of Hasidism, Wiesel is still attempting the near insurmountable task, "to turn a tremendous amount of despair into a chant, into a prayer."

His all-encompassing effort to comprehend the evil of the past has kept Wiesel from expressing himself specifically on contemporary Jewish issues. What views he has voiced have had their foundation in the holocaust and are perhaps weak superstructures.

Wiesel has made it plain—though never directly or specifically—that the anti-Semitism of the holocaust was merely different in intensity and scope from that of earlier varieties. In *Gates of the Forest,* the hero depicts his Hungarian childhood as filled with assaults by other children on Jewish youths. In various articles in *Le Chant des Morts,*[7] he comments bitterly on European anti-Semitism and sees significance in Hitler's choice of Poland as the site of the extermination camps. Wiesel also seems to suggest religion as the prime basis of anti-Semitism although he never dwells on the theory. The anti-Semitic attacks he describes are invariably followed by shouts of "Christ-killer." In *Gates,* Wiesel answers the charge through his own treatment of the Judas theme, hinting that the passion of Christ has been dwarfed by that of the Jews, a passion mercilessly repeated throughout the centuries.

Similarly Wiesel's vision of Jewish history has the holocaust as its vantage point. He cannot forget or forgive that all doors were closed to Jews. The Evian Conference had made it plain to the Nazis that no one wanted the publicly lamented Jews and that they could safely proceed with the Final Solution. He believes Eichmann's recorded statement that even if he had agreed to sell Jews for a fixed amount, there would have been no buyers. Jews simply were not popular and were dispensable, marginally human elements in the Christian world of the Diaspora. Wiesel's resentments may be gleaned from an occasional remark on the subject, but nowhere is Christianity or even Germany a prime target of protest. The permanent and mysterious significance of the holocaust alone has preoccupied Wiesel, not its transient facets rooted in time and place.

Like others hurt by the sharp edges of anti-Semitism, Wiesel was drawn to Zionism from the first. The thought of a Jewish home was a comfort to him in the dark days of the crematoria. Wiesel welcomed the establishment of a Jewish home, has lived in Israel and remained a correspondent for one of its major dailies. In a mood half playful and half serious, Wiesel has recently said that the coming of the Jewish state when it did was in part a misfortune. It provided the outside world with a quick palliative for its guilty conscience when a lengthy wrestling with this conscience would have yielded the greater long-range moral benefit.

But unlike most Jews acutely aware of anti-Semitism, Wiesel has never attributed Jewish survival to the stresses and insecurities of the Jewish condition. While he concedes that Judaism has flourished under stress, he reminds Jews that this stress was imposed, not chosen. He leans almost to the opposite view that Jews managed to oppose persecutions and stress an affirmation of life and in fact the sanctity of life.

More than any other writer Wiesel is entirely wrapped

up in Jewish tradition. The outside world, he confesses, barely existed for him in his Hungarian youth. It appears to occupy even now an insignificant role. He may feel that enough writers are feeding on the Western Christian tradition without a Jewish writer interpreting the same experience. Little surprise, therefore, that in his ceaseless investigation into the holocaust, Wiesel has been singularly unconcerned with the executioners and all the more with their victims. To be sure, he has displayed a lively interest in the moral apathy of the witnesses to the executions, whom he seems to condemn more than the executioners themselves. But again it is not the practical, temporal dissociation of the witnesses which prompts his remarks, but his own growing realization of the responsibility of one human to another.

The double moral imperative that history must not repeat and that Man cannot be a silent witness to injustice has driven Wiesel out of his tower of mystical speculation to enmesh himself in the destiny of Russian Jewry. In this one area of external relations, Wiesel's voice has been heard loudly and clearly and in characteristically Wiesel language. Thus he has called Russian Jews the "Jew of silence."[8] On a visit to Russia, Wiesel was struck by the remarkable vitality of Russian Jews four decades after the Revolution and despite determined efforts to eradicate any group characteristics and loyalty. He was equally astounded that Russian Jewish youngsters, Communists like all others their age, could yet sing and dance and rejoice in Hebrew and Yiddish on a Jewish holiday. Wiesel has called for a determined effort on the part of world Jewry to use its total influence in behalf of even limited Jewish survival in the Soviet Union.

Wiesel's attitudes toward Jewish external problems are

only vaguely defined. His attitudes toward the Jewish heritage is not. He worships at the shrine of Jewish literary
traditions which have served him more than any other
Jewish writer as the source for creative endeavor. He continues to read Talmud with regularity and, especially in
his last two novels, has employed its sayings, parables and
tales to release the development of plot and action. The
Talmud is for him the very symbol of the Jewish people.
Burned countless times by non-believers, it has yet managed to survive and overcome. But it represents more than
part of Jewish history. It contains the will and dedication
to live, which Wiesel—so long in the shadow of death—
has come to regard as the essence of Judaism.

But no facet of the Jewish tradition has lured Wiesel
more than the Hasidic. Just as he is a perennial student of
Talmud, he has become a frequent visitor to the Hasidim
of Williamsburg. The significance of Hasidism for this
Auschwitz graduate finds expression in this impassioned
statement by the Hasidic Rebbe in *Gates of the Forest:*

> The man who goes singing to death is the brother of the
> man who goes to death fighting. A song on the lips is worth
> a dagger in the hand. I take this song and make it mine.
> Do you know what the song hides? A dagger, an outcry.
> Appearances have depth of their own which has nothing to
> do with the depth. When you come to our celebrations
> you'll see how we dance and sing and rejoice. There is joy
> as well as fury in the hasid's dancing. It's his way of pro-
> claiming. "You don't want me to dance; too bad, I'll dance
> anyhow. You've taken away every reason for singing, but
> I shall sing. I shall sing of the deceit that walks by day
> and the truth that walks by night, yes, and of the silence
> of dusk as well. You didn't expect my joy, but here it is;
> yes, my joy will rise up; it will submerge you."[9]

It is not only the Hasid's stubborn affirmation of life that attracts Wiesel, but also his tales. He has been intrigued with their curious blend of realism and suggestions of transcendence which he has transformed into significant sections of his own books.

Wiesel's language is suffused with phrases and images from Hebraic literature, especially its mystical segments. For example certain expressions recur with particular frequency. These Wiesel endows with special attributes. Thus, on the folklore of death: Death has no hair—it has only legs. A dying man listens only to his stomach. There are girls who like to make love only to men obsessed with death. Dead souls have more to say than living ones. God is in the graves to make men and women warm. The sea makes one think of death. Death and life are juxtaposed. Following his accident, the hero of that novel comments:

> I . . . thought of myself as dead. I thought I was dead and that in a dream I imagined myself alive. I knew I no longer existed, that my real self stayed there, that my present self had nothing in common with my other self, the real one.[10]

Even life doesn't want to live. For life is really fascinated with death.

Invariably the lore surrounding these words is modified by Wiesel's own aphoristic style. To use another high-frequency word, suffering. Here the man Wiesel and the experiences of brutal reality break through the net of Jewish lore and mysticism. But even there his words retain their aphoristic potency and essentially biblical quality. Suffering does not lead to saintliness. It brings out the lowest and most cowardly in man. There is a phase of suffering beyond which man becomes a brute and is pulled hopelessly away from other humans. Suffering dehumanizes and makes moral contact impossible.

But lore and man are reunited in the highest frequency word of all, God. Wiesel has been called a God-besotted writer and one critic commented that it is as natural for a Wieselian character to ask, "Do you believe in God?" as it is for most mortals to inquire, "Do you smoke?" He speculates ceaselessly about His intent and purpose, always within the context of Judaic lore. At times He is a God of chaos and impotence, sometimes capable of committing the most unforgettable of crimes—to kill without reason. But perhaps God is condemned to eternal solitude and compulsively amuses Himself by using Man as a toy. But he always surprises by extending signs of friendship, as when he speaks in dreams. The existence of this God is tied to ours. The obsession with Him never ceases, being funneled every few pages into new speculative moods.

Wiesel's Jewish sources have, of course, suffered the influence of some Western sophisticated philosophical ideas. Slightly detectable are the influences of Camus and Sartre and perhaps that of Dostoyevski. Jewishly he has been under the wing of Abraham J. Heschel more than any other contemporary thinker. Add the personal experience of the holocaust and two of Wiesel's primary themes, madness as lucidity and silence as true communication, which are the slightly expectable compounds of this rather odd concoction.

Dostoyesvski's quote, "I have a plan to go mad," serves as the motto for *Town Beyond the Wall*. The hero strives for a metaphysical madness which would enable him to understand what normal lucidity veils from him. In several novels it is the *mad* man or woman to whom God re-

veals himself and who perceives most clearly the true character of events. In *Night* it is the town madman who has
escaped from captivity to warn his unsuspecting fellow
Jews, only to be cast aside as insane by the rational fools. In
the cattle-train to Birkenau a mother, beserk with grief over
separation from her husband, sees fire in her trances and
Cassandra-like she prophesies their doom in the ovens.
Again and again the insane, the drunks, the discarded have
grace, justice and truth on their side. "Lucidity," writes
Wiesel in *The Accident,* "is fate's victory, not man's. It is
an act of freedom that carries within itself the negation of
freedom. Man must keep moving, searching, weighing,
holding out his hand, offering himself." In *Town,* the
hero's father explains why he seeks out the company of
Mad Moishe:

> Moishe—I speak of the real Moishe, the one who hides be-
> hind the Madman—is a great man. He is far-seeing. He sees
> worlds that remain inaccessible to us. His madness is only
> a wall, erected to protect us: to see what Moishe's bloodshot
> eyes see would be dangerous.[11]

Wiesel has stated that madness began to interest him
because it was madness that swept through the world from
1939 to 1945, resulting in what Buber has called "The
Eclipse of God." Similarly, his concern with silence has its
roots in the same period which taught him the horrible
failure of language, its inability to express this eclipse, to
explain the mystery of the holocaust, to lend itself to such
crimes as labeling selection and resettlement the worst
crimes in history. Wiesel regarded Arthur Miller's *Incident at Vichy* a major failure because of its refusal to employ the maximum of silence, and its audacity to assume
that such horrendous events lend themselves to the use

of words.[12] Wiesel is acutely conscious that he himself has
been forced to employ words to present his ideas and has
thus partly failed in his protest against language. But he
has consciously attempted "to inject as much silence in his
books as possible, a silence between and within his words."

Wiesel has carried the experience of the holocaust from
a simple yet overpowering documentary report in *Night*
through the agonies of readjusting to a life that has become incomprehensible as well as insufferable. In having
his hero travel the long road back to psychological and
moral integration, Wiesel has undertaken the most ambitious and difficult assignment of interpreting the whole
trauma of the 1940's and its aftermath. In the process he
has supplied twentieth-century Jewry—and indeed contemporary man—with exemplary, yet realistic, prescrip-
tions of hope and determination. This hope and determination achieve meaning and purpose only through the
involvement of man in the destiny of others, in action and
commitment that favor justice and humanity, in the joy
of living. Streamlined Hasidism, as reflected in Buber and
perhaps even more in Heschel, provides more meaningful
answers to life than the rational line pursued by earlier
thinkers. Wiesel has succeeded in blending Jewish philosophy, mythology and historical experience. In this respect
he must be placed alongside two other practitioners of
Jewish fiction in the front ranks of the art. One of these
is André Schwarz-Bart whom Wiesel overshadows as a
weaver of ideas, but whom he cannot match in warmth
and humanity; the other, the much older Isaac Bashevis
Singer, who employs many ingredients similar to Wiesel's,
but whose mixture appears less varied even as his narrative skill is superior. Among the top American Jewish

writers, Wiesel bears a greater resemblance to Malamud than to either Bellow or Roth.

There are flaws in Wiesel's novels. Often the action of the story does not directly lead to the philosophical conclusions of the end. (*The Accident* is perhaps the most seriously flawed in this respect.) His work also bears the heavy introspective stamp of many twentieth-century French novels which unquestionably have greatly influenced him. If Wiesel's work has caught on in America only with select few, it is because the intellectual novel is still rare in this country and the intellectual hero trying to solve religious-spiritual problems is even less common. In Elie Wiesel we may well have the brightest young hope on the Jewish literary horizon.

12

Arnold Zweig:
From Zionism to Marxism

THE DECISIVE INFLUENCE in the life of Arnold Zweig was the experience of World War I. It affected in a major way both his Jewish attitudes and social outlook. His fiction centers almost exclusively about it. World War I was to supply, besides the physical setting, a series of shattering insights the effects of which were never to weaken or subside. It instilled in him the firm conviction that war denied the very meaning of human existence; that only those who stood to benefit by it economically and psychologically wanted it, and sought to perpetuate it. From here it was but one step to conclude that the ruling groups, consisting of greedy industrialists and rabid militarists, were responsible for most inequities and constituted the chief hurdles in man's forward movement toward greater moral, social and economic justice. Jews had championed these constructive goals in modern history; the perennial forces of power, joined in each epoch by different allies

194

and transferred his emphasis to philosophy, economics and psychology. His first major publishing effort came in 1909 with the appearance of *Aufzeichnungen über eine Familie Klopfer* ("Notes About a Family Named Klopfer"). According to Moritz Goldstein, writing on Zweig in 1926,[1] this early book already suggested Zweig's future striving for absorption in things Jewish and European. Peter Klopfer, Zweig's first fictional alter ego, is an ardent Zionist whose Jewish national convictions propel him to the shores of Palestine. It was Zweig's second novel, *Novellen um Claudia,* which first attracted nation-wide interest. In this book, so different from all others, Zweig peers unashamedly into a bridal chamber in which an inhibited Claudia gradually yields to her primeval instincts. Although Goldstein believed to recognize in the over-refined, cultured, somewhat precious Claudia a Jewish type—in a much later novel she and her husband were to reappear as Nazis—this is one of few novels which completely bypasses Jews and their problems. But in two plays soon to follow, *Abigail* and *Ritual Murder in Hungary,* Zweig not only returned to Jewish themes, but treated them with an aggressiveness rare even among the Jewish publicists of the time. The stage version of an actual occurrence—an accusation of ritual murder in Hungary—the second play insists that Jewish suffering must no longer be taken passively, but fought with determination and vigor. *Das Ostjüdische Antlitz* ("The Face of Eastern Jewry") was to distinguish him sharply from other German-Jewish intellectuals, ashamed and fearful of showing off the poor Jewish relatives from the East. Zweig portrayed warmly and sympathetically the lives of Polish and Russian Jewry, a subject to which he was often to return. To be sure, as an emancipated, educated Western Jew, Zweig could not fully identify with his impoverished Eastern cousins, but he felt for them at all times a genuine empathy.

Had Zweig's work ended here, it is doubtful that it would be remembered. It took *The Case of Sergeant Grischa* to inscribe his name indelibly on world literature. Reflecting Zweig's own personal experiences as a non-combatant soldier before Verdun—which, to use his own words, gave him his first direct view into human society—the novel mercilessly followed a helpless human being being ground to death by an impersonal, overpowering machine of war. It was a depressing, sordid view, yet infinitely constructive in its virulent anti-war, anti-militaristic, trans-national point of view. But Zweig also set forth here values which early marked him as a favorite target of German nationalists everywhere. Unperturbed by the abuse which was heaped upon him by the German Right, he was to describe himself as follows:

> He [Zweig] . . . had underscored, even from his first book on, that here was a Jew writing in the German tongue and one who would not let anyone prescribe any limits for him which he was able to reach; in a book, *Caliban or Politics and Passion,* in 1926, he tried to make clear . . . his attitude as a conscious Jew and Zionist, as a European intellectual and German writer.[2]

Outspokenness such as this was flaunting the elements then rising to power in Germany and whose designs and mentality he had exposed in *Young Woman of 1914, Education Before Verdun* and *Crowning of a King.* When these forces finally achieved control under the Nazis, Zweig was compelled to emigrate at once. Where most writers grounded in European culture chose France, Switzerland or the United States as their new home, Zweig rather uniquely opted for Palestine. Here he wrote what critics justly derided as a weak and inconclusive novel on the emerging Arab-Jewish struggle, *De Vriendt Goes Home.* Yet later events were to disclose with uncomfortable clarity how this novel reflected his nascent doubts about Jewish nationalism—how, in fact, it stands at the crossroads of Zweig's development as a Jew. In between novels he evolved a long and courageous tract on German Jewry, *Bilanz der deutschen Judenheit* ("Balance-Sheet of German Jewry"). But life in exile, even in the Palestine he had fought for as a Jewish home, proved arduous and difficult to bear for a European intellectual lacking the capacity to grow new roots. In the late 1940's he resolved to return to Germany where the Eastern intellectual elite welcomed him with wide open arms. Here in East Berlin he has dedicated himself exclusively to the struggle for peace and it is evident that he is convinced of the sincerity of Communist peaceful intent. To him the Communist World has evidenced the greater and more genuine determination for warlessness. In the West he suspects behind the scenes the same forces which decimated first Germany and then Europe. But as Zweig has coveted salvation from the cult of Communism, he lost his erstwhile interest in Jewish affairs. A closer scrutiny of Zweig's attitudes toward Jews and the "Jewish question" clearly point to an explanation of the victory of Marx over Herzl.

Zweig's theoretic exposition of Jewry is to be found mainly in *Caliban* and *Bilanz,* but also in essays that have appeared in journals over the years. His less conscious views are expressed in the Grischa novels, which are heavily populated with Jews. They appear in uniform and civilian garb: as officers and privates, as business magnates and they have listened more to the scholar than the man of wealth.[3] Owing to their long cultural history and their Mediterranean origin—which Zweig again and again places above a Nordic one—and their special development in the nineteenth century, Jews have demonstrated an intellectual drive and force which have specifically affected the *Weltbild.* Together with the Arabs, the Jews (in other words the Semitic mind) have unveiled a pronounced and individualized capacity for the abstract, especially for mathematics. As patent and tangible proof of the creative energy of Jews, Zweig submits a seemingly endless list of German culture heroes of Jewish extraction. It is they who have always militated against war and the use of force in settling disputes; since time immemorial Jews have demonstrated respect for the worth of the individual and for the preservation of the cultural heritage of all peoples. Throughout all history they have steadfastly aligned themselves against barbaric retrogressions. The German Jew, exploiting fully the unique opportunities which the past century opened for him, had shown promise by 1933 of becoming the prime representative of Western European culture on the German intellectual scene.[4]

In his books on the Jewish question, Zweig addressed himself in the main to Gentile readers. He confides to them his utter bewilderment that a people with such distinguished traditions—which perhaps more than others had earned the right to survive—should have been singled out for continued attempts at rape and destruction. As an explanation for the phenomenon of anti-Semitism Zweig outlines certain psycho-sociological concepts of prejudice, many of which were to find vast approval in the United States after World War II. A form of ethnocentrism (*Zentralitätsaffekt*) with all its corollaries and implications, has caused the Jews, as a perennial minority, to be exposed everywhere to the whims of a dominant group.[5] Zweig is aware that other groups have constituted minorities over periods of time without encountering the miseries and perils that have befallen Jews. The answer lies in the very nature of the contributions which Jews have been wont to make. Endowed with a powerful tradition of justice and *Zedaka,* and being a forward looking, progressive people with strong democratic leanings, the Jews have time and again offended the ruling classes who could not, and would not, accept these standards. Standing for civic liberty, intellectual progress, the continuation of peace, Jews became the very symbol of all that these ruling elements hated in life and by which they felt themselves threatened. This, of course, is not Zweig's sole explanation of anti-Semitism, but it synthesizes well the views of an ardently national-minded Jew and of a budding Marxist.

Consonant with this appraisal is Zweig's readiness to measure the state of civilization by the degree of the Jew's acceptance into the host society. In 1934, Zweig wrote, "The German is as he behaves toward the Jews . . . a warning to everyone . . . our [Jewish] weakness is the measuring stick of the real maturity and strength of the others."[6] Thus Zweig could warn in good faith and with conviction that anti-Semitism was potentially as dangerous to the Gentile as to the Jew.

Zweig was pessimistic concerning the Jewish future; he thought it essentially insecure. History was replete with examples of retrogression; and each such period, by its nature, constituted a threat to the Jew, who was entirely too available and suitable a victim for ethnocentric sentiment, especially in periods of vile reaction. To those nurtured on anti-Semitism the Jew can be at once cap-

italist and freemason, all in the same person; to them he is
intellectually superior and even demoniac in his clever-
ness. Ht is an apt victim, for he is conveniently devoid
of power, but suspected of possessing vast secret quantities
of it; he lives in one's country and yet has numerous international links; he is a strange, accursed, visible figure, yet
has been suspected of diabolical dealings since time immemorial.[7] Jews are the hapless victims of the myths spun
about them over centuries; they are the pitiable products
of their social and religious apartness, whether self-imposed or not; they are the embodiment of the Eternal Jew.

For Zweig the Nazis were merely the latest to exploit
the many-sided vulnerability of the Jew. There would be
others after them! The chief effect of the Hitlerite episode
was the destruction of the illusion of the German Jew's
security, his unrealistic reliance upon human rights and
education, his faith in constitutions and written docu-
ments.[8] How easy it had proven to abrogate the emancipation agreement with the Jews and to restore, at the
majority's convenience, the medieval situation, with modern methods of torture and persecution skillfully super-
imposed. But this emancipation, Zweig knew well, had
never been so complete as Jews had imagined. It had been
forgotten that emancipation had been granted to Jews as
individuals and not to *Jewry as a whole;* also that it had
not been granted for the sake of Jewry, but almost in spite
of it. Now, under the Hitlerite terror, this fact began once
more to reassert itself in a moment of ultra-reaction.

The establishment of a Jewish home and state impressed
Zweig as the most obvious and pressing solution. He had
been a disciple of Zionism long before Hitler's rise had
hardened his conviction. Zweig saw no conflict between

his Jewish nationalism and his pronounced general hostility to all nationalisms. In the 1920's and 1930's, the
Zionist brand of nationalism seemed different to him. He
compared it to the liberal nationalism of the early nineteenth century—an aspiration to statehood characterized by
the desire of a group with reasonably common background
to determine its own common destiny. Any segment of
the human species, Zweig felt, could be assured of continued existence and progress when it existed on its own
soil—without foreign domination, naturally, and without
doubts and complexes, but with concern for the free
formation of the group self. Zionist nationalism was
founded on this assumption.[9] It was thus unaggressive in
nature: not rooted in any exclusive, divisive tribalism or
racism. Nor was it encumbered by any romantic or mystic
trappings. Zionism was a response to the self-preservation
instinct of the Jews, but one which also tended to secure
future Jewish productivity. For Jewish creative potential
to be realized, Jews required their own territory, their own
language—especially the latter, since it was needed to
facilitate communication among immigrants. Zweig used
the term "productivity" in the physical-economic sense as
well as the cultural. Zweig did not comment on the likely
effect the stress on physical productivity would have on
intellectual output, especially as the pressures of exile and
conflict diminished.

Like most other writers, Zweig envisaged the Jewish
home state as a distinct psychological need, a revitaliza-
tion of Jewish energy. In the Diaspora he had painfully
observed the Jew's pathological self-consciousness, his lack
of naturalness, even his self-hate. Too often he was at war
with himself: internally torn, his emotional apparatus de-
fective. His thinking on essential matters was vacillating

and undirected: now leaning toward the rejection of his Jewish heritage, now eager to integrate it. A new land of his own, living amidst fellow-Jews would normalize his situation. It was the only way of aligning Jews with other peoples having their own soil and nation.

But as Zweig looked at Western Jewries, they did not appear to have the aspect or shape of a people or nation. There were elements to unite them, but these Western Jewries had assumed too much the habits, ways and colorings of the host people to continue effectively as a distinct group. A Jewish Frenchman was no more distinguished from the dominant Frenchman than a Breton, a Norman or Provençal. But assimilated though they were, their status was still that of an unprotected minority. With a Jewish state these Western Jewries would acquire, more psychologically than legally, the status of naturalized citizens or of men constituting a national minority. Thus a Jewish state would bring about tacit recognition of the Jews as a people having a stationary minority represented in the various lands. This minority would be legally and psychologically strengthened in this fashion.

In adopting this view Zweig veered sharply from the majority stance of German Jewish intellectuals, who everfearful of their position as Germans, were determined to talk low as Jews. Zweig painted a glowing portrait of this species as European intellectuals, but a considerably darker one as Jews. Zweig was alternately amused and horrified by those German Jews whose unfairness toward the non-German extended to the Jews of other lands. So deeply imbedded was their Teutonic ethnocentrism that not even murder of fellow-Jews or persecution and defamation by Germans could basically shake their faith in German ways and institutions. In Palestine, where Germanic judgments of superiority were applied to Eastern Jews, the situation struck him as especially ludicrous and painful. Zweig recognized the ghetto Jew's "inferiority" in accepted Western manners and sophistication, polish and correctness, but he placed higher than this external distinction the Polish or Russian Jew's humanity, capacity for work, and spirit of sacrifice.

Because of his pathological preoccupation with *Deutschtum*, which permeated all layers of Jewish society from Zionists to religious Jews, the German Jew was unable to live with himself peacefully as Jew. Herein lay his real tragedy. Oblivious to any positive values in Judaism, he considered birth into the latter as a cross to bear. Yet for personal or family reasons he hedged over the ultimate step of conversion. He came to hate this Jewishness of his as he hated himself. Because of this psychological factor especially, Zweig dwelt at length on the need for positive Jewish education for all children. Here again Jewish national reconstitution would facilitate a vital task.

Zweig thus idealized in the 1930's a Jewish liberal nationalism structured on the psychological, social and political needs of Jews. This variety of nationalism appeared to him wholly consonant with his international, humanitarian and pacifist ideals. Zweig anticipated no real clash between his Jewish-national and generally antinational, or perhaps supra-national, thinking. Yet, not too long after, there appeared the first signs of doubts, the first seeds of caution. The murder in Palestine of Dr. Arlosoroff, as well as certain Jewish policies and actions in that country, prompted the initial reappraisal. Would Jewish nationalism succumb to the temptations of other nationalisms? Would it fail the test? His one Palestinian novel, *De Vriendt Goes Home,* which relates the murder of a conciliatory Jew (Arlosoroff), showed him to be remarkably friendly to the Arabs and not at all willing to forsake their legitimate interests, for whatever reason. This novel clearly set his Zionism apart from the more rabid political species which, however, became increasingly dominant. Policies of the Jischuw in succeeding years, his frequent personal protests notwithstanding, disclosed a trend toward the tribalism he had so condemned. Writing some thirty years later, Zweig commented with the benefit of hindsight and a new Marxist orientation: "Even then [in 1932] the Zionist solution seemed conceivable to me only on a democratic-socialist basis and so I belonged since its foundation to Hapoel Hazair. My friendship with Dr. Ch. Arlosoroff dated back to my student days. . . . Arlosoroff was murdered by Jewish terrorists of ultra-nationalist viewpoints, because he was striving for a reasonable solution of Jewish-Arab relations through negotiations with the then Emirship of Transjordan. After my arrival in Jaffa, on December 21, 1933, I immediately tried to shed light on this murder and its motives and to prove the responsibility of the supporters of the Jabotinsky wing of Zionism. . . ."[10] Zweig became ever more disillusioned with the trends of the Zionist experiment, its new emphases, tactics and alleged subterfuges.

Owing partly to the inability of an aging European writer to thrive on foreign soil, to his personal disillusionment with Yishuw policies, the evolution of Zionism on Palestinian soil, his increasingly Marxist socialism, Zweig gradually but clearly put physical and intellectual distance between Israel and himself. Jewish salvation, he felt in the post-Nazi world, had to be sought not in the Jewish national idea, but in the broader solution of a socialist world—i.e. a more meaningful social order which would achieve liberation from the vicious circle of national and individual egoisms. This socialist foundation was also the prerequisite for the final extirpation of anti-Semitism, itself the consequence of group selfishness and ethnocentrism. With the dawn of the Socialist era would come the softening of all tribal instincts. Whether his decade of propinquity to the Marxist paradise has not brought him another grave disappointment, especially in the light of Soviet anti-Semitism, cannot be accurately assayed at this time.

The Jewish history of Arnold Zweig is a tragic one. He had never been attracted to Judaism as a religion, an abnegation which had remained with him since childhood days. Nevertheless he had been closely identified with Jewish peoplehood and ethical-cultural traditions. Through a Zionism of the stamp of Hapoel Hazair he had battled for Jewish land as the prime hope for normalizing Jewish life. Then, to use his words, the road to Zion proved an illusion. The policies of the new state of Israel totally repelled him as his hope for Jewish-Arab coexistence disappeared.[11] With no religious attachments to bind him to Judaism, with loyalty to the Zionist cause turned to bitterness, Zweig's detachment from Jewish questions—and the Jewish people—became virtually complete. His embrace of Marxism was a further cause of total alienation.

Zweig's conversion to Marxist Socialism could not come as a total shock to those who had followed the neat straight line of his intellectual evolution since 1916. But there had always been enough balance in Zweig, enough of the Western liberal tradition, to keep him from taking the final plunge. Even as in the 1920's and 1930's he depicted the conspiracies of industrialists and generals, even as he had thundered against the exploitation of the masses and registered his discontent with the feeble and fearful actions of German's liberal democracy, he had stoutly upheld the freedom and dignity of the individual, the security of his person, the right to stand freely and boldly before other men and authority. Thus, when socio-economic concerns seemed to propel him eastward, political and philosophical considerations kept him grounded in the West. And above all, he appeared firmly tied to his Jewishness. Yet as post-war events have clearly demonstrated he was less strongly attached to the Jewish pole than to the Marxist. Without a religious base, and lacking also a specific commitment to the Jewish heritage, Zweig's Jewishness could not withstand the "failure" of his one area of full Jewish participation: Zionism. With the Zionist dream destroyed the Marxist chimera absorbed his surviving hopes. After World War II it shone more brilliantly than ever on Zweig's generally darkened horizon.

Yet, despite it all, it remains difficult to comprehend how Zweig, so ardent an advocate of political freedoms (see his condemnation of the Nazis for violating them) could turn into an apologist for the Communist version of socialism. Personal motives aside, it could only be that the author of *Grischa*, the inveterate foe of exploitation and war, was completely persuaded by the Russians' sundry peace offensives and that he needed to plug the hole created by the vacancy left by alienation from Zionism. All his pro-Communist writings extol the Eastern emphasis on peace as opposed to Western saber rattling.

How Zweig felt about the Soviet Doctor's Plot and other known persecutions of Jews, and how he reconciled these with the Marxist-Socialist solution, is difficult to say. If he was as truly removed from Jewish problems as he has indicated, obstinate silence must yet have proved a difficult course. In any case it is tragic that the erstwhile apostle of strong Jewish identity, the former fighter for the Jew's proud right to be a Jew, could only envision the end of anti-Semitism through the end of Judaism.

But it is possible that an old, long silent voice demanded to be heard at the end of the Six-Day War. Apparently the violently anti-Zionist and sometimes anti-Jewish policies of the Socialist governments angered the erstwhile Zionist and conscious Jew. According to various press reports, Zweig wrote a letter to the Israeli Writers' League in which he vehemently attacked the attitude toward Israel and Jews of the East German government he had so loyally served. This same government may well have applied pressure on Zweig who has since denied having condemned the East German outbursts. Whatever the mystery—for such it remains—the now octogenarian is not likely to risk persecution once more, or pack up his belongings one last time, by publicly reversing himself. If Zweig has had any second thoughts on the capacity of socialism to solve the Jewish problem, he may well be condemned to keep them strictly and painfully to himself.

13

The More Recent Writers

NEVER IN THE two thousand year history of the Diaspora has the remarkable resilience of the Jewish people been demonstrated more convincingly than in our time. From the crushing blows dealt them by the Nazi hordes, they have emerged psychologically stronger than at any time in the post-ghetto period. For if our era has witnessed the most disastrous crisis in Jewish history, it has also been treated to its most promising developments. Even as Jews were counting their losses in Europe, they were battling for the establishment of the promised Jewish homeland and building in America one of the strongest Jewish communities ever assembled in the Diaspora.

These achievements have done much to sustain the debilitated Jewries of Europe. The new Jewish state has instilled in them a generous source of pride. Israel has enabled them to substitute the image of conquering hero for that of hunted refugee, of positive achievement for continued failure. If Israel has helped bring about inner restoration and a better self-image, the wealthy, charitable community across the seas has increased the chance of physical and cultural survival.

Despite all this, when the balance sheet of contemporary European Jewry is drawn, it will yield the distressing fact that European Jewries—what is left of them—have lost something they can never regain. Perhaps it is innocence or optimism or undiluted hope. Perhaps it is merely the safety derived from numbers, the knowledge that there are many others like oneself. Outside the Soviet Union, where Jewish life is largely clandestine and has a limited future under a hostile regime, only France and England can boast of a fair-sized postwar Jewish community. But the French community, consisting largely of survivors or refugees from other countries, offers only modest promise for Jewish recrudescence. According to all available reports, the Jews of Paris, the residence of most of the survivors, are not strongly affiliated with Jewish life. Even with support from Israel and the United States the outlook for the development of a healthy French-Jewish community is not especially bright.

But on the basis of the efforts of French-Jewish intellectuals, this pessimistic view is not wholly justified. The majority of the surviving French-Jewish writers have expressed Jewish attitudes which their more universalist fathers never shared. Even those young men who had not felt themselves Jewish prior to 1940, or were ambivalent, have been driven by the debacle to a renewed interest in things Jewish or identified with Jews. Their Jewishness may have been mainly reaction intent upon protest against an unjust environment which violated human rights and decency. But even these Jews by reaction have demonstrated a greater willingness to examine the Jewish heritage. Occasionally this examination brought about the realization that what they had judged as atavistic, crude survivals of an ancient culture was pregnant with meaning for modern times. Some, of course, had not needed the catastrophic events to create this awareness.

In general, it may be said that some of the positions analyzed in the preceding chapters may also be found in the newer writers. The shadings are different and certainly the emphases have changed. But underneath the new words are many of the old doubts, the old conflicts, the old actions and reactions. Yet something has been added to the portrait of the post-Hitlerite European Jewish writer. Instead of the former caution in the face of the Christian world, there is now greater defiance of it, open distrust, which at times borders on contempt. This younger generation is saying, in fact, that Christians, or those who passed for such, have struck down an entire people, violated the Jew in the most inhuman of ways and thus bear on their conscience the greatest guilt in history. There is nothing they can now do to frighten Jews. The inhumanity of others has somehow dehumanized Jews as well.

Nevertheless, both Julien Benda and Emmanuel Berl have their assimilationist progeny today, just as Fleg and Spire have been succeeded by Jewish-oriented writers. Past patterns appear to repeat themselves, with only some variations which lend them a new texture.

The most talented of the young writers in France has also been the most publicized. André Schwarz-Bart's own life story is exceptionally rich in human interest and his one Jewish novel is probably the most ambitious French-Jewish fictional effort of all times. Schwarz-Bart is in no way the spokesman for Jewish intellectuals today, but his mood—and that of his novel—is in a way their mood. His novel telescopes the experiences of many others.

Schwarz-Bart was only thirty-one when *The Last of the Just* was published and awarded the coveted Goncourt Prize. He was born in the Lorraine city of Metz, the son of poor Polish immigrants. His father had extensive rabbinic training in Poland and he sought to pass on to his seven children his considerable Judaic learning. Their poverty was such that André could not even attend elementary school with regularity. When war intervened it brought for André the usual heartbreak: flight, arrest, escape, separation from family, guardianship of surviving children (when he, himself, was not yet fifteen), a seaman's apprenticeship aboard a trawler, renewed arrest, clandestine employment on a farm, and following the Liberation, service in the French Army. At seventeen Schwarz-Bart finally sought to educate himself—no mean task because he worked nine hours a day in a factory. He began with fifth and sixth grade readers, then graduated to mysteries. One day he discovered *Crime and Punishment,* believing it to be a mystery. According to an interview in *L'Express,* this book was a revelation. He began to read more intensively than ever and gained admission to the Sorbonne.

Only two weeks of university experience were enough to disillusion him. He returned to the factory, writing in his spare time, "to communicate almost anything." After another year he gave the Sorbonne another try; this time the experience proved successful. He wrote *Le Dernier des Justes* over a four-year span, rewriting it five times in all.

Schwarz-Bart's mood is one of gentle grief over Jewish suffering, especially that part which he himself witnessed. Very rarely does this grief turn into acrimony. Only when he speaks ironically of the Jesus of impossible love does he turn bitterly against others, implicating Christianity in the history of anti-Semitism and underscoring its unreal aspirations against a record of failure. Far more important than Schwarz-Bart's indictment of the Jew-haters of all time is his reaffirmation of the Jewish "mission," what French mystics have called the mystery of Israel. By enveloping his novel in the legend of the Lamed-Wow, Schwarz-Bart has supplied Jewish folklore as its frame and the ethical tradition as its theme. Stylistic and structural weaknesses notwithstanding, *The Last of the Just* ranks without a doubt among the great Jewish novels of all time.

Schwarz-Bart regards suffering as the distinctive feature of Jewish destiny and the actions of the non-Jewish world as responsible for this suffering. Whether it is England in the Middle Ages, Renaissance Prague, Poland in succeeding centuries and Germany or France in our time, the persecutions have always been the same, essentially forced by the same agents, with only the grounds for persecution altered in each time or place.

Schwarz-Bart has publicly declared that there is no Jewish existence independent of Jewish religion. This factor, more than peoplehood or culture, constitutes the real common denominator for Jews everywhere. Nevertheless, *The Last of the Just* is perhaps not a full-blown religious book. It is, to be sure, rich in Jewish lore; its customs and ceremonies are presented authentically; its ideas fit into the mainstream of the Jewish tradition. Yet its major modern characters are not mainly inspired by the Torah. The last two generations depicted in the novel, including Ernie Levy, the last of the just, were neither schooled in the Law nor particularly conscious of their heritage. They are peripheral Jews: Jews by habit or by reaction to outside threat. They are the Jews of today, not strongly aware of any positive quality to their faith, yet unconsciously living it and suffering for it. In their personalities and outlook, especially in Ernie Levy, there is a marked Jewish sensibility which can be felt, but not analyzed. There are moments when through the suffering heart of Ernie Levy there shines the glowing light of the Hasid. But Ernie Levy, the last of the just, is also, and rather curiously, a Christlike figure who can be fitted as easily into a Christian as into a Jewish tradition. As Pierre Aubéry, a distinguished French critic, has put it: Schwarz-Bart's entire vision of Jewish fate comes closer to the Christian punitive concept than the Jewish prophetic vision. On the whole, Schwarz-Bart's religious view of Israel, as it emerges from this novel, must still be judged as vague and ill-defined.

Finally, in 1967, Schwarz-Bart published a second book, *Un Plat de porc aux bananes vertes* ("A Dish of Pork with Green Bananas"). This new novel does not deal with Jews, but with the Negroes of the West Indies. Schwarz-Bart wrote it jointly with his wife, Simone, herself a West Indian Negress. In this new novel Schwarz-Bart is still dealing with his old themes of suffering and oppression, but he has given them a new setting. Christian villains in relation to Jews have been supplanted with white villains vis-à-vis Negroes. The preoccupations of *The Last of the Just* have been applied to the downtrodden of other races. It is apparent that Schwarz-Bart's future work will be to keep chronicling the story of the West Indies, only begun in this novel, which fails to be wholly convincing.

Roger Ikor, Schwarz-Bart's senior by nearly a generation, was the first postwar Jewish Goncourt laureate, (1955). Where Schwarz-Bart's book was bitterly assailed by

Christian critics, Ikor's suffered a similar fate at Jewish hands. Less epic in sweep than *The Last of the Just,* *Avrom's Sons* is nevertheless an important, even powerful book;[2] but also one that is understandably controversial. In his straight, unadorned, realistic narrative Ikor reveals the marked influence of Emile Zola. Despite the attention lavished on minute detail, Ikor at times lapses into sloppy research. In his treatment of Jewish festivals and customs and even his references to Jewish lore, he has often been careless and guilty of both half-truths and falsehoods. It was this disregard for accuracy in reporting the tradition, his lack of respect for important facets of it, which aroused the ire of Jewish critics. But Ikor's occasional carelessness with fact was hardly the only and perhaps not even the real reason for Jewish anger. French Jewry still felt itself too close to the accusations of the Hitler era to cherish inclusion in Ikor's novel of Jewish pimps, prostitutes and crooks among his Eastern immigrant family. While his critics conceded the artist's right to paint any characters he wanted to portray, they were yet indignant. The number of Jewish pimps and prostitutes in France was too small to justify inclusion in a book professedly realistic. After all, claimed the critics, the book purported to be more than the life of a *single* immigrant family.

Ikor is probably less involved in Jewish destiny than Schwarz-Bart. Perhaps more significant than his carelessness in reporting Jewish customs, his sarcastic treatment of Jewish orthodoxy and formalism, and perhaps the absence of concern for the consequences of his book has been the casualness and emotional distance suggested in his account of the Nazi years. Ikor was, of course, playing the role of the dispassionate, naturalistic writer seeking to detach personality from the events recorded. The very fact, however, that he succeeded so well hints at a remoteness from the events which is surprising. Certainly Ikor felt little of the anger, the sorrow, the grief, the hatred, the rage which characterizes the treatment by other Jewish artists. Unlike Schwarz-Bart, Ikor writes from experience rather than vision; in the relative shelter of a German prisoner-of-war camp, he neither saw nor was close to the disintegration of families, the tortures, or the deportations. In any case, the impact is less.

It would be foolish to claim that Ikor was not incensed by the Nazi crimes. However, to him they were crimes not so much against Jews, but, far worse, crimes against humanity. Ikor was not writing mainly as a Jew, but as a Frenchman and European, viewing the Nazi era as an outrage against Man and a general blot on the human race.

Ikor's apparent lack of sympathy was noted by those critics who regarded *Avrom's Sons* as an assimilationist novel. Ikor introduces three generations of Jews, each representing a stage in the decline of modern Judaism. Avrom, the patriach, represents the traditional brand: timeless, placeless, unmoved by both good and evil things that fortune may bring. Paris disinterests him and the son's attempt to show him the City of Light ends in hopeless failure. For Avrom the universe is bounded by the limits of the Jewish world. Beyond it there exists no other. Unlike other patriarchs in Jewish fiction, Avrom possesses ludricrous features that make him detestable if not repulsive. Ikor finally packs him off to Palestine; but his letters to France stamp Avrom an alternately absurd and even unpleasant creature.

Avrom's son, Yankel, is the novel's central character. He is the first to leave the Lithuanian village when pogroms have made life there intolerable. Unlike his father, Yankel

falls in love with Paris, with France, with all the glitter
and polish of the Western world, with all that lets him
forget the ghetto. Within a year after his arrival in France,
Yankel contemplates marriage to his Christian boss' daughter—willing to abandon the wife still waiting in the ghetto.
But conscience and memory jar him back to reality when
a letter from his wife reaches him despite his anonymity.
Yankel's wife arrives in France and proves poorly adapt-
able to French ways. It is this fact which finally keeps
Yankel unhappily mired in a Jewish milieu. But frequently Yankel peers enviously beyond the gates of the
new ghetto. Yankel has become the ambivalent Jew with
a strong penchant for the ways of others, but also being
pulled toward the ancestral ways.

The assimilation process is completed with Yankel's son.
The Judaism he has observed in Yankel's home has not
appealed to him. As a result he is powerfully attracted to
the Christian world. Little by little, Jewishness loses all
meaning for him. Simon falls in love with—and marries—
a farmer's daughter on the Ile de France, the most French
of French locations. (The farmer, incidentally, has never
met a Jew before and Judaism to him evokes only biblical
images.) Yankel's son does not insist on the circumcision
of his son. He is fully accepted into the French family. In
the words of Ikor's French title, "The Waters Have
Mixed."

It is obvious that, of the two extreme characters—Avrom,
the full Jew, and Simon, the assimilated one—Ikor feels
greater sympathy for the latter. But neither character is
fully drawn—the former is a caricature and the latter's
portrait is one-dimensional. It is in Yankel, the ambivalent,
undecided Jew that Ikor scores his artistic success.

Ikor understands Yankel. He knows what Yankel knows;

he senses what Yankel senses. He comprehends the desire to go beyond the confines of a Jewish life often too narrowly conceived, even more narrowly practiced; at the same time, he recognizes why it is difficult to go beyond these confines. Although it is Simon, Yankel's son, who takes this final step, Ikor himself is unable to get inside the skin and mind of this character. One cannot help suspecting that intellectually Ikor accepts the assimilationist view, while emotionally he is still a distance removed from it.

If Ikor has reacted differently to the Jewish tragedy of our time, he also had been affected differently by the Jewish triumphs. Ikor can best be explained as an extension of those universalist thinkers who go beyond time and place and who judge events like the Hitlerite episode and the establishment of a Jewish state against the total background of history. His universalism demands that individual groups merge with others to become a larger unit: the ultimate such unit being the Human State. Unable to see in Judaism the intrinsic merits that would justify continued suffering, he is more willing than most to urge "a mixing of the waters."

Albert Memmi fits into the dominant pattern of postwar Jewish attitudes. Memmi is a Tunisian rather than a French Jew, but he expresses himself in French and has obviously imbibed richly of French culture. The son of an Italian-Jewish father and a Berber mother, Memmi grew up in the dingy, unwholesome atmosphere of the Tunisian ghetto. Unusually gifted, he was fortunate to find a "benefactor" whose generosity enabled him to enter the French schools. The intense conflict produced by multiple minority status in a variety of milieux provides the chief interest of his autobiographical first novel *La Statue de Sel* ("The

Pillar of Salt"). A Jew among the Arabs, an Arab Jew among the Frenchmen, a Frenchman among Tunisian Jews, Memmi was more ideally than happily equipped to write the novel of the multiply divided Jew. With marginal status in every group, the hero of *Pillar of Salt* suffers in the end a kind of cultural crackup, a decomposition of identity which leaves its hero little more than a sense of despair. He has abandoned whatever faith he has held. Islam, Judaism, Western agnostic, France are all found wanting as the hero seeks solace in a mythical, enigmatic, allegedly all materialistic Argentina.

Both in this initial novel and the much inferior *Agar* ("Hagar") Memmi showed only moderate respect for Judaism and even less for the behavior patterns of its prac- ticants. If he yet identified solidly and firmly with them, it was mainly by reaction, spite and protest.

The superstitious, formalistic, primitive Judaism Memmi encountered in the Tunisian ghettos could not be expected to attract the brilliant youngster trained in Cartesian thought by the very rational French schools. However, these schools had also taught something about the rights of men and minorities. If the Jews of Tunisia, out of ignorance or conviction, chose to remain Jews, then they were entirely within their rights. Memmi insisted on active association with those—his own people or others— whose rights were being restricted. Benillouche, the hero of *Pillar of Salt,* becomes emphatically Jewish only in the internment camp when his Jewishness is assailed and at- tempts made to besmirch it. It is only then that he iden- tifies wholly and unstintingly with his people.

These elements come to the fore again in Memmi's more recent *Portrait of a Jew,* to which he has promised a sequel.[3] In this volume, which cannot quite make up its mind whether to reveal a Jewish personality or generalize about the condition of Jewishness, some of the earlier cultural neuroticisms come more clearly into focus. Despised by Arabs for being a Jew, by Jews for not being fully a Jew, by Frenchmen for being a colonial subject and a Jew, a human personality bears indelibly the stamp of the experience. *Portrait of a Jew* is largely a detailed analysis of oppression. The mature teacher of philosophy sees three types: oppression of the Jew (of any majority), of women (by men), of colonial peoples (by colonizers). Memmi recognizes in Jewish oppression a broader tendency of mankind. His outlook becomes correspondingly gloomy.

His reaction to Jewish oppression has now driven him to a strongly Zionist position. After youthful enthusiasm for Zionism he had later rejected it as just a Western Jew's passion for the Orient—a passion, which he, as a North African, could not share. But it was his study of oppression—the full, almost pathological sense of Jewish exposure —which sent him reeling back into the Zionist camp. Comprehension of the dynamics of prejudice could only lead to the conclusion that oppressed groups were insecure groups, its members denied the status of human beings. Hence their psychological development was stunted and even warped. In his homeland, the Jew would cease to be insecure. Until the day arrived when differences among people can be respected instead of vilified, the weaker must always seek maximum security. This the Jew could find only in his own nation of Israel.

Thus Memmi's Jewishness and Zionism are devoid of internal (Judaic) content. It is the practical Jewishness born of conflict with a hostile environment. This conflict, in his judgment, was bound to continue. Memmi stubbornly refuses to look at the situation of U.S. Jews for either a refutation of his pessimism or even a faint glimmer of hope. Whether he believes the experience of U.S. Jewry too young and atypical Memmi has chosen not to explain. In the absence of such an explanation it may be difficult to give full credence to his theory of perennial and ubiquitous oppression.

Equally angry, morose and disheartened—but much less withdrawn—is a minor writer, Isidore Isou. Highly talented, but unable to discipline this talent, he has engaged in what Henri Peyre, a distinguished critic, has labeled a holy war against the Christian world. Through the utter violence of his outbursts, unrestrained, vituperative, even a bit blasphemous, Isou may have voiced the secret, innermost feelings of Nazi victims vis-à-vis those who stood idly by. Isou's revolt has none of the gentleness of Schwarz-Bart or the anger and protest of Memmi; instead, it is best described as lucid unreasoning, or reasoned destructiveness. Some have judged it as devil-may-care folly.

This bright young immigrant from the East has made his major contribution to poetic theory. But it is in his long novel (or is this a misnomer?) *L'Agrégation d'un Nom et d'un Messie* (The Growth and Fusion of a Name [Isou's] and of a Messiah [Isou?] that his views on the Jewish dilemma are presented. Penned in the late war and early postwar years, it mirrors the pent-up fury of young European Jews during the cataclysm. This novel, written against the backdrop of untold suffering and humiliation, contains the most ruthless and devastating attacks to which the Christian world has been subjected in modern times. ". . . they have the murder of Jews in their blood like an hereditary syphillis."[4] In his insistence on Christian responsibility there is a suspicious racism in reverse. The fusion of Auschwitz despair, irrational vengeance and Marxist dogma have prompted Isou to assail unsparingly the very bases of Christian dogma and practice. His outbursts reach such venomous proportions that Robert Kemp, a moderate French critic, has labeled Isou a most dangerous young man. Isou's pathological radicalism is at least partly the result of his persistent and nagging fear that anti-Semitism will again be on the upgrade in France, that it is an eternal phenomenon, co-terminal with a pathologically Jew-hating Christian world. Isou is haunted by the never-ending possibility of a repeat of Auschwitz. The image of more Jews passively led to slaughter unleashes in him a swell of hatred which borders on madness.

It is then that Isou's Jewishness becomes fanatically assertive. "I am entirely, in every fault and weakness, in every sense, in every emotion, in every move, in every silence, a Jew. . . . I am so much of a Jew that it is perhaps the only word in my life which I will spell with a capital letter. . . . I would like to be known as Isou the Jew."[5] Isou forgets his Marxist atheism long enough to develop a "System of Judaism" in which he extols both past achievement and the present condition of Judaism. While his "argumentation" and "explication" contain some extravagant claims and characteristically immoderate statements, they also expose many original observations. It is only before Zionism that Isou recoils. Like Brod and Zweig before him, Isou fears that a Jewish state will cause Jews to be cast in the same mould as other peoples and thus lose both their individuality and their unique and peaceful mission: that of giving the world great men. Zionism will depress the quality of Jewish life and offer a threat to Judaism infinitely greater than either persecution or assimilation.

Thus, a holy war against the oppressor and persecutor,

a fanatical Jewishness by protest and revolt, a vision of Jewish life being distinctively different and capable of producing genius, and a ruthless anti-Zionism characterize the Jewish attitudes of this strangest of young French-Jewish writers.

A more moderate reaction to the Nazi experience was that of Jean Bloch-Michel, political analyst and sometime novelist. Bloch-Michel grew up in an assimilated home which perhaps was not anti-religious, but certainly disinterested and detached. Until 1940, the year of chaos, being a Jew was totally devoid of significance for this young, liberal, democratically oriented writer. "Judaism," he wrote, "had exerted no recognizable influence on either my manner of thinking or living."[6] Religious convictions he had none; his consciousness was entirely French, his views those of the moderate Left. Jewishness was a trivial accident of birth.

Then came the fatal forties and this Jewishness, so incidental before, was forcefully brought home to him. As a resistance leader Bloch-Michel had been captured by the Gestapo, tortured, and escaped with his life only through a miracle. In *Witness,* his most powerful novel, in *La Fuite en Eygpte* ("Flight to Egypt") and *Un Homme Estimable* ("A Respectable Man") these frightening experiences of war and persecution and their psychological and moral import have found artistic expression. Physical and spiritual survival, courage in all its phases, individual and social commitment to justice, have been the obsessive concerns of Bloch-Michel.

Bloch-Michel also fits into the postwar tradition of Jewishness by anger, revolt and honor. Even now Judaism does not represent for him a special message or ethical-spiritual quality. Nor does he see in Israel either a fatherland or a religious home. He does profess, however, a somewhat vague respect for those rabbinical ancestors of his "who made me what I am." The real source of his postwar Jewishness lies in this defensive reaction: ". . . as soon as anyone speaks of persecuting a Jew, I am a Jew."[7] Stalinist anti-Semitism in the early fifties prompted the declaration that, for the second time in his mature years, he felt compelled to shout out loud he was a Jew. The first time had been in 1940 when France was being defamed by collaborators and he—internationalist that he had been—felt himself a patriotic Frenchman; just as Jewish martyrdom that year had made him identify proudly as a Jew. Both his patriotism and his Jewishness were thus the result of protest and anger, of the need to declare his solidarity with the underdog, of the yearning for a just world and one of human brotherhood. His protest Jewishness thus had Western humanistic and cosmopolitan sources which largely excluded any rapprochment to a more positive Judaism with its sectarian aspects.

The peculiar quality of his reactive pattern is illustrated by a wartime anecdote Bloch-Michel relates in *Les Grandes Circonstances* ("The Great Events") . He had just recently been admitted to the Resistance and was to see an underground leader capable of arranging transport for him to London. This leader, who turned out to be a professor of Canon Law, conducted the interview with great care, gradually steering it into unexpected channels. Condemning racism in firm tones, the resistance leader then expounded on the number of his Jewish friends. One of them was particularly dear to him, he said, a former comrade-in-arms, whom he had met under similar circumstances. Yet he, too, had been converted. Bloch-Michel comments, "As it turned out, I failed to understand. We left each other without getting together. I never again saw this amiable proselytizer." Amused, Bloch-Michel adds, "Perhaps I was wrong. London was well worth a Mass."[8]

Of a different hue and shade is the Jewishness of Arnold Mandel. He was born in the Jewish stronghold of Alsace. Even before the debacle Mandel never minimized the permanence or severity of the threat to Jews. As an Alsatian Mandel may have been especially aware of anti-Semitism. It had been here that the dream of postemancipation equality had first been shattered by anti-Semitic outbursts, shortly following the act of emancipation itself. Again, it was among Alsatian Jews that the Dreyfus Case had underscored the lesson of permanent danger, even if the Jew was attired in the uniform of a French officer. In his youth Mandel often overheard the worried remarks of his elders and with maturity he was forced to adopt them himself.

Mandel has been the outspoken foe of assimilation, acidly casting doubt on "the mirage of security." As long as Hitler had left the world alone, Jews were sacrificed with the tacit assent and knowledge of the world. Mankind became involved in his assault upon Jews after he had attacked the Danes and the Dutch, the Belgians and the French. His treatment of Jews then became a convenient wartime propaganda weapon. Suddenly his doings became very reprehensible.

In his evaluation of Jews and their heritage, Mandel appears to draw a clear line of demarcation. His Jewish characters are often unlikeable and even obnoxious. But while he is unkind to individual Jews, he tends to idealize the Jewish past. He is proud of the record of Judaism in terms of its ethical development and its contributions to both individual cultures and the welfare of mankind. Mandel belongs among the few French Jewish intellectuals who have demonstrated a genuine affection for Yiddish literature. (He has undertaken several translations from Yiddish into French.) He has been charitable in rationalizing the attitude of French Jews toward their Eastern brethren. He admits that the French Jew is often cruelly amused by the lack of polish and sophistication of the Eastern Jew. Nevertheless, he claims that this same Eastern Jew will be warmly received into the French-Jewish home and be helped wherever possible.

In his opposition to assimilationism, Mandel resembles André Spire.[9] Like him he has lucidly and effectively described the failures of the assimilationist viewpoint, characterizing it as puerile and reflecting the child's desire to be like others. The non-Jew, to the assimilationist, is like the "big shot" who sets the tone for all the others. Such imitation is futile and foredoomed because of the different natures of the groups involved.

Jews can find their true place in society by remaining true to themselves. Because of history and heritage they have developed an individuality of their own. Rather than attempting to shed this difference, they should preserve it for their own good and proper development. Again and again Mandel has cautioned against the loss of identity and the lure of "coyping" and absorption.

Arnold Mandel has searched resolutely for the positive and meaningful in Judaism. Because he has judged his search to have been fruitful, he is deeply worried about the ineffective manner in which the spiritual and ethical content of Judaism has been transmitted, especially in

France. The French Rabbinate, he charges, has consistently shied from relating the Jewish heritage to the weighty problems of today. The result is a comfortable but meaningless envelopment in ritual and ceremony, a formalism which is unattractive to the youth of the nation, ever eager for the bold and the imaginative.

With Judaism hampered by this failure to put its message across, to establish its significance and appeal, French Jewry appears to be sliding gradually into a Jewishness by habit. Zionism, which had given it a source of pride during the fighting years before statehood, has now lost most of its ideological power and appeal. "The present difficulties of Israel, the end of the 'heroic' phase, and a sort of acceptance of the *fact* of Israel—all these have reestablished the traditional attitude born of Jewish emancipation in France, an attitude to which many Jews have returned with a real sense of relief: 'We backed Israel in her struggle; our prayers continue to accompany the builders and defenders of the Holy Land; but we are still French, and we must not lose ourselves in the affairs of the young state with so many troubles.' "[10] Needless to say, Mandel deplores this attitude which must be honestly faced if it is to be overcome.

The problem of the French Jew, as Mandel sees it, has been different from that of the German Jew. The latter, through a Wassermann, had evolved a conscious doctrine of assimilation. Assimilation took place in France also, perhaps even more widely, but it just happened, never evolving as purposeful design. In a country in which the non-religious values of the Enlightenment had become part of republican doctrine, there was no compelling need to indulge in conversions, such as happened across the Rhine. On the other hand, there never developed a Franco-Jewish culture. France and her Jewish community never made excessive demands upon each other, dispensing with the necessity of a new synthesis. Instead a symbiosis was possible which did not lead to new cultural combinations, as it did across the Rhine.

Mandel does not appear overly optimistic about the future development of a strong Jewish community in France. Even the Eastern immigrants, he feels, are gradually succumbing—unlike prewar years—to the integrationist temptation. Perhaps this is not altogether true of the older generation of immigrants, but it certainly seems to apply to the youngsters. For native French Jews the outlook is even less bright. Yet Mandel wants no part of despair. European Jewry—or what remains of it—is not in the process of liquidation. The insecurity which has led some Jews to abandon Judaism has led others to reaffirm it more vigorously. A number of intellectuals have pointed the way to a return to Jewishness, making this a respectable choice instead of an option for atavistic primitivism. Finally, the abandonment in France—since the advent of De Gaulle—of the politico-philosophical complex of assumptions derived from nineteenth-century religious skepticism has raised the chances for a religious revival from which Judaism would surely not be excluded.

Two other writers merit inclusion in any account of current French authors. Both have dealt creatively with the holocaust. Neither, however, has developed—as have Wiesel and Schwarz-Bart—a comprehensive view of Jewish destiny.

Anna Langfus, who died suddenly in the summer of 1966, was the third French-Jewish writer in less than a decade to receive the much coveted Goncourt Prize. (Ikor won it in 1955 for *Avrom's Sons* and Schwarz-Bart in 1959 for *Last of the Just*). Miss Langfus' 1962 Goncourt winner, *The Lost Shore,* failed to achieve the critical acclaim of previous laureates. Her own first novel, *The Whole Land Brimstone,* possessed greater scope and depth than her prize-crowned work and French critics felt a sadistic need to punish Miss Langfus by enveloping her final novel, *Saute, Barbara* ("Jump, Barbara"), in a silence that must have embittered the last few months of her life. She died in Paris at forty-six.

The protagonists of Mrs. Langfus' three novels are all grappling with the psychological need to rid themselves of the ghosts of departed loved ones and reconnect their own lives with a humanity that had lost its essence of being human. Mrs. Langfus, on the whole, generated more warmth and compassion than bitterness, though the latter is not absent from her work. Partly because of this—and perhaps because she offered no answers to the broader questions of the holocaust—her novels have not been accorded the broad interest that was aroused by Wiesel's work.

Piotr Rawicz has written only one novel, but acclaimed by some as the only artistic treatment of the Nazi horror. In *Blood in the Sky* dissociated images and ideas flash across his pages in such a manner as to suggest the break with continuity, the violence done to reality, in those years of impossible horror.

It should be noted that the three most talented novelists of the holocaust—Wiesel, Langfus and Rawicz—were themselves former victims of Nazi persecutions and chose France as their new home. They were foreigners writing in a strange idiom, often about events that defied the imagination. It is also important to point out that the bulk of French-Jewish novels bears the indelible mark of the holocaust, which serves them either as point of departure or arrival. In a broader sense, it suggests the very great physical and spiritual proximity of the European Jewish writer to these events. Both British and American authors have been able to use the Jew in discussing problems of universal import; few such novels have issued from continental Europe. As yet no Malamud or Bellow appears in sight on the European literary horizon.

Two authors have continued to write in German, though not from a German home base. Two books, *Soul of Wood* (1962) and *Sidewalk in Concrete* (1966) have sufficed to establish for Jakov Lind a most enviable reputation. Influenced distantly by Franz Kafka and very immediately by Günther Grass, Lind's imagination shows the bloody marks of the Hitler era. Writing from London, his two books have centered more about the evil of executioners than the sufferings of victims. Nor is Lind one-sided in the treatment of Nazi crimes. In the title story of *Soul of Wood* he deals with the curiosities of evil, while in *Sidewalk in Concrete* he stresses its banality.

Lind himself only narrowly escaped death at Nazi hands, much like the crippled son of "Soul of Wood." But his parents, again like the boy's, did not make it and probably "were taken off the train by men in uniform and cremated the same day." Lind peoples the first half of the novella with wooden-legged men, paralytics, epileptics; the second half with mad, obsessive Nazi doctors and sane but helpless patients. Better than most writers Lind grasped the truth that the Nazi monsters and their *Mitläufer* defied realistic description and could be presented only as grotesques. His Nazi doctors, SS men and the solid citizens have built into them a comic streak which serves only to accentuate their monstrosity.

The author's vision is that of a man who can no longer weep over humanity but only laugh over its cruel and ludicrous ways. "Soul of Wood" deals with the machinations of an Austrian male nurse to whose care deported parents entrust the welfare of their crippled child. As a reward, they offer him their apartment. He in turn abandons the crippled youngster on a mountain top and sets off to negotiate for the sale of the apartment to a Nazi bigwig. The latter has him committed to an insane asylum where two maniacal doctors, in deadly competition with each other, seek his services as a spy and informer. With the end of the war, the crippled Jewish boy, miraculously alive, is needed by all as proof of their good-will toward Jews. Lind's irony is skillful in this story as, indeed, in most others.

Lind has not expressed himself on Jewish questions beyond their victimization in World War II. His work to date suggests a deep rootlessness, which may well be one of the sources of his creativity.

Better known than Lind, but bearing some resemblance to him, is Peter Weiss, controversial for both his original theatre and Marxist theses.

Peter Weiss has been a painter, a film-maker, a novelist, poet and playwright. He has attracted the most acclaim as playwright and it is in this role he is likely to be remembered. In two widely-hailed plays, *Marat/Sade* and the more recent *Investigation,* Weiss has firmly established his reputation for providing visually exciting and original theatre. Vague in their ideas, but rich in imagery and suggestion, these two plays summarize best his other talents. They also show up his weaknesses.

All critics have commented on the descent of *Marat/Sade* from Artaud's theatre of cruelty. The nightmarish, ghoulish atmosphere of the asylum of Charenton with its broad selection of psychotics, its flagellations and other perversions, its gross deformed images of reality reveal the wild abandonment of the imagination found especially in Günther Grass, Jakov Lind and others haunted by Auschwitz and Hiroshima. It is hardly astonishing that this first play of terrifying ugliness and cruelty should have been followed by another. But where *Marat/Sade* is all the result of a human imagining *The Investigation* is anchored entirely in fact. In a real sense, it is a reportorial, microscopically realistic play, for which the author has supplied little more than the frame and point of view. Even the language is the language of reality, the peculiarly treacherous, innocent language of concentration-camp administrators, guards and "ignorant" witnesses.

The *Investigation* is the most brutal play of the horrors of Auschwitz. But curiously the chief victims of Auschwitz, its murdered Jews, are only once mentioned by name. All this despite the fact that Weiss himself suffered because of his impure racial origins—he had a Jewish father—and that this fact provided him with his favorite literary themes, exile and emigration. But Weiss, now in his middle years, has steadfastly refused to look upon Auschwitz in terms of a Jewish disaster or upon the Jewish question as truly a Jewish question. The phrase "Jewish question" to him is not real. It should be supplanted by "human question," with the Jews being merely the prototypes of the weak everywhere and their tormentors the representatives of the strong. If he has shown any sympathy for Jews —and he has scrupously abstained from even expressing himself on Jewish issues—it has been concern for the perennial underdog, whatever the label. Weiss has declared that being a Jew means only to be persecuted and threatened.

It has no other meaning for him, positive or negative. "I have never understood differences in races," he wrote recently. "Christians, Jews, Negroes, Chinese, Indo-Chinese people are just one human race to me." Anyone oppressing any group is ipso facto his enemy. The roots of oppression he finds largely in economics, with a goodly share of ignorance and prejudice mixed in. Weiss claims that prior to the advent of "the strong" and "the patriots" he was almost unaware of being Jewish in any sense. He had no Jewish education and was wholly integrated into the surrounding society.

Some two years ago, Peter Weiss publicly declared his solidarity with the Socialist bloc. As a result, he has tried, with exaggerated loyalty to dogma, to blame the whole of Hitlerism on Big Business. He has also sought to prove, too assiduously, that West Germany is governed by the criminals of yesterday. His adherence to party line has evidently blinded him to the other side of the coin. East Germany has admitted a considerable number of former Nazis into its governing ranks, with no greater requirement than a new totalitarian loyalty to supplant the old. Weiss' protest against Nazis is in the name of humanity, with the emphasis on the executioners and their crime, and little thought to the victims. With his universalist point of view and stress on executioner, Weiss is at the opposite pole of Elie Wiesel whose viewpoint is intrinsically Jewish and whose thought goes out to the victims and their survivors.

Weiss has arrived at many of the same conclusions as the much older Arnold Zweig, like himself a darling of the East German regime. The Jewish problem is reduced to the extension of the Marxist formula of the weak being exploited by the strong, the outs by the ins, the have-nots

by the haves. It must therefore not be treated by any med-
icine by or for Jews but by the Socialist prescription. Unlike the older Marxist, Weiss has never been attracted to
Zionism—which he would dismiss, were he to comment,
as just another divisive element in a broad, unlined humanity. Nor has Weiss ever been drawn to the Jewish religion, or for that matter any religion. More than Toller
and Tucholsky, more than Stefan Zweig, Weiss has acknowledged no smaller loyalty than that to Man. In this
universalist religion, so prevalent among Jewish intellectuals before Hitler, but approached more cautiously since,
Weiss has found an entirely secular complex of gods.
Among the younger writers growing to maturity after
Auschwitz, Weiss appears to be the only major figure to
have remained with—or returned—to this pre-Hitlerian
cult.

Yet, when all is said and done, Weiss has displayed a
remarkable understanding of the Jewish condition. The
reason may be simple. The one overwhelming experience
of his life has been his emigration and forced exile. While
he has not specifically linked these up to his own origins,
he has been more preoccupied with these themes than any
other. His two novels, *The Leavetaking* and *Der Fluchtpunkt* abound with the search for self and identity in un-
accustomed surrounding. In *The Leavetaking* he wrote:

Emigrating had taught me nothing. Emigrating was for me
a confirmation of the not belonging that I had experienced
from my earliest childhood. I had never possessed a native
soil.[11]

Had he not earlier identified with the Jewish condition?

I thought of Friederle (a friend), who was to become an
example of the heroic defense of the Fatherland, and at once

I was entirely on the side of the underdog and the outcast, but I did not yet understand that this was my salvation. I still only grapsed my lostness, my uprootedness. I was still far from taking my fate into my own hands and making the fact of my now belonging a source of power for a new independence.[12]

Man's alienated position in exile even forms the themes of *The Mirage,* one of his movies. Here he shows alienated man crushed underfoot by the weight of a hostile civilization. In *Fluchtpunkt,* probably in large measure autobiographical, he shows how difficult it is for the banned and exiled to behave in civilized fashion.

The *Marat/Sade* play with its inconclusive argumentation between free and self-seeking individualism and an idealistic, though fanatical collectivism, suggests the possibility that Weiss' commitment to the Socialist bloc is less intellectually firm than his pronouncements would suggest. The indecisiveness of the ideas and the refuge into visual artistry at least hint that Weiss has not yet found a permanent spiritual home. His own search for the roots of oppression will lead him sooner or later to find oppression where he has refused to see it. With this greater realism may also come a reappraisal of other issues, of which the "Jewish problem" might indeed be one.

of spiritual conversion, like Bergson and Werfel, refrained from fear of dishonoring the people from whom they issued. Many men turned almost aggressively to their origins and against their oppressors. Jewish identification ranged from quiet reaffirmation with some to noisy flag-waving with others. Toward the outside world, which had either actively participated in the crimes or silently stood by during their commission, the attitudes fluctuated between gentle anger or disdainful resignation with a few, and loud contempt and devil-may-care insults with others. Ghetto-fears, subservience, and doglike appeasement suddenly gave way to unrestrained denunciation. This outside world had refused to consider them as human beings, worthy of human treatment? All right; but this did not reflect on Jews, only on them! It reflected on Christian failures, an unrealistic and even hypocritical system of ethics! The Christian world regretted what had happened to the Jews? Lip service! The Christian attitude had never changed! The burden of proof to the contrary rested squarely on their shoulders. Anti-Semitism had revealed itself as much a Christian as a Jewish problem. From the courageous yet circumspect Feuchtwanger, deeply steeped in history, the old and gentle Fleg, the yet older and aggressive Spire, to the young and gentle Schwarz-Bart, and the somewhat older and outspoken Mandel, the policy of appeasement and deference was being reappraised and denounced. It had failed, clearly and beyond doubt. In presenting their arguments in the future, Jews must speak from courage and a sense of justice and not from fear and the desire to please. More and more, they agreed with a viewpoint expressed much earlier by André Spire: do not bother to open your wallet; instead, clench your fist!

Assimilation, too, was subjected to reevaluation and

found wanting by most. Of the older generation only Benda and Berl persisted in it, while substantially less secure of their ground; among the younger men, Koestler offered it as a legitimate alternative to settlement in Israel. Ikor admitted it as a likely course for Western Jews to follow. But those who had previously been anti-assimilationist found further support for their views in the holocaust. Some were moved by anger and action to rebel against any notion that would make them more similar to the oppressor. All had new doubts about human rights asserting themselves sufficiently to overcome the backlog of prejudice, hatred, and the belief in the right of the stronger.

Jewish identification was strengthened by the horror, as it had earlier been by the Dreyfus episode; yet relatively few of the writers bothered to authenticate their identity. Often their Jewishness resembled a pose, a stance vis-à-vis the unfriendly and unjust world which had permitted such crimes to occur. The act of defiance often proved an end in itself. As might be expected, it was the younger generation which resorted the most readily to this gesture. Neither Koestler nor Memmi nor Isou nor Bloch-Michel accorded genuine merit to the Judaic tradition; some rejected it in toto. André Schwarz-Bart, Arnold Mandel and Elie Wiesel have found creative inspiration in the Jewish past. But some of the older men were attached enough to this tradition for it to be of comfort and solace during the hours of trial. Of none is this more true than Edmond Fleg, the poet who cruelly lost both sons.

Even if identification by protest failed to bring about a meaningful appreciation of Judaism, it did provoke some thought about the Jewish people. Here, many found features in which to take pride. With some, the record of peace or the number of great men produced; with others, the absence of coarseness and brutality. In any case, they discovered a history with qualities they admired. Besides, these qualities lent themselves well to integration into their socialist-internationalist-humanitarian Weltanschauung. They were broadening, liberal features far removed from the narrow parochialism they detested.

There is some evidence, also, that the Jewish tradition was not well understood by some. For Koestler and Döblin, for example, Judaism was too closely identified with unhappy personal impressions to get a clear and unbiased hearing. Others were guilty of the error first made by Heine, of putting Judaism and Christianity into the same basket of otherwordliness and supernaturalism. Still others were intellectually too steeped in Western rationalism and modernism not to be suspicious of an Eastern doctrine four thousand years old. The fault does not lie with the writers alone. Communications between Judaism and its practicants were faulty. Men like Fleg, Brod, and Jehouda, who stood for a vigorous, vibrant Judaism expressed dismay over the failure of Judaism to reach its adherents. The intellectual, especially, was prone to conclude that he was dealing with an atavistic, alien doctrine. Too often Judaism seemed arid, uninspired, and relying heavily on authority.

To summarize, then, the holocaust brought about a clear resurgence of Jewish awareness. But the awareness had in it an element of spite and protest; it resembled in some respects a stance before a hostile world; it did not lead to a strong inner commitment to Judaism. Greater awareness automatically meant suspicions of assimilation. Whether this type of greater awareness is likely, in the long run, to offer a sufficient bulwark for Jewish survival in the West is seriously open to doubt. Yet, there are some, like Elie Wiesel, himself a near victim of the holocaust, who have been moved to search deeply for its meanings. Wiesel has found his answers in a mystical neo-Hasidism which insists on singing and dancing as a triumph over the life one is made to live. But Wiesel may be one of the exceptions. Given a prolonged period of peace, prosperity, a gradual extension of human rights through education, it is entirely probable that the Jewish intellectuals will slide back into the mainstream of attitudes permitted by emancipation, and the universalist, democratic optimism which followed it.

The other pole of modern Jewish experience has been the fact of a Jewish state. Most of the writers examined have been Zionists at one or another time of their life. Only the assimilationists who have minimized their Jewishness, and Isidore Isou who has frantically proclaimed it, have abhorred participation in the statehood enterprise. The reasons, of course, differed: the assimilationists wished nothing to impinge on their Frenchness or their *Deutschtum*. Isou, on the other hand, feared for his Jewishness. But not even these writers objected to a refuge for oppressed Jews, especially not in the postwar years. They did object to the ideologies which accompanied statehood.

The majority of writers remained loyal to a Zionism they already embraced in their youth. Fleg, Spire, Brod, Feuchtwanger, Jehouda and Mandel recognized early in life the need for normalizing the Jewish situation, for assimilating Jews, in this sense, to other peoples. Like others, Jews needed a homeland to advance their culture, to give free reign to their nature, a chance to defend themselves against attack. Through Zionism they aspired to a psychological conditioning of the Jewish people which would improve their mental and physical health. Like others, Jews should become conscious of their heritage; instead of despising themselves for their differences as a minority group, they should recognize these differences and convert them into a source of strength. Above all, they should deepen and strengthen their cultural and spiritual roots in Israel. These roots could grow to become a source of nourishment even to Jews in the Diaspora.

The heroic phase of the Zionist movement ended in 1948 with the proclamation of a Jewish state. To religiously oriented writers this act was the realization of an ancient prophecy and to others a modern dream come true. It also became a source of immense pride. Jews had triumphed and demonstrated a courage which neither they nor their foes had discovered before—a courage in the face of numerous perils. Jews were well on the road to normalcy. A revolution had been achieved in the two-thousand-year history of the Dispersion. Only emancipation, 150 years before, had been an event of comparable historical significance.

But the materialization of an old dream signifies the confrontation of a new reality. Once the joys had been tasted, the problems had to be faced. What about future relationships between the Diaspora Jew and the new nation? Should he look upon the new state with the satisfaction born of achievement and rest on his laurels? Did he owe further obligations to this child he had helped into existence? And would his relations to this child get him into hot water with others—with his mother country, for example? Finally, was this child developing as he had hoped?

Not all the writers expressed themselves on each of these issues; some shunned them altogether. Brod alone of all

Zionist writers chose Israel as his residence. Fearful, at one time, of a Western style political nationalism in a Jewish state, he was prompted by postwar events to minimize this fear and justify strong national action in the search for legitimate Israeli objectives. His ethical nationalism, while still desirable, has been diluted by political realities. André Spire never had serious qualms about powerful action by Jews or their state: the attitude of a hostile world legitimized vigorous Jewish defense and the full use of the tools of state, despite his avowed anti-nationalism. Edmond Fleg, more specifically concerned with the spiritual heritage, remained fearful that this heritage might be lost in a welter of political or military concerns. Feuchtwanger, too, had qualms which only the war helped him to overcome. Like the Brod of old, he has dreaded the possibility of Judaism being sacrificed to the exigencies of national demands. Nevertheless, he regards Israel as a hope and continued promise. Jehouda, most integral of Jews, has shared Fleg's worries and has demanded the subordination of political Zionism to the cultural and ethical varieties. Thus, at least a few of the writers have been mindful that Jewish statehood might weaken the substance of traditional strengths and values. These might be lost before more urgent needs: stress on physical virtues, on courage, bravery, heroism; on political skill and the public morality it authorized; the inevitable materialism which would develop with physical growth.

Only Arnold Zweig has been sufficiently displeased with the new state to abandon the ship of Zionism. After loyal commitment to the Zionist program for over three decades, Zweig emigrated to Palestine, only to find himself in conflict with nascent policies. An internationalist and Socialist, Zweig could not reconcile himself to the extremist positions taken vis-à-vis the Arabs. In the murder of one of his friends, a moderate, at the hands allegedly of rabidly nationalist Jews, he perceived the first bad omen. The later attitudes prevalent in official quarters reminded him of the belligerent nationalism he had fought all his life. Zweig concedes that his personal ill fortunes in Israel contributed to his decision to depart, but his disillusionment with Jewish nationalist programs was the primary reason. Zweig's fears were similar to Fleg's and Jehouda's; their starting point was Judaism, however, not as with Zweig's, Socialism and Western culture.

Perhaps more significant is Koestler's vision of the changed relationship between Israeli and Diaspora Jew. The Jewish dilemma has been simplified by the new state. Israel has finally given the Jew who is a Jew a place to go. If the Jew does not feel the urge to live there, then only one course is honorably and intelligently open to him: the course of assimilation. It is an either–or choice which Koestler imposes on Diaspora Jews. This proposition, one may suspect, will be restated at some future time. Coming from someone less controversial as an extremist it is likely to attract greater attention than achieved initially. Helped by Israeli statesmen who will stake immigration as a challenge to the Jewishness of Diaspora Jews, the proposition may become more meaningful than it is at the moment. Conflict over double loyalty may also revive it at some future time.

It is significant that Zweig and Koestler, both ardent Zionists who once chose to live on Palestinian soil—were the chief defectors from the Zionist cause. Both were perhaps temperamentally unsuited for life in a Near Eastern nation and felt culturally displaced. But there may be other reasons. Ardent Zionists though they were, their

Zionism was not backed by any attachment to Judaism. Koestler had almost a distaste for Judaism. His Jewishness tended to be exclusive, with a strong dislike for any form which was not Western. Zweig was not religiously Jewish, but neither was he very negative toward Judaism. Also, from a distance, at least, he admired the Jews of the East, especially for their authentic Jewishness. Without any religious affiliation and even antipathy for Jewish culture in one, and no strong sympathy for it in the other, the Zionism of both men was ill equipped to withstand the rigors or disappointments of Palestinian existence. The reserve strength was missing, as the political facet alone was found wanting.

The same problems which have threatened Jewish survival in the nineteenth-century are still largely unsolved today. Left unsolved too long, they may become cancerous. The problems involve two distinct and yet interrelated elements. First, it is the craving, itself perhaps a concealed by-product of Jewish ethics, for a human community characterized by social justice and human brotherhood. Long confined to the Jewish community itself, this ideal was permitted free expansion by the French Revolution and the liberalism that issued from it. This universalist ideal has tended to exclude as too parochial or atavistic the teachings of Judaism. The other element is the disorder, as Max Brod put it, in the dogmatic garden of Judaism. It is this disorder, this confusion, which has made it difficult for a strong unifying voice to be heard in Judaism. It is such a voice which might attract the intellectual to Jewish studies. Otherwise, guided often by ineffectual teaching in his youth—which stresses formalistic practice, ritualism, endless do's and don'ts—he is liable to dismiss

Judaism as an antiquated, narrow and parochial set of rules. The door to Judaism may well be shut forever.

The strong unifying voice must be identified and heard. To be attractive to the Western intellectual with an open mind, it needs to synthesize the eternally competing tendencies between universalism and particularism. Pure universalism carries within it the destruction of Jewishness by sliding the Jew ever more into assimilation. Pure particularism is unattractive to the modern intellectual and runs contrary to the mainstream of modern thought. The problem of choice with which the Jewish intellectual and writer has been faced since emancipation can only be solved by adherence to a vigorous Judaism which reconciles the two tendencies within it.

Notes

CHAPTER 1

DRIVE TOWARD SAMENESS

1. See Hermann Marggraff *Deutschlands jüngste Literatur—und Culturepoche* (Leipzig, 1839) for reactions of Germans to the appearance of Jews on the German literary scene. Interesting also are the remarks of the important, but anti-Semitic critic, Wolfgang Menzel.

2. The inner conflicts which plagued many of the post-emancipation German writers and, in fact, those of later generations are depicted with admirable restraint in Sol Liptzin's *Germany's Stepchildren*.

3. For Heine's specific positions on Jewish questions, at different periods of his life, as well as the numerous contradictions, see Hugo Bieber, ed. *Heinrich Heine: A Biographical Anthology* (Philadelphia, Jewish Publication Society, 1956). Also, by the same author: *Heinrich Heine: Bekenntnis zum Judentum (Confessio Judaica)*, (Berlin, Welt, 1925).

4. Many of the men of the second post-emancipation generation were, like Heine and Boerne, satirists of distinction. (Saphir, Robert) As a result, wit and satire, rare commodities in Prussia, came to be associated with Jewishness,

admired at first, but then condemned as alien, irreverent and unGerman. Marggraff, *op cit.*

5. See note 1, above.
6. Tchernoff, Iouda. *Dans le creuset des civilisations,* t. III. *(De l'Affaire Dreyfus au Dimanche Rouge de Saint-Pétersbourg),* (Paris, Rieder, 1937), p. 25.
7. Léon Blum in his *Souvenirs sur l'Affaire* is explicit in his denunciation of the French Jewish bourgeoisie, which had been shocked by the anti-Semitic outbursts and became ever more fearful of hostile sentiments, pp. 25 ff.
8. Siegfried Thalheimer in *Macht und Gerechtigkeit: Ein Beitrag zur Geschichte des Falles Dreyfus* (Munich, C. H. Beck, 1958) stresses the speed with which anti-Semitic feelings could now be spread and the consternation this caused among many Jews.
9. Léon Blum, *op. cit.,* p. 25.
10. Bernard Lazare, *Le Fumier de Job* (Paris, Rieder, 1928—posthumous publication, written about 1900), p. 169.

CHAPTER 2

SAMENESS RECONSIDERED

1. The degrees of self-hate and its sources differed considerably among these men. See Hans Kohn's *Karl Kraus—Arthur Schnitzler—Otto Weininger: Aus dem jüdischen Wien der Jahrhundertwende* (New York, Leo Baeck Institute, 1962); also the chapter on Kraus in Harry Zohn's *Wiener Juden in der deutschen Literatur,* (Tel Aviv, Olamenu, 1964).
2. Sol Liptzin, *Germany's Stepchildren,* Chapter XII, "Jewish Aryans," deals extensively with the phenomenon of self-hate. For a detailed and balanced treatment of Kraus, see note 1 above.
3. Sol Liptzin, *op. cit.,* p. 184.
4. Max Brod details the friendly interrelationships among the young Prague writers in *Der Prager Kreis* (Stuttgart, W. Kohlhammer, 1967).

5. For a full and rich discussion of the writers who achieved eminence in Germany, see Sol Liptzin's *Germany's Stepchildren*. The author has relied heavily on this volume and herewith wishes to acknowledge his debt.

6,7. Wassermann's characterizations of Jews are found at close of the prelude to *Die Juden von Zirndorf*, (1897).

8. Jakob Wassermann, *Lebensdienst* (Leipzig, 1928), p. 158.

9. Wassermann first expressed this view in the early *Die Juden von Zirndorf* (The Jews of Zirndorf) (1897), reiterated it in *My Life as German and Jew*, (1933) (German ed., 1921) and stated it once more in *Lebensdienst*, 1928.

10. When Hitler burned his books and continued Jewish existence seemed threatened, Wassermann finally and resolutely returned to his origins. He attempted to record Jewish history through a monumental work of fiction, a work interrupted by his death.

11. Stefan Zweig, *Der begrabene Leuchter*, (Vienna, 1937), p. 34.

12. Ernst Toller, *Eine Jugend in Deutschland*. (Amsterdam, 1933).

13. Harry Zohn, ed., *The World as a Comedy: A Tucholsky Anthology*, (Cambridge, Sci-Art Publishers, 1957), p. 39. Professor Zohn's introduction to Tucholsky is still the best study available in English.

14. *Ibid*, p. 50.

15. See Liptzin's article on Beer-Hofmann in the *Columbia Dictionary of Modern European Literature* and Harry Zohn's chapter on him in *Wiener Juden in der deutschen Literatur*. Liptzin's full length study, *Richard Beer-Hofmann*, (New York, Bloch, 1936) is especially valuable for an insight into Beer-Hofmann's Jewish attitudes and positions.

16. This view was first expressed through the mouth of Beer-Hofmann's Jewish hero in *Der Tod Georgs*.

17. The most complete and authoritative work on French-Jewish writers, a book at once informative and objective, is Pierre Aubéry's *Milieux Juifs de la France contemporaine*. Organized into chapters outlining the sense of difference, political attitudes, anti-Semitism, concepts of suc-

cess, etc., Aubéry's book is of outstanding value and far more deserving of attention than it has received to date.

18. Daniel Halévy, *Trois Epreuves: 1870, 1914, 1940* (Paris, Plon, 1941), p. 133.

19. Pierre Aubéry, *op. cit.,* p. 191. Quoted from Nina Gourfinkel, *L'Autre Patrie,* (Paris, Seuil), pp. 229 ff.

20. Crapouillot, ed., *Dictionnaire des contemporains,* (Paris, 1949), no. 8, p. 24.

21. Léon Blum, *L'Histoire jugera,* (Paris, Diderot, 1945) p. 330.

22. Maurice Sachs' autobiography and "confessions" were published in this country as *Witches Sabbath,* (Stein and Day, 1964).

EMMANUEL BERL

1. *Méditation sur un amour défunt,* (Paris, Grasset, 1925), pp. 138–139.
2. *Ibid,* p. 139.
3. *Sylvia,* p. 10.
4. *Présence des morts,* (Paris, Gallimard, 1956), p. 118.
5. *Ibid,* p. 119.
6. *Prise de sang,* (Paris, Laffont), p. 141.
7. *Sylvia,* p. 10.

JULIEN BENDA

8. *Jeunesse d'un clerc,* pp. 49–50.
9. *Ibid,* p. 41.
10. *Un Régulier dans le siècle,* pp. 131, 145.
11. *Jeunesse d'un clerc,* p. 14.
12. *Ibid,* p. 43. Perhaps the best known of the brothers was Salomon Reinach (1858–1932) who achieved considerable fame as a philologist and historian of art. The others were Joseph (1856–1921), writer and statesman and Théodor (1860–1928), jurist and philosopher.
13. *Ibid,* pp. 43–44.

14. *Ibid,* pp. 44–45.
15. *Ibid,* p. 49.
16. *Ibid,* p. 171.
17. *Ibid,* p. 30.
18. *Précisions, 1930–1937,* (Paris, Gallimard, 1937) , p. 38.
19. *Jeunesse d'un clerc,* p. 51. For his strongly anti-Zionist stand, as just "adoration de leur sang" (adoration of one's blood), see *Un Régulier dans le siècle,* p. 220.
20. *Un Régulier dans le siècle,* p. 126.
21. Not many critics agree that Benda's account of the episode is wholly accurate and that anti-Semitism was the actual cause for his failure to win the prize.
22. Chapter 7 of *Le Rapport d'Uriel* sets forth Benda's analysis of anti-Semitism and his defense against it.
23. *Ibid,* p. 96.
24. *Un Régulier dans le siècle,* p. 146.
25. *Le Rapport d'Uriel,* p. 101.
26. *Exercice d'un enterré vif, juin 1940—aout 1944,* p. 172.
27. *Ibid,* pp. 173 ff.

MAX BROD

1. Much of Brod's fictional work has medieval or modern Prague as its setting. See especially his autobiography *Streitbares Leben* and the very recent *Der Prager Kreis* for his intimate involvement with this city.
2. *Im Kampf um das Judentum,* p. 51.
3. *Ibid,* p. 40, 51.
4. *Ibid,* p. 42.
5. *Ibid,* p. 61.
6. For Brod's discussion of Jewish peoplehood, see *Im Kampf um das Judentum,* p. 37 and especially pages 71–80.
7. *Ibid,* p. 76.
8. *Rassentheorie und Judentum,* pp. 48 ff.
9. *Im Kampf um das Judentum,* pp. 78–79.
10. *Ibid,* p. 54, 63.
11. Even Reubeni, the false Messiah hero of his historical

novel, *Reubeni, Prince of the Jews,* is obsessed with the idea of Jewish physical strength and vigor and sees it as an important solution to the Jewish problem.

12. *The Redemption of Tycho Brahe,* pp. 260 ff.
13. *Heidentum, Christentum, Judentum,* v. I, pp. 28 ff.
14. *Ibid,* pp. 118–119.
15. *Ibid,* p. 120.

ALFRED DÖBLIN

1. For these and other biographical data, see *Schicksalsreise,* pp. 155 ff.
2. *Ibid,* p. 156.
3. *Ibid,* p. 157.
4. *Ibid,* p. 158.
5. *Ibid,* p. 164. For an account of this trip, see *Reise in Polen,* (Berlin, S. Fischer, 1926).
6. See *Flucht und Sammlung des Judenvolkes,* p. 34, from Döblin's reconstruction of the mental attitudes toward their Jewishness of so many German Jews.
7. *Ibid,* pp. 48 ff. for Döblin's version of the "emancipation-pact." Döblin frequently returns to this theme, especially in *Jüdische Erneuerung.*
8. *Flucht und Sammlung,* pp. 105 ff.
9. *Ibid,* p. 38.
10. *Ibid.*
11. *Ibid,* p. 37.
12. Döblin never ceases to point out the differences between Eastern and German Jewry. See especially *Reise in Polen.*
13. *Flucht und Sammlung,* pp. 27–33.
14. *Ibid,* p. 27.
15. *Ibid,* p. 108.
16. This remains the overriding consideration of Döblin's Zionism as expounded in *Flucht und Sammlung* and *Jüdische Erneuerung.*
17. *Jüdische Erneuerung,* p. 49. Döblin was much more attracted to the idea of Jewish soil and land than to Jewish

nation. Hence, he vigorously supported for a long time the Territorialist solution.

18. *Schicksalsreise,* p. 269. See this and other passages in the same book for the meaning of the crucifix during his months of peril and flight in 1940.

LION FEUCHTWANGER

1. *Power,* pp. 165–166.
2. Ralph Friedman, "A Visit with Feuchtwanger," in *Chicago Jewish Forum,* v. 17, no. 2, Winter 1958–59, p. 86.
3. "The Jew's Sense of History," in *Jewish Heritage,* v. 1, no. 1, Fall–Winter, 1957.
4. *Ibid,* p. 13.
5. Speech given by Lion Feuchtwanger on the occasion of the World's Fair opening of the Palestine Pavilion in 1940. A copy of this brief address was made available to me through the generous cooperation of Mrs. Martha Feuchtwanger, the author's widow.
6. "The Jew's Sense of History," *loc. cit.,* p. 15.
7. Ralph Friedman, "A Visit with Feuchtwanger," *loc. cit.,* p. 86.
8. *The Devil in France,* p. 179.
9. *Success,* p. 773.
10. Victor Klemperer, "Der zentrale Roman Lion Feuchtwangers," in *Lion Feuchtwanger zum Gedenken,* Karl Dietz, ed. (Greifenverlag, 1959), pp. 37 ff.
11. *Moscow, 1937.*

JOSUE JEHOUDA

1. This volume has recently been published in English by Thomas Yoseloff under the title *The Five Stages of Jewish Emancipation,* (South Brunswick, 1966).
2. From a mimeographed publication available from the Center for the Study of Monotheism, Geneva.
3. *De Père en fils,* p. 35.

4. *Miriam,* p. 228.
5. *De Père en fils,* p. 31.
6. *La Famille Perlmutter,* p. 187.
7. *De Père en fils,* p. 91.
8. *La Famille Perlmutter,* p. 30. See also *Le Royaume de justice,* pp. 161 ff. for Jehouda's Hasidic commitments.
9. Jehouda's book on anti-Semitism is one of his most original and its basic ideas are summarized in a brief statement prepared by him in 1959 and translated by Eva Jackson as "Monotheistic Messianism and Anti-Semitism." I have relied heavily on this document.
10. Jehouda, of course, is a political realist. In the 1930's he insisted loudly on a united Jewish crusade against the Nazis. Obviously, he understands the need for the state of Israel to use the customary tools of state.
11. Jehouda discusses "Jewish traits" in *La Famille Perlmutter,* pp. 34, 129 and 150. See also *Le Royaume de justice,* especially Chapter VII.

ARTHUR KOESTLER

1. *Dialogue with Death* relates Koestler's stay in a Franco jail while under sentence of death.
2. *Arrow in the Blue,* p. 90.
3. *Ibid,* p. 95.
4. *Ibid,* p. 110.
5. *Ibid,* pp. 110–111.
6. *Ibid,* pp. 112–114.
7. *Ibid.*
8. *Thieves in the Night,* p. 55.
9. At one point, Joseph writes in his diary, "Sometimes I think that the Dead Sea is the perfect symbol for us. It is the only big inland lake under sea-level, stagnant, with no outlet, much denser than normal water . . . oversalted, overspiced, saturated . . ." *Ibid,* p. 261.
10. *Ibid,* p. 170.
11. For some interesting remarks between theoretical and practical egalitarianism, see *Scum of the Earth,* which de-

tails Koestler's experience in French detention camps in the early phases of World War II.
12. *Arrow in the Blue*, pp. 113–114.
13. *Ibid*, p. 114.
14. *Ibid*. In reference to his subsequent adoption of Communism, Koestler was to use almost identical language. Again, he wanted to "build and construct."
15. *Thieves in the Night*, p. 153.
16. *Arrow in the Blue*, p. 205.
17. *Ibid*, p. 119.
18. *Promise and Fulfilment*, p. 335.
19. *Ibid*.

ANDRE SPIRE

1. The biographical data have been gleaned mainly from various articles in *Hommage à André Spire* (Paris, Lipchutz, 1939), and Stanley Burnshaw's *André Spire and His Poetry*. I have had some helpful correspondence with Spire in his final years and access to two important letters written to another French writer of distinction.
2. *Poèmes juifs*, p. 33.
3. *Ibid*, introduction to the 1919 edition.
4. "Irons-nous à Jérusalem?" *Pages libres*, October 29, 1904, p. 356.
5. See Spire's article on Weininger, *Quelques Juifs et demi-Juifs*, v. I, pp. 165–200.
6. "Valeurs spirituelles du sionisme," in Daniel-Rops, ed., *Les Juifs*, (Plon, 1937).
7. *Quelques Juifs et demi-Juifs*, v. I, Avant-Propos, V. XVII, also v. II, note, p. 183. See also Spire's "Préface" to *Bilan Juif* (*Confluences*, nouvelle série, 1947, no. 15–17), pp. 8–10.
8. *Les Juifs et la Guerre* (Paris, Payot, 1917). See especially the chapter "Germanisme contre Judaïsme."
9. *Quelques Juifs et demi-Juifs*. See note 7 above. *Ibid*.
10. *Ibid*.
11. I had access to a letter written by Spire to an eminent

French Jewish writer in which Spire expressed continued skepticism about the Christian attitude toward Jews, at the very moment that the Vatican Council was debating specific changes in the Catholic position toward Jews. Also, in *Bilan Juif* (see note 7 above), Spire wondered whether the old anti-Jewish prejudices would not live as long as Judaism itself.

12. *La Libre Parole* was the virulently anti-Semitic paper edited by Edouard Drumont.

13. Extract from text of Spire's will, written on the eve of his duel. Quoted from Stanley Burnshaw, *op. cit.*, p. 30.

14. *Bilan Juif*, p. 9.

15. *Quelques Juifs et demi-Juifs*, Avant Propos, p. VII. Spire's ideas were derived largely from Maurice Barrès, *Un Homme libre* (Paris, Plon), p. 15.

16. For the influence of Zangwill's *Chad Gadya* on Spire himself, as well as some other young French Jewish intellectuals, see *La Renaissance religieuse: Les Problèmes juifs dans la littérature* (Paris, Alcan, 1928), pp. 108, 109, 111, 112. See also *Quelques Juifs et demi-Juifs, Avant-Propos*, pp. VII–VIII and, in the same work, the study devoted to Zangwill, pp. 1–164, but especially 9–16.

17. *Ibid.*

18. Spire was often accused of using the whip on his co-religionists. But he castigated them only for one weakness: foolish assimilation, which made them lose their identity, and the lack of stamina this showed.

19. In this early pronouncement "Irons-nous à Jérusalem?" *loc. cit.*, Spire expressed his fear of Orthodox Jewry taking over a Jewish state and depriving "heretic" Jews of their freedom of thought and action. Yet he would rather have this oppression than the variety growing in the Diaspora.

20. "Exode," *Poèmes juifs*. Several of Spire's Jewish poems have been translated and may be found in Stanley Burnshaw's *André Spire and His Poetry*.

21. *La Renaissance religieuse: Les Problèmes juifs dans la littérature*, (Paris, Alcan, 1928), pp. 107–108.

ELIE WIESEL

1. *Dawn*, p. 86.
2. *Ibid*, p. 21.
3. *The Accident*, p. 105.
4. *Ibid*, p. 117.
5. *The Gates of the Forest*, p. 225.
6. *Ibid*, p. 226.
7. See especially "Notre Commune Responsabilité" and "Plaidoyer pour les morts" in *Le Chant des morts*.
8. See Wiesel's book of the same title. (New York, Holt, 1967).
9. *The Gates of the Forest*, p. 198.
10. *The Accident*, p. 48.
11. *The Town Beyond the Wall*, p. 14.
12. *Hadassah Magazine*, March 1965.

ARNOLD ZWEIG

1. Moritz Goldstein. "Arnold Zweig" in G. Krojanker, ed., *Juden in der deutschen Literatur*, p. 243.
2. *Bilanz der deutschen Judenheit*, p. 140.
3. *Ibid*, p. 152. For other Jewish traits, see *Ibid*, pp. 113 ff., also 120 ff.
4. *Ibid*, p. 115. In the same volume, see pp. 214 ff. for a description of the overall intellectual achievements and contributions of Western Jewries.
5. This whole concept of "Zentralitätsaffekt," a form of ethnocentrism as a source of anti-Semitism, is discussed briefly in *Bilanz*, pp. 61 ff. and at very great length in the earlier *Caliban* which evolved complex theories of anti-Semitism.
6. *Bilanz*, p. 309.
7. *Ibid*, p. 95.
8. *Ibid*, p. 6. In the same volume, pp. 311 ff. Zweig analyses

the faulty conditions of emancipation and how German Jewry misconstrued the agreements and their rights.

9. *Ibid,* pp. 306 ff.
10. Quoted from a letter by Arnold Zweig to the author.
11. *Ibid.*

THE MORE RECENT WRITERS

1. *L'Express,* no. 437, October 29, 1959.
2. Critics for right-wing journals, traditionally unfriendly to Jews, enthusiastically commended Ikor for drawing an "accurate" portrait of alien influences in the French body.
3. This sequel appeared early in 1967. *The Liberation of the Jew* (New York, Orion) develops further the theses of the earlier book. Like the earlier work, it is a highly personal work, stems from his own complex Jewishness, and has more interest than validity for Western and, especially, American Jews.
4. *L'Agrégation d'un Nom et d'un Messie,* pp. 279 ff. and 418 ff. for Isou's blatant denunciation of the role of Christianity in anti-Semitism.
5. *Ibid,* p. 209.
6. *Journal du désordre,* p. 51.
7. *Evidences,* January–February, 1953, p. 8.
8. *Les Grandes Circonstances,* p. 80.
9. *L'Homme-Enfant,* p. 92.
10. Mandel's views, often repeated, are to be found in various journals such as *Evidences* (now defunct) and *L'Arche.*
11. *The Leavetaking,* p. 134.
12. *Ibid.*

Selected Bibliography

The following does not aim to provide a complete listing of each author's literary output, but only certain key works that have relevance to his Jewish positions. It is hoped that the interested reader can be led to those books which will deepen his understanding of the writer's Jewish thinking.

Most works have not been translated into English and the reference is given for the work in the original language. Where a translation is known to exist, the reference given is to the translation.

GENERAL

ANCHEL, ROBERT. *Les Juifs en France*. Paris. 1946
AUBERY, PIERRE. *Milieux Juifs de la France contemporaine.* 1946
BLUM, LEON. *Souvenirs sur l'Affaire*. Paris. Gallimard, 1935
KOCH, THILO. (Ed.) *Porträts zur deutsch-jüdischen Geistesgeschichte*. Köln. DuMont, 1961
Leo Baeck Institute Annual. Essays in the history of the Jews in Germany. 1956–1967. London, East and West Library.
LIPTZIN, SOL. *Germany's Stepchildren*. Philadelphia. Jewish Publications Society, 1944
WASSERMANN, JAKOB. *My Life as German and Jew*. New York. Coward McCann, 1933

LENGTHY STUDIES

Julien Benda

NOVELS

L'Ordination. Paris, 1911. Cashiers de la Quinzaine, 9ᵉ cahier de la 12ᵉ série.

PHILOSOPHICAL, AUTOBIOGRAPHICAL—JEWISH

Betrayal of the Intellectuals. Boston. Beacon, 1928. New ed. 1955
Belphégor. New York. Payson and Clarke, Ltd., 1929
Discours à la nation européenne. 10ᵉ ed., Paris. Gallimard, 1933
La Jeunesse d'un clerc. Paris. Gallimard, 1936
La Grande Épreuve des démocraties. New York. Editions de la Maison française, 1942
Exercice d'un enterré vif. Genève, Paris. Editions des Trois collines, 1945
Le Rapport d'Uriel. Paris. Flammarion, 1946
La Crise du Rationalisme. Paris. Editions du Club Maintenant, 1949
Mémoires d'infra-tombe. Paris. R. Julliard, 1952
Un Régulier dans le siècle. Paris. Gallimard, 1938

Emmanuel Berl

Sylvia. 5ed. Paris. Gallimard, 1952

Max Brod

NOVELS

Arnold Beer: Das Schicksal eines Juden. Berlin. A. Juneker, 1912
Jüdinnen. München. K. Wolff, 1922

The Redemption of Tycho Brahe. New York. A. A. Knopf, 1928

Reubeni, Prince of the Jews. New York. A. A. Knopf, 1928

Die Frau, nach der man sich sehnt. Berlin. P. Zsolnay, 1928

Die Frau, die nicht enttäuscht. Amsterdam. A. deLange, 1934

Unambo: Roman aus dem jüdisch—arabischen Krieg. Zurich. Sternberg, 1949

The Master. New York. Philosophical Library, 1951

Mira, ein Roman um Hofmannsthal. München. Kindler, 1958

Jugend im Nebel. Berlin. Eckard, 1959

Die Rosenkoralle; ein Prager Roman. Berlin. Eckart-Verlag, 1961

PLAYS

Eine Königin Esther. K. Wolff, 1918

AUTOBIOGRAPHICAL—JEWISH

Im Kampf um des Judentum. Wien. R. Löwit, 1920

Das gelobte Land. München. 1921

Heidentum, Christentum, Judentum. München. K. Wolff, 1922

Rassentheorie und Judentum. Prag. J. A. Verb "Barissia", 1934

Diesseits und jenseits. Winterthur. Mondial-Verlag, 1947

Franz Kafka; A Biography. New York. Schocken, 1947

Heinrich Heine; the artist in revolt. 1st U.S. ed. New York. New York University Press, 1957

Streitbares Leben; Autobiographie. München. Kindler, 1960

Der Prager Kreis. Stuttgart. W. Kohlhammer, 1967

Alfred Döblin

NOVELS

Alexanderplatz, Berlin. New York. Viking, 1931; also New York. F. Ungar, 1958

AUTOBIOGRAPHICAL—JEWISH

Reise in Polen. Berlin. S. Fischer, 1926
Jüdische Erneuerung. Amsterdam. Querido, 1933
Flucht und Sammlung des Judenvolkes. Amsterdam. Querido, 1935
Schicksalsreise. Frankfurt a.M. J. Knecht, 1949
Der unsterbliche Mensch: ein Religionsgespräch. Freiburg. München. Herder, 1959

Lion Feuchtwanger

NOVELS

Power. (Jew Suess). New York. Viking, 1927
Success. New York. Viking, 1930
Josephus Trilogy. New York. Literary Guild
   1. *Josephus*. New York. 1932
   2. *The Jew of Rome*. New York. 1936
   3. *Josephus and the Emperor*. New York. 1934
The Oppermanns. New York. Viking, 1934
Paris Gazette. New York. Viking, 1940
Double, Double Toil and Trouble. New York. Viking, 1943
Simone. New York. Viking, 1944
Raquel, The Jewess of Toledo. New York. Julien Messner, 1954
Jephta and His Daughter. New York, Putnam, 1958

AUTOBIOGRAPHICAL—JEWISH

The Devil in France. New York. Viking, 1941

Edmond Fleg

NOVELS

The Life of Moses. London. V. Gollancz, 1929
The Life of Salomon. New York. Dutton, 1930
Jesus; Told by The Wandering Jew. New York. Dutton (definitive ed. 1953)
L'Enfant Prophète. Paris. NRF. (19e ed.) 1934

PLAYS

La Cloison (Un acte). Paris. Molière, 1906
Le Juif du Pape (4 actes). Paris. F. Rieder, 1925
Les Dieudieux (Moralité en 3 actes). Paris, G. Baty, 1931

POEMS

The Wall of Weeping. New York. Dutton, 1929
Ecoute, Israel. Paris. Gallimard, 1945

GENERAL

The Jewish Anthology. New York. Harcourt Brace, 1925

AUTOBIOGRAPHICAL—JEWISH

The Land of Promise. New York. Macaulay, 1933
Israel et moi. Paris. Gallimard, 1936
   with "Pourquoi je suis juif" and "Ma Palestine"
Why I am a Jew. New York. Bloch, 1945

Josué Jehouda

NOVELS

Under collective title: *La Tragédie d'Israel*
Le Royaume de Justice. Paris. Lipschutz, 1923
De Père en Fils. Paris. Grasset, 1927
Miriam. Paris. Grasset, 1928
La Famille Perlmutter (with Panat Istrati). Paris. Nouvelle
   Revue Française, 1927

PHILOSOPHICAL   (AUTOBIOGRAPHICAL—JEWISH)

La Terre Promise. Paris. Rieder, 1924
La Vocation d'Israel. Genève. Editions Synthesis, 1947
Le Monothéisme, Doctrine de l'unité. Genève. Editions Syn-
   thesis, 1952

Sionisme et Messianisme. Genève. Editions Synthesis, 1954
La Leçon de l'histoire. Genève. Editions Synthesis, 1956
L'Antisémitisme, Miroir du monde. Genève. Editions Synthesis, 1956
Le Marxisme, Face au Monothéisme et au Christianisme. Genève. Editions Synthesis, 1962
The Five Stages of Jewish Emancipation. South Brunswick. Yoseloff, 1966

Arthur Koestler

NOVELS

The Gladiators. New York. Macmillan, 1939
Darkness at Noon. New York. Macmillan, 1941
Thieves in the Night. New York. Macmillan, 1946
The Age of Longing. New York. Macmillan, 1951

NON FICTION—JEWISH

Scum of the Earth. New York. Macmillan, 1941
Dialogue with Death. New York. Macmillan, 1942
Insight and Outlook. New York. Macmillan, 1949
Promise and Fulfilment. New York. Macmillan, 1949
Arrow in the Blue. New York. Macmillan, 1952
The Invisible Writing. New York. Macmillan, 1954
The Yogi and the Commissar. New York. Collier, 1961
The Act of Creation. New York. Macmillan, 1964

André Spire

POEMS

La Cité présente. Paris. Société d'Editions littéraires et artistiques, 1903
Et vous riez! Paris. Cahiers de la Quinzaine, 1905
Versets (Et vous riez! Poèmes Juifs). Paris. Mercure de France, 1908
Vers les routes absurdes. Paris. Mercure de France, 1911
Poèmes juifs. Genève. Kundig, 1919

Samael (Poème dramatique). Paris. Georges Crès, 1921
Poèmes d'ici et de là-bas. New York. Dryden Press, 1944
Poèmes d'hier et d'aujourd'hui. Paris. José Corti, 1953
Poèmes juifs (édition définitive), collection "Présences du Judaïsme," Editions Albin Michel, 1959

AUTOBIOGRAPHICAL—JEWISH

Israel Zangwill. Paris. Cahiers de la Quinzaine, 1909
Quelques Juifs. Paris. Mercure de France. Paris, 1913
Les juifs et la guerre. Paris. Payot, 1917
Refuges. Paris. Editions de la Belle Page, 1926
Quelques juifs et demi-juifs (deux volumes). Paris. Grasset, 1928
Souvenirs à bâtons rompus. Paris. A. Michel, 1962.

Elie Wiesel

NOVELS

Night. New York. Hill and Wang, 1960
Dawn. New York. Hill and Wang, 1961
The Accident. New York. Hill and Wang, 1961
The Town Beyond the Wall. New York. Atheneum, 1964
The Gates of the Forest. New York. Holt, 1966
Le Chant des Morts. Paris, Seuil, 1966 (stories and essays)
The Jews of Silence. New York. Holt, 1966

Arnold Zweig

NOVELS

The Case of Sergeant Grischa. New York. Viking, 1928
Claudia. New York. Viking, 1930
Young Woman of 1914. New York. Viking, 1932
. . . De Vriendt goes Home. New York. Viking, 1933
Education before Verdun. New York. Viking, 1936
The Crowning of a King. New York. Viking, 1938
The Axe of Wandsbek. New York. Viking, 1947
Die Feuerpause. Berlin. Aufbau, 1954
Die Zeit ist reif. Berlin. Universitas and Aufbau, 1959

PLAYS

Die Sendung Semaels. München. K. Wolff, 1920
Die Umkehr des Abtrünnigen. Berlin. Potsdam. G. Kiepenham, 1927

AUTOBIOGRAPHICAL—JEWISH

Das ostjüdische Antlitz. Berlin. Welt, 1920 *
Caliban; oder, Politik und Leidenschaft. Potsdam. G. Kiepenheuer, 1927
Juden auf der deutschen Bühne. Berlin. Welt, 1928
Herkunft und Zukunft: Zwei Essays zum Schicksal eines Volkes. Wien. Phaidon, 1929
Bilanz der deutschen Judenheit. Amsterdam. Querido, 1934

BRIEFER STUDIES

Jean Bloch-Michel

NOVELS

The Witness. New York. Panthéon, 1949
The Flight into Egypt. New York. Scribner, 1955
Le Visage nu. 5ed. Paris. Gallimard, 1959

AUTOBIOGRAPHICAL—JEWISH

Les Grandes Circonstances. Paris. Gallimard, 1949
Journal du désordre. 2nd ed. Paris. Gallimard, 1955

Albert Memmi

NOVELS

Agar. Paris. Corres, 1955
The Pillar of Salt. New York. Criterion, 1955
Strangers. New York. Orion, 1960

AUTOBIOGRAPHICAL—JEWISH

Portrait d'un Juif. Paris. Gallimard, 1962

Isidore Isou

L'Agrégation d'un nom et d'un Messie. Paris. Gallimard, 1947

Peter Weiss

NOVELS

The Leavetaking. New York. Harcourt, 1962
Exile. New York. Delacorte, 1968

PLAYS

Die Ermittlung. Frankfurt a/M. Suhrkamp, 1965

Index

Action Française, 45
Ahad Ha-am, 142
Amitié Chrétienne-Juive, 120
Arlosoroff, Charles, 205–206
Aubéry, Pierre, 44, 215
Auschwitz, 54, 82, 177, 180, 223, 233

Baeck, Leo, 81
Balfour Declaration, 174, 179
Barrès, Maurice, 172
Baruk, Henri, 129
Beaumarchais, Pierre-Augustin, Caron de, 95
Beer-Hofmann, Richard, 41–42
Bellow, Saul, 193, 231
Benda, Julien, 52–67, 212, 237, 239
Bergson, Henri, 42, 43–44, 45, 170, 199, 239
Berl, Emmanuel, 23, 212, 237
Bernard, Tristan, 42, 44, 45
Bernstein, Henri, 26, 45–46
Bloch, Jean-Richard, 26, 46–47
Bloch-Michel, Jean, 224, 237, 239
Blum, Léon, 26, 44, 47–49
Boerne, Ludwig, 19–21
Borchardt, Rudolf, 30–31

Brecht, Berthold, 105
Brod, Max, 32, 68–82, 113, 144, 223, 240, 241, 242, 243, 245
Buber, Martin, 127, 142, 191

Camus, Albert, 190
Center for the Study of Monotheism, 129, 130
Chagall, Marc, 124
Chateaubriand, Francois René de, 160
Clement VII, 121
Crémieux, Adolphe, 19

Dauerflucht, 91
De Gaulle, Charles, 229
Descartes, René, 56
Desjardins, Paul, 162
Deutschtum, 31, 39, 88, 205, 241
Doeblin, Alfred, 83–94, 112, 240
Dostoyevski, Fyodor Mikhailovich, 96, 190
Dreyfus, Alfred, 25ff, 117
Dreyfus Case, 25ff, 45, 47, 116, 163, 165, 167, 226, 239
Drieu La Rochelle, Pierre, 54
Dumas, Alexandre (père), 95

Ecole Normale Supérieure, 116

269

Eichmann, Adolf, 186
Einstein, Albert, 155, 199
Enlightenment, 15, 20
Evian Conference, 185
L'Express, 15, 20

Feuchtwanger, Lion, 95–110, 238, 241, 243
Final Solution, 156
Fleg, Edmond, 26, 29, 42, 111–126, 144, 160, 212, 238, 239, 240, 241, 243, 244
Fould family, 19
French Revolution, 7, 15, 16, 17, 18, 21, 23, 58, 245
Freud, Sigmund, 155, 199

Ghandi, Mahatma, 105
Giniewski, Paul, 167
Goldstein, Moritz, 196, 231, 232, 233
Goncourt Prize, 61, 213, 215, 229
Gourfinkel, Nina, 44
Goya, Francisco, 95
Grass, Günther, 231, 232, 233

Halévy, Daniel, 44
Hapoel Hazair, 207
Hasidism, 176, 178, 185, 188ff, 192, 241
Hebrew University, 104
Heine, Heinrich, 9, 21–24, 41, 97
Heine, Salomon, 21
Herzl, Theodor, 27–28, 36, 37, 42, 117, 142
Heschel, Abraham J., 190
Hess, Moses, 28
Hiroshima, 177, 180, 233, 235
Hitler, Adolf, 29, 37, 39, 48, 53, 95, 97, 98, 156, 202
Hölderlin, Friedrich, 86
Hugo, Victor, 118

Ikor, Roger, 215–219, 229, 239

Indifferentism, 70ff.
Irgun, 156
Isou, Isidore, 222–224, 239, 241
Israel, State of, 73, 77, 82, 103, 115, 118, 125, 157, 158, 179, 186

Jabotinsky, Vladimir, 157, 206
Jaurès, Jean, 48
Jehouda, Josué, 127–145, 176, 240, 241, 243, 244
Jesus, 112, 214
Joan of Arc, 106
Johanan ben Zakkai, 102, 104
Josephus, 95, 98, 102
Jud Süss, 96, 98, 99, 105
Judentum, 88

Kafka, Franz, 31–33, 68, 82, 231
Kemp, Robert, 223
Kibbutz, 148
Kierkegaard, Soren, 86
Kleist, Heinrich von, 86
Koestler, Arthur, 69, 73, 78, 90, 93, 146–159, 239, 240, 244, 245
Kraus, Karl, 30–31, 82

Lamed Wow, 214
Langfus, Anna, 229–230
La Palestine Nouvelle, 174
Lazare, Bernard, 26, 28
Lenin, Vladimir Ulyanov, 105
Lessing, Gotthold Ephraim, 15
Leven (Narcisse) Foundation Prize for Jewish Literature, 127, 130
Lewisohn, Ludwig, 123
Ligue des Amis du Sionisme, 174
Lind, Jakov, 231–232
Liptzin, Sol, 42

Mahler, Gustav, 78
Malamud, Bernard, 193, 231
Malraux, André, 146

Mandel, Arnold, 226–229, 238, 239
Mann, Heinrich, 97
Mann, Thomas, 97
Maritain, Jacques, 50
Marranos, 89
Maurois, André, 42, 43, 45, 46, 52
McCarthy, Joe, 107
Memmi, Albert, 219–222, 239, 241
Mendelssohn, Moses, 15, 17
Milhaud family, 19
Miller, Arthur, 191
Molcho, Salomon, 121
Munich Pact, 54

Napoleon I, 21
Neue Freie Presse, 37
Nietzsche, Friedrich Wilhelm, 96
Nordau, Max, 142

Péguy, Charles, 163
Pétain, Marshal Henri, 43, 44, 46
Peyre, Henri, 222
Pinsker, Leo, 142
Pro Causa Judaica, 128
Prophets, 65
Proust, Marcel, 27
Prussian Edict of Emancipation (1812), 16

Racine, Jean, 53
Rathenau, Walther, 106
Rawicz, Piotr, 230
Reinach Brothers, 26, 59
Renouvier, Charles, 56
Reubeni, David, 121
Revue Juive de Genève, 129
Riom Trials, 48
Rolland, Romain, 37, 56, 195
Rosenberg, Alfred, 54
Roth, Philip, 193
Rothschild, family, 19

Rousseau, Jean-Jacques, 95, 106

Sabras, 155, 158, 160
Sachs, Maurice, 49–50
Sartre, Jean-Paul, 190
Schwarz-Bart, André, 192, 212–215, 222, 229, 238, 239
Schwarz-Bart, Simone, 215
Scott, Sir Walter, 95
Shylock, 172
Silone, Ignazio, 146
Singer, Isaac Bashevis, 192
Six-Day War, 209
Sorel, Georges, 163
Spinoza, Baruch, 56
Spire, André, 26, 29, 42, 44, 160–175, 212, 227, 238
Streicher, Julius, 54

Territorialism, 174
Titus, 98
Toller, Ernst 39–40, 235
Tucholsky, Kurt, 40–41, 235

Unitas, 149

Varnhagen, Rahel, 19–21
Vespasian, 98
Voltaire, François-Marie Arouet de, 106

Wandering Jew, 125–126, 179
War of Liberation, 125
Wassermann, Jakob, 33–37, 43, 45
Weimar, 95
Weininger, Otto, 30, 171
Weiss, Peter, 232–235
Weizmann, Chaim, 157
Weltsch, Felix, 77
Werfel, Franz, 32, 43, 239
Wiesel, Elie, 176–193, 229, 230, 234, 239

Yiddish, 150–151, 187, 227

Zangwill, Israel, 165, 171, 172–173

Zionism, 28, 34ff., 61, 66, 75ff., 93ff., 102ff., 109, 122ff., 141ff., 147, 153ff., 174ff., 186ff., 221, 223–224

Zohn, Harry, 41

Zola, Emile, 216

Zweig, Arnold, 29, 69, 78, 97, 102, 108, 147, 194–209, 223, 234, 243, 244

Zweig, Stefan, 33, 37–39, 171, 195, 235

DATE DUE

GAYLORD			PRINTED IN U. S. A.